# INHERITING AGILE

SANDPRINT PRESS

1120 Berkeley St.
Durham, NC 27705

ISBN: 979-8-9891496-0-5 (paperback)
ISBN: 979-8-9891496-1-2 (ebook)

Library of Congress Control Number: 2023922176

Ordering Information:
Special discounts are available on quantity purchases by corporations, associations, and others. For details, contact www.roblineberger.com

Publisher's Cataloging-in-Publication Data:
Names: Lineberger, Rob, 1973- author.
Title: Inheriting agile: the IT practitioner's guide to managing software development in a
    post-agile world / Rob Lineberger.
Description: Durham, NC : Sandprint Press, 2024.
Identifiers: LCCN 2023922176 (print) | ISBN 979-8-9891496-0-5 (paperback) | ISBN 979-8-
    9891496-1-2 (ebook)
Subjects: LCSH: Agile project management. | Agile software development--Management. |
    Computer software--Development--Management. | Software engineering. | Information
    technology. | BISAC: COMPUTERS / Business & Productivity Software / General. |
    COMPUTERS / Software Development & Engineering / General. | COMPUTERS /
    Information Technology.
Classification: LCC QA76.758 .L56 2024 (print) | LCC QA76.758 .L56 2024 (ebook) | DDC
    005.1/2--dc23.

# INHERITING AGILE

## AGILE

### THE IT PRACTITIONER'S GUIDE TO MANAGING
### SOFTWARE DEVELOPMENT IN A POST-AGILE WORLD

ROB LINEBERGER

WHAT TO DO WHEN IT IS YOUR CIRCUS AND THOSE ARE YOUR MONKEYS

Dedicated to the brave ones who peer into the whirling cogs at the heart of their organization and dare to reach a hand inside.

# TABLE OF CONTENTS

# PART 3: THRIVING IN THE BLUR BOX    231

# YOU'VE INHERITED AGILE. NOW WHAT?

DO YOUR SOFTWARE DEVELOPMENT EFFORTS SUCCEED IN THE WAY you hope and expect them to? If so, please accept my congratulations, and thanks for stopping by.

If not (or if you are just starting out), get comfortable, because I have a story for you. It is about a tragic comedy of errors 50 years ago that led modern software development astray. Our shared past is like a circus train wrecking in slow motion, and we've inherited the chaos. I'm going to show you why many people take the exact opposite approach they should—convinced the whole time that it is the responsible way to work. I'm going to show you why the rule book we follow does not match the realities of a highly iterative process. With the absolute freedom that comes from the necessity of reinventing the rules, I'll give you a comprehensive overview of considerations to help you make the right choices in constructing and managing a software development effort. Finally, I will reveal the (sometimes embarrassing) choices I made in my own 25 years of developing software.

By the end of this story, you will know, with absolute clarity, how we got into this mess, how iterative software development actually behaves, and what you can do to make it work for your unique circumstances.

For now, here is a teaser of why the typical arguments of "waterfall vs. agile" (the two prevailing approaches to software development) are actually a sideshow to a deeper problem that influenced both approaches—and why that leaves us in an awkward (yet great) position to move forward.

Have you ever skimmed a book and written a book report on it, only to find out you'd completely missed the point of the book? Your teacher found out you hadn't read it at all? If you have, chances are the worst consequences were a failing grade and a lingering sense of shame. But in 1983, some people skimmed a groundbreaking computer engineering article, mistook its cautionary tale as sound advice, and turned it into the predominant software development methodology in the world. That tragic mistake has cost us trillions upon trillions of dollars and led to pervasive failure in the information technology profession.

People have tried to fix this—primarily, those involved in writing the "Manifesto for Agile Software Development," (commonly referred to as the Agile Manifesto) which describes a different way of working on software. If you're in the software development industry, chances are you have heard the term "agile." If you love thinking about agile approaches, or you're curious how to effectively manage an iterative process, welcome! You're going to love this book.

Perhaps you are wary of the what the term agile represents. The movement has gone from scrappy upstart to widespread adoption and is now headed toward caricature. The popularity of agile certifications, frameworks, and buzzwords has exploded to the point where there is now a growing backlash against them. In some ways, it has become a circus. And to be fair, agile proponents such as myself are so vocal, you could be forgiven for never wanting to hear the word "agile" ever again.

I definitely forgive that sentiment. The agile approach had a lot of success at the software project level. Since then agile has moved outside of a project context altogether and is considered an organization-level initiative. Agile is also expanding beyond software, to reach all aspects of the organization. Some people have cranked out meaningless certifications and soured the word "agile." Many agilists bash other approaches in a tribalistic show of solidarity, which isn't helping very much. In short, the word "agile" is everywhere—and used loosely. The context, agenda, and impact of people who use the word "agile" are all over the map, creating hope, confusion, and even chaos.

An agile circus, if you will.

Ron Jeffries, one of the Agile Manifesto coauthors, bemoans the state of this misapplication of agile in his post "Developers Should Abandon Agile": "It breaks my heart to see the ideas we wrote about in the Agile Manifesto used to make developers' lives worse, instead of better. It also saddens me that the enterprise isn't getting what it could out of the deal, but my main concern is for the people doing the work."[1]

In the last few months, I've gone on a personal quest to understand the current state of agile and do a gut check of whether the advice in this book is sound. I traveled across North America to talk with people face-to-face and learn their successes and challenges. I've spoken in person or direct message to hundreds of people across Mexico, the United States, and Canada in these last weeks, including:

- Young developers just starting their careers, some of whom have inherited agile (willingly or no) and are overwhelmed.
- A few of the Agile Manifesto coauthors and other established names in the agile movement who didn't sign but were just as involved.

---

1    Ron Jeffries, "Developers Should Abandon Agile," *Ron Jeffries* (blog), May 10, 2018, https://ronjeffries.com/articles/018-01ff/abandon-1/.

- Seasoned agile coaches who are training clients in a wide array of fields and company sizes at different states of maturity.
- Value Management Office (VMO) founders at large companies who are over ten years into their agile transformations.
- Project managers from all over the world who specialize in agile approaches.

The people I've talked to have ranged from 18 to 80. An inspiring community that spans all generations, genders, colors, personalities, and years of experience. The two things that unite every person I spoke with—myself included—is we're each a little overwhelmed by what agile has become, and we're each passionate about what it can be.

No matter what your disposition is toward the term "agile," studying iterative management techniques is critical to the health of your software development efforts. Sorting through the buzz is easier once you are empowered with the information I'll present in this book.

Don't take my word for it. Jim Highsmith, one of the coauthors of the Agile Manifesto, recently wrote in an article titled "Agile on the Precipice," "After 20+ years of growing influence, Agile appears to be standing on the precipice of irrelevance. In this time, Agile has spread wider than we Manifesto authors dreamed, but failed to spread as deeply as needed. … Agile, in the form of Agile Methodologies, may be on the precipice, but the need for *agility*, at all levels of enterprises, remains critical to surviving and thriving."[2]

At the time of this writing, there is also a new initiative being launched at reimaginingagile.com by experts in the field. It's called "Reimagining Agile: Making agility accessible to all." The key overlap between this book and that initiative is this: "First, it is time to reimagine agile by clarifying

---

2    Jim Highsmith, "Agile on the Precipice," LinkedIn, January 2, 2023, https://www.linkedin.com/pulse/agile-precipice-jim-highsmith/.

and strengthening agile fundamentals, making them more accessible."[3] I'm thrilled to see that perspective presented so openly and responsively. If fortune is kind, by the time this book goes to press there will be some synergies between what you're about to read and what the agile community produces in response to that call to action by Heidi Musser, Jon Kern, Sanjiv Augustine, and Jim Highsmith.

In fact, those very same concerns are the reason why I wrote this book in the first place. I originally titled it *The Blur Box: Escaping the Bear Trap of Managing Agile Software Development.* But as I have talked to more people, from the newest hires to seasoned professionals, and learned new perspectives, *Inheriting Agile* emerged as a more descriptive title. Some people say agile is thriving, some say it is dead, and some say it was never fully realized in the first place. I'm more in that latter bucket.

The more people I talk to, the more convinced I am that we're in the middle of a monumental shift in the industry. In a post from 2019 titled "Post-Agile Thoughts," Manifesto coauthor Alistair Cockburn summarizes the transition:

We are now in the "post-Agile" age.

> "Post"-something means that we are in an in-between period, where one thing has been incorporated into our culture and the next thing has not yet formed to the point of naming. The period of horseless carriages preceded the age of cars; indeed, even "automobile" is an in-between word, indicating only that a vehicle moves itself.

> We have not yet noted and named whatever happens after fully absorbing Agile. What we can see is that Agile development has crossed the chasm from innovators to the early majority, moved

---

3    Heidi Musser et al., "Reimagine Agile: Back to Basics, Forward to the Future," Agile Alliance, November 14, 2023, https://www.agilealliance.org/reimagine-agile-back-to-basics-forward-to-the-future/.

from the early majority to the late majority, and is starting to pull on the laggards.[4]

The post goes on to describe the lasting positive impacts made by the agile philosophy. I recently followed up on this post and asked Alistair what is next for the agile community of practitioners:

> I don't make predictions about the future; none of my past predictions ever came true. However, we are already in the "post-agile" era, whereever people just grow up with it and don't know anything else, and old stuff seems just nonsense to them. All that notwithstanding the holdouts. What's next? No idea, but agile is now mother's milk, so who knows what the next "better" upgrade will be.[5]

No one else knows what is next, either. The early response to the Reimagining Agile initiative is controversial. For example, here is an articulate alternate take on the issue by Thomas Meloche, who posted his predictions for what is next on LinkedIn and cautioned that agile may not be in the picture at all:

> "Embrace Change," Kent Beck encouraged … well, change is about to embrace you. There will be no next new version of agile. Agile will not be reimagined. Agile will be eliminated.

> We stand on the brink of a transformative era powered by artificial intelligence; it's time to be honest about the fate of Agile methodologies. Agile has been a force in project management and software development, guiding teams through incremental and iterative work cadences. But, as history teaches us, no methodology is immune to obsolescence.

---

4     Alistair Cockburn, "Post-Agile Thoughts," *Heart of Agile*, April 22, 2019, https://heartofagile. com/post-agile-thoughts/.

5     Alistair Cockburn, personal communication, October 27, 2023.

Much like the buggy whips became redundant with the advent of the Ford Model T, Agile is approaching its twilight."[6]

In my opinion, agile principles are sound, but the century of experience that led to predictive approaches in our industry also has merit. Agile proponents are admitting that agile has not penetrated as deeply as it should have, and waterfall proponents are quietly squirreling away the agile ideas that seem reasonable. The core ideas of the Manifesto have lots of vitality, while various factions are digging in their heels—and paradoxically opening their hearts to opposing viewpoints.

I did not write *Inheriting Agile* because agile is the hot trend, nor due to any of the increasingly loud talking points on both sides that, as of this writing, are dominating the agile discussion. No, I wrote this book because the entire "agile vs. other" debate is a sideshow to a deeper problem. A horrible misunderstanding has led to widespread failure in the software development industry, regardless of which methodology you use. Everyone involved in software development, from the staunchest waterfall conservative to the bleeding-edgiest agile adopter, is suffering from the aftermath.

We are in an invisible bear trap, right now. If you are anything like me, you probably aren't even aware of that. I didn't realize it until recently, and I've been studying agile for decades. By taking a step back and looking at iterative development in context, you will see your own agile circus for what it is now, and what it could ideally become. You'll be empowered to form effective strategies.

That's the intent of this book: to reveal the past mistake, help you filter the agile buzz that has erupted ever since, and arrive at a pragmatic solution that is always attacking the problem. Because the problem of how to adapt to an iterative process exists, no matter how we feel about things or how many buzzwords fly around.

---

6    Thomas Meloche, "A Future Without Agile," LinkedIn, November 21, 2023, https://www. linkedin.com/feed/update/urn:li:activity:7132714275269210112/.

Speaking of feelings, I feel like someone who has stepped out of a time machine and is wondering how we arrived in the current timeline. It puts me in a unique position to talk about the current agile landscape. See, I contributed in a modest way during the formation of the agile mindset 25 years ago with a conceptual model called the blur box, then put my head down and used agile methods happily ever since. Now I'm peeking my head up. I see a lot of frustration on all sides of an argument that is really about the same goal: how to deliver quality software in a way that sustains your enterprise.

Let's decipher that noise together.

# CHAPTER 1

# WE CREATED THE BLUR BOX TO SAVE OURSELVES AND IT CAN SAVE YOU, TOO.

What's up with that time machine comment? My agile journey began in 1999. All things considered, 1999 was absolute mayhem in terms of what was going on with software development. The looming Y2K deadline caused widespread apprehension that dominated every technical enterprise. Code repositories were not a widespread practice: merging code was a group affair of nervous people hovering around a single computer to manually combine their contributions. Linux had not yet proliferated. Apple had barely crawled back from the brink of bankruptcy. Microsoft was mired in an antitrust lawsuit with the federal government. Mobile development was unknown.

Against that backdrop, the proliferation of the waterfall project management approach had peaked. Agile development principles had not yet been codified into the Agile Manifesto. Project Management Institute's *PMBOK Guide, 2000 Edition,* was on the cusp of publication. The divide in philosophy between traditional management and agile had barely been articulated, but the discussions were heated. The books *Agile Software Development with Scrum*[7] and *Extreme Programming Explained*[8] had not yet been released.

That was the environment in which the blur box originated.

I had recently left Subaru's just-in-time delivery environment to join a 10-year initiative at Purdue University to convert legacy student systems to a new object-oriented backend written in Smalltalk. My chief architect, Gary Yates, and I would have long conversations about software development methodologies. What would be the most efficient approach for a cross-specialized team of users, managers, business analysts, developers, and testers all hopping from one thread of work to another as needed? Our brains were shorting out from the strain of knowing what we knew (which was that the current management approach would definitely fail for the new approach we wanted to take) and figuring out how to communicate that in a digestible way.

Purdue is a fairly conservative engineering school, having successfully launched a bunch of astronauts into space. So us telling them to let go of their road maps and work allocation charts, to just embrace the thrilling ride of iterative software development, was not going over very well.

One day Gary told me he'd come up with something interesting. Gary is a very skilled and modest person, so that might as well have been a mic drop. He'd come up with a series of drawings illustrating "The Standard Approach You Want Us to Use" and another series of drawings of "Why Those Drawings I Just Showed You Are Going to Fail."

OK, he didn't really call the drawings that, but that's what it amounted to.

As it happened, I was getting my master's degree in information technology. I asked Gary if I could run with the idea. So for the next two years, I started hanging out on bulletin board chat rooms with people like Martin Fowler, Ron Jeffries, Kent Beck, and Scott Ambler. We'd discuss the best

---

7   Ken Schwaber and Mike Beedle, *Agile Software Development with Scrum* (Prentice Hall, 2002).
8   Kent Beck, *eXtreme Programming Explained*, 2nd ed. (Boston, MA: Addison-Wesley, 2005).

way to develop software. Hand in hand with developing software is talking to other people about how you are going to develop software.

Then we all went off and did our own things. Some of the people I followed, and a handful of other people, went on to draft the "Manifesto for Agile Software Development,"[9] which changed software development forever. Scott went on to write the groundbreaking *Agile Modeling: Effective Practices for eXtreme Programming and the Unified Process.*[10] I went on to get my master's degree and make a modest splash in the rising flood of agile discussions. Gary and I had presented "Why Those Drawings I Just Showed You Are Going to Fail"—rebranded as the blur box—a few times internally at Purdue University. Now I was about to fly to Nashville with Kevin Dittman to present it to the 2001 PMI International Symposium (now known as the Global Summit). I stepped onstage and presented an early version of what you are about to read.

Then I got mobbed—literally. They had to interrupt the proceedings and ask me and my new friends to exit the room. That led to a brief stint traveling the country for a year or so giving talks on the blur box, then I presented again at the 2002 PMI International Symposium. The traveling didn't fit very well with my day job. So I stepped away from giving talks, hopped into the time machine, and spent the next two decades leading software development teams.

Decades later, people still reach out to ask me to write a book based on those talks. So I popped up to take a look at the current agile landscape. I don't like what I see. The visionary authors of the manifesto are being lauded and attacked in equal measure. Misinformation is proliferating from both agile proponents and dissidents.

There's lots of great information too! As a software development professional, I think this is a wonderful time to be in the business. You have a

---

9    "Manifesto for Agile Software Development," Agilemanifesto.org, 2001, https://agilemanifesto. org/.

10    Scott W. Ambler, *Agile Modeling: Effective Practices for eXtreme Programming and the Unified Process* (New York: John Wiley and Sons, 2002).

wealth of resources handy—as long as you have a solid conceptual framework to help you sort good advice from bad.

That's why I wrote this book: to provide that solid conceptual framework for understanding iterative development. I've seen the same mistakes repeatedly. I've used the same successful patterns over and over. And I've seen that "The Standard Approach You Want Us to Use" is still kicking around, alive and well.

Understandably so. Some of the standard management techniques are excellent ideas, in many cases. They have worked their magic time and time again and steered many projects successfully. But predictive management approaches are usually unproductive in iterative development.

The key is knowing what applies well and what does not.

CHAPTER 2

# WHAT DOES "INHERITING AGILE" MEAN?

This book is meant to help those who are facing an agile process for the first time and need some advice on how to do it. Or those who want to convince their organization to implement an agile process, but are facing cultural hurdles. There are different interpretations of what it means to "inherit agile." Let's hear from some real people now about what it means to them to inherit agile:

**Gina Williams, Customer Support Manager**
When I think of inheriting, I think of receiving or coming into something (money or property). I know agile is a project management method. So I would guess that "inheriting agile" means coming into a situation where agile is already set up and now it's mine. I know nothing about agile, but I am willing to learn. As for what the term "inheriting agile" means to me … I know agile is a project management method and that's about it. So the confusion is how to apply agile to my project. I remember from school that there is a waterfall and iterations, but that's it. How to apply them to this project is confusing to me.[11]

---

11    Regina Williams, personal communication, November 22, 2023.

### Sydney Taylor, Business Analyst

To me, inheriting agile means coming into a new team and having to be agile in the way the team is vs. the real meaning of agile.[12]

### Baxter Crabtree, Software Developer

I have been working in agile shops since 2008. Most of the agile that I've been exposed to I've inherited from visionaries, thought leaders, and passionate agilists who implemented those systems. They also inherited their agile methods from the "OG" agile signers, some of them directly! What it took me years to realize is that even the signers of the Agile Manifesto inherited their methods from others who came before. What was the common thread? Each of the human beings operating within a system of constraints was compelled to be creative, adaptive, iterative … and productive! Agile systems are not pure, though there is an odd perpetuation of them as distilled and pure things. What they are, more than anything, is a codified way of behaving when the going gets tough, when crap hits the fan, and when the industry you're working in needs constant change. What's important to think about when inheriting agile from those who came before us is that they also were doing it all by the seat of their pants with the best information they had at hand. Good luck to all of us.[13]

### Tim Draegen, Chief Technology Officer

Based upon 30 years of experience within the software development world spanning most roles—from QA, development, architecture, customer support, operations, evangelism, product management, hiring, process design, through CTO—to me, the term "inheriting agile" means "figuring out what to do with today's software development dogma."

---

12    Sydney Taylor, personal communication, November 25, 2023.
13    Baxter Crabtree, personal communication, November 22, 2023.

Twenty years ago, agile filled a methodology void in the very young discipline of software engineering management. Since then, agile has grown to dominate how modern software engineering teams are organized, with dedicated conferences, trade organizations, and professional marketing providing accessible career paths into software team management. Unfortunately, software—and the teams that create it—is incredibly diverse. This diversity reflects the composition of teams, the environment a team works in, the problem being solved with software, changing customer needs, and the complexity of a team's larger organization.

To "inherit agile" means you'll need to understand that agile is one of many ways to manage software development, and that to pick what works for you in your unique context will require an ability to recognize agile for what it is: a simple approach from an earlier time that is now getting in the way of effective software development.[14]

### Chris Correale, Developer

Inheriting agile to me means casting out old directive based, *command and control* ideas and adopting a much more disciplined *inspect and adapt* mindset where failures are viewed as learning opportunities, and ownership is distributed across an empowered workforce. This essentially is a major cultural shift in people's mindset and behavior toward thinking for themselves with minimal to no oversight from management.

### Tiffany Schneider, Agile Coach

Regarding "inheriting agile," the first thing that comes to mind is you are walking into someone else's Agile landscape. That could be a good thing. That could be a icky thing. It depends on wherever they are in their journey with agile.

---

14    Tim Dragen, personal communication, November 22, 2023.

When I got started as a scrum master, it was with a company who was very mature in their agile journey. They'd been doing it for 11+ years. So I was inheriting their agile. I was being taught their agile, their scrum, their SAFe™ version.

I didn't know anything else. The more comfortable that I got in my scrum master journey, the more that I questioned (in a good way) why were they implementing some things? Why were they having us do these certain types of reports? Teams were going along with it because that's what they were told they had to do.

Once I left that mature environment for a company who was just starting to implement agile, I was taking something that I'd learned from this experience over here, putting it into another company where they want to be agile, but it looks different.

**Bob Galen, Agile Coach**

I began explore agile ways of working in 1995–96, inspired by the Scrum paper shared at OOPSLA 1995. Someone asked me: "I want to capture advice from experienced agilists as to if they were just starting out now in agile, based on their experience, what would they tell their younger selves?" And in no particular order, here is my answer:

- The journey is a marathon, not a sprint.
- Build and activate your trusted partner (friend, colleague, mentor, and cheerleader) network.
- Remember, agile is an inside-out job.
- Mindset is a thing; an important thing!
- Certifications are a complacency trap.
- When in doubt, trust your teams.
- Leave something positive behind, a legacy.

- Agile is bigger than software; change the world!
- Respect people … including leaders and managers.
- Continuously build your personal brand.
- Take better care of yourself (self-care)!
- Take the time to build better relationships.
- And … you ROCK! Trust your gut.

CHAPTER 3

# YOU'RE IN THE BLUR BOX—WHETHER YOU LIKE IT OR NOT

This book presents a visual model for anyone who wants to learn or implement an agile approach to iterative software development. The blur box model was designed to be visually compelling and metaphorically strong so that the idea sticks with you and provides a jumping-off point for discussion.[15]

I wouldn't ask you to jump without giving you a few reasons to trust me, so here are my bona fides. This book is part project management, part technology, and part psychology. I'm versed in all three. I've presented agile project management topics at three Project Management Institute (PMI) Global Summits and many local PMI chapters across the U.S. I have a master's degree in managing information technology, 25 years of software development experience, and have taught IT courses at Purdue University. I have also taught introductory psychology at Virginia Tech as a graduate instructor, been published in one of the most prestigious journals from the

---

15    Robert E. Lineberger and Kevin C. Dittman, "The Blur Box: A Conceptual Model for Understanding Iterative Development" (paper, Project Management Institute Annual Seminars & Symposium, Nashville, TN, 2001).

American Psychological Association (APA), and presented my findings at an invited roundtable talk at the 105th annual proceedings of the APA. So when I throw a folksy mixture of psychology, management, and technology at you, rest assured I have deeply studied these topics—both academically and in the field.

Enough about me. I expect the people reading this book will see themselves in one or more of these categories:

- Brave (i.e., risk-taking) stakeholders—or those who had no choice and have been put on the spot—in organizations that are about to embark on an agile approach to software development. They want to ensure their best chances of success. That means instilling the right practices and also avoiding common pitfalls due to not understanding the agile process.

- Project managers who are stuck between a rock and a hard place. When I say "you" in this book, I'm often addressing project managers wrestling with an iterative software development process.

- Dispirited project leaders in organizations that have already implemented an agile approach that has not worked to their expectations. They think they've done everything "the right way," but success eludes them.

- Developers who are excited to use an agile or lean approach in a traditional engineering culture. They might want to convince upper management to adopt agile

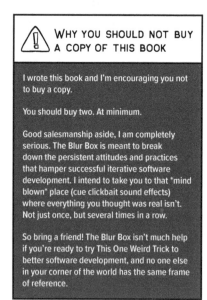

**WHY YOU SHOULD NOT BUY A COPY OF THIS BOOK**

I wrote this book and I'm encouraging you not to buy a copy.

You should buy two. At minimum.

Good salesmanship aside, I am completely serious. The Blur Box is meant to break down the persistent attitudes and practices that hamper successful iterative software development. I intend to take you to that *mind blown* place (cue clickbait sound effects) where everything you thought was real isn't. Not just once, but several times in a row.

So bring a friend! The Blur Box isn't much help if you're ready to try This One Weird Trick to better software development, and no one else in your corner of the world has the same frame of reference.

practices so they can get some relief from traditional approaches that bog down the process.

- Upper managers who are looking for an edge when implementation failure is but one missed decision away.
- Professors in university technology departments (particularly graduate programs) who want to provide a solid foundation of how to approach software development.
- Consultants or agile coaches who want an understandable metaphor to share with clients.

Essentially, this is for anyone who wants to adopt an agile approach to software development but is being hampered by instincts that go against that approach. It doesn't matter whether they are your own instincts as a manager or part of the corporate culture you have to work within.

Why would you want to adopt an agile approach? There are lots of reasons. Probably the most succinct comes from my colleague Glen Alleman, who asks people, "How long are you willing to wait before you find out you're late?"[16] Agile gives you the answer in a matter of weeks, or even within one day if you're really on point.

But a shorter feedback cycle is not the only benefit to an agile process. Scott Ambler and Mark Lines, the creators of Disciplined Agile (DA™, formerly known as Disciplined Agile Delivery), have done the math. Scott has been tracking metrics on this for as long as I've known about his work, which is about 24 years. In their early work, *Disciplined Agile Delivery: A Practitioner's Guide to Agile Software Delivery in the Enterprise*, Scott and Mark summarize the benefits of agile:

> Teams following either iterative or agile processes have been shown to produce higher-quality solutions, provide greater return on investment, provide greater stakeholder satisfaction, and deliver

---

16 Glen Alleman, "Project Manager and Agile," *Herding Cats* (blog), June 29, 2011, https://herdingcats.typepad.com/my_weblog/2011/06/project-manager-and-agile.html.

these solutions quicker as compared to either a traditional/water-fall approach or an ad hoc (no defined process) approach.[17]

There's a lot more to be said on the matter, and I assure you that Scott and Mark back up those statements. Read about DA™ if you really want to get into the metrics that show the value of agile. DA™ isn't prescriptive—rather, it's a toolkit that gives options and the trade-offs of how teams implement metrics to measure their own effectiveness. For example, to learn the trade-offs of how to organize a team-based metrics strategy, check out the "Organize Metrics" overview at PMI's Disciplined Agile site.[18] To learn what to potentially measure at the software team level, see "Measuring Outcomes."[19]

The model presented in this book is designed to challenge the assumptions of anyone who wants to apply traditional engineering management approaches to iterative software development. I've presented this model to thousands of people and seen how effective it is in getting points heard in both directions.

By the way, this seems like another good place to tease the big reveal in part 1, which is that Agile vs. Waterfall is a myth. The waterfall is an established software development management methodology where a project is broken down into sequential phases. This methodology is inherently predictive, dictating the schedule and deadlines in advance. It's often referred to as "the traditional project management approach" because this is what most project managers were taught.

The truth is, not all predictive approaches are waterfall, and they're not necessarily traditional. And agile techniques are not always implemented in a truly iterative way. So these terms are nebulous. I, too, fall prey to reducing predictive, traditional, and waterfall into one ill-fitting bucket and

17    Scott W. Ambler and Mark Lines, *Disciplined Agile Delivery: A Practitioner's Guide to Agile Software Delivery in the Enterprise*, 1st ed. (Indianapolis, IN: IBM Press, 2012).

18    "Organize Metrics," Project Management Institute, January 2023, https://www.pmi.org/disciplined-agile/ongoing-goals/organize-metrics.

19    "Organize Metrics."

classifying agile as a reaction to that bucket. The reason I perpetuate this shorthand is because, as you will see later, this discussion on terminology is ultimately a sideshow. And people in the software industry generally know what you mean when you say waterfall vs. agile. A better characterization is probably "predictive vs. adaptive" project management approaches. But few people use those terms, so let's suffer through.

Just as agile proponents like me will try to encourage you to leave predictive practices behind, those of you who use them have valid reasons based in experience. The ultimate goal is to produce an optimal project management approach based on your management goals while facing the uncomfortable realities iteration brings. The recommendations I provide are best embodied by one question: what happens when the hard truths of iteration meet the demands of established management practices?

Each team and culture are different. So when I tell you my best practices in the context of the blur box, it's my good faith effort to show you how I gnawed myself out of the bear trap, in hopes that the thought process might shed some light on your own personal escape journey.

I cannot promise you success. But I can promise that if you and whoever you're trying to discuss software development with both read this book, you will have more productive conversations and avoid some major pitfalls.

CHAPTER 4

# STATEMENT OF PROBLEM: SEEING WHAT'S HOLDING YOU BACK

You are in a bear trap.

At the time the blur box model was created in 1999, according to Gartner, over 2 trillion dollars were being spent on information technology projects, and about half of those projects failed.[20] But a lot has happened in twenty years. The spend has gone way down, and we're close to a 100% success ratio.

Right? *Right?*

Far from it. Spending has doubled, and the failure rate has increased. Gartner estimates 2023's worldwide spending on software will be 4.6 trillion dollars.[21] Standish Group's annual *CHAOS Report* for 2020 states that 66% of technology projects fail either partially or totally.[22] It is bad. You already know it. That's probably why you're reading this introduction right now.

---

20    D. Reiber, "Bucking the Project," *Enterprise Solutions* (July/August 1999): 16–18.
21    "Gartner Forecasts Worldwide IT Spending to Grow 5.5% in 2023," Gartner, April 6, 2023. https://www.gartner.com/en/newsroom/press-releases/2023-04-06-gartner-forecasts-worldwide-it-spending-to-grow-5-percent-in-2023.
22    Frank Faeth, "IT Project Failure Rates: Facts and Reasons," March 22, 2022, LinkedIn, https://www.linkedin.com/pulse/project-failure-rates-facts-reasons-frank-faeth.

Something has to be done about it. With the release of the Agile Manifesto in 2001, methodologies such as scrum and the scaled agile framework (SAFe™) have risen up to promise transformative solutions. And agile methods have made some truly staggering improvements.

But not in all cases. Some companies apply agile methodologies and fail. Some, like Amazon, Uber, and Spotify, achieve agile successes so stunning that they make waves, tantalizing the rest of us. Now there are half a million books, consultants, and buzzwords about agile, causing information overload. Agile advocates and established management practitioners have each dug in their heels, telling the world how their approach is the right way. It's getting heated. The noise-to-signal ratio is pretty high right now.

My description of the agile landscape in 2002 is eerily prescient of this current state of affairs. When presenting to the 2002 PMI International Symposium, I described four stereotypes of people who talk about agile methods. Today I prefer not to stereotype or divide people into buckets because the overall complexity of the problem is so high, and everyone has a unique perspective. Even so, there is some truth in my twenty-year-old Exhibit 1: Agile Viewpoint Stereotypes:[23]

| | Agile Proponents | Agile Opponents |
|---|---|---|
| Good | Accomplished, technologically savvy managers and senior developers who are comfortable with complex technology and/or require speed and flexibility in software development; development teams that are comfortable taking the risks and responsibility for successful implementation. AKA: Trailblazers | Accomplished, technologically savvy managers and senior developers who take a conservative approach or have been burned by hasty bandwagon jumping in the past; those in industries where a formal process is critical because of massive team size, dispersed business units, or government regulations. AKA: Captains of the Guard |
| Bad | Code hackers who want to escape the discipline and constraints of a formal process; consultants with little real experience to capitalize on the "hot" new trend. AKA: Exploiters (Hackers) | Managers and business people who are comfortable with the status quo; existing processes are culturally difficult to incorporate; people who are either unwilling or unable to perceive the benefits of taking "drastic" steps to lighten existing processes. AKA: Camels |

23   Robert E Lineberger, "The Blur Box Explored: Solutions for Integrating Adaptive Processes" (paper, Project Management Institute Annual Seminars & Symposium, San Antonio, TX, 2002).

Agile definitely holds the answer for many of you. But that answer is obscured by more than ideological arguments, corporate culture, lack of expertise, or marketing hype. In the next chapter, I'll discuss a little-recognized but widespread lie that has grown like a snowball and dominated our industry for decades. The entire debate and promise of agile is completely reframed if you recognize the aftermath of that lie. If you do, and you learn a different way of looking at iterative software development, you'll gain the insight needed to make iterative development work for your organization.

CHAPTER 5

# WHY WE NEED A NEW APPROACH

A critical shortcoming in the IT industry is a grasp of IT-specific management principles, which some attribute to information technology's continued reliance on the engineering body of knowledge. The gist of it is that engineering management practices put humans on the moon and made semiconductors and stuff. Those same management practices should apply to software development too, because it deals with facts and data and computers and therefore is governable by the same approaches.

But software development is actually about human relationships, fostering both communication and collaboration. It's about culture and soft skills, involving far more than the programmers writing the code in the basement. But software development is actually about human relationships, fostering both communication and collaboration. It's about culture and soft skills, not programmers writing code in the basement. Less about mass production, and more about innovation and creating novel solutions.v

With the best of intentions, we incorrectly apply engineering approaches to software development. We create must-have documents, like contracts or road maps. But governing iterative software development through predictive means, such as schedules, contracts, timelines, and work breakdown structures, is like trying to hold sand in an iron fist. The harder you tighten your grip, the faster the sand falls through.

From start-up to Fortune 500, we often make the same mistakes, which are versions of "But we really need to have [insert predictive approach here]." We say something like "It's ridiculous to think that a serious project wouldn't have [insert predictive approach here]." Then we wonder why our iterative software effort just failed when we did everything "the right way."

This book mostly comes from a standpoint of single teams on IT projects. Agile has progressed far beyond that lens. Beyond one team. Beyond projects. But a small IT team on a single project is an easily graspable context. Such a context makes sense to discuss the basics, which can hopefully scale to larger implications.

One of the major complications IT development projects face is the highly cyclical, recursive nature of project stages (a.k.a. iterative processes), which invalidates many of the traditional management principles IT managers apply. Predictive techniques are not inherently bad.

They're indicators that you are confident that you know where things are headed. Iterative processes make no such claim. Their strength is in discovery and immediate refinement in the face of discoveries. As such, predictive artifacts are at best baggage, and at worst, they will spring the bear trap.

A scene in *The Karate Kid* perfectly captures this situation. Mr. Miyagi is explaining commitment to his student, like so:

> Daniel-san, must talk. Walk on road. Walk right side, safe. Walk left side, safe. Walk middle, sooner or later, get squish, just like grape. Here, karate, same thing. Either you karate do, "yes," or karate do, "no." You karate do, "guess so," [makes squish gesture] get squished. Just like grape.[24]

My experiences suggest you can be successful following very controlled and regimented processes—if your culture values specification and documentation (a.k.a., protection) at the expense of efficiency. There are cases where that trade-off is valid, such as highly specialized teams with siloed skill sets or large-scale deployments. You can also be successful going the opposite direction, which is a completely fluid process such as kanban.

If you walk in the middle of the road while adopting an agile process, sooner or later, you'll get squished. Mike Griffiths, who led the writing team for the new PMI Agile Practice Guide and helped create the PMI-ACP certification, creates a similar metaphor in his work. He compares agile to a baked tuna entrée and predictive approaches to a chocolate cake. You can dine on fish and then enjoy cake for dessert, but combining them won't work because "no one likes a tuna-chocolate cake."

My upcoming, highly biased pronouncements that certain approaches will fail are meant to highlight ingrained, instinctual, "right-way" approaches we've internalized that will threaten your project. In a flexible methodology, system design is revisited continually as development takes place. This process should clarify requirements as the project moves forward, and

---

24    *The Karate Kid*, directed by John G. Avildsen (1984: Columbia Pictures), DVD.

the customers should be highly involved as iterations of design take place. However, this approach is not as successful if predictive management strategies are applied to the complexities of iteration.

An iterative process demands a project approach that embraces the changeability and flexibility of IT so that we can fully exploit the benefits of IT. Given the tremendous time demands of the internet economy, creating a parsimonious project methodology becomes more vital than ever.[25] With that in mind, this book presents a conceptual model, called "the blur box," for understanding iterative processes such as object-oriented development, rapid application development, iterative software development, devops, or complex integrations.

The blur box is not a methodology. It doesn't tell you what to do. It simply describes how things are. It's a structured way of looking at iteration so you can make informed business decisions when managing such a project. It's akin to *The Mythical Man-Month* by Fred Brooks, another example of a book about project management that isn't a methodology either but a critique or analysis. The blur box is a business communication tool that you can use in many ways: convincing upper management that certain documents are unnecessary, showing new project managers what they are in for, or explaining to the customer that the random nature of communications they'll receive is not haphazard but preferable.

That last sentence is really the crux of this whole agile movement and what I'll be writing about in this book. The Agile Manifesto lists it as the first of its four values:

*Individuals and interactions* over *processes and tools*[26]

Agile is a mindset that seeks a more realistic way of working with human beings in a technical enterprise. As I read the ever-burgeoning mountain of books and articles about agile, one encouraging trend stands out to me: Authors are using words like "learning," "humility," "culture," "dynamics,"

---

25   Lineberger and Dittman, "The Blur Box."
26   "Manifesto for Agile Software Development."

"communication," and "bravery" much more often than we used to. The acknowledgment that software is about people instead of code has moved from implicit to explicit. As you read this book, always keep your organization's culture in the back of your mind.

For example, think about your team dynamics. What tacit penalties are in place for being brave, agile, or iterative? Almost every organization of even modest maturity has a certain conservatism baked in. They're biased toward the status quo and avoid taking unnecessary risks. There are excellent reasons for this. Your future success is probably based on your past success. But if you are embarking on an agile or iterative venture for the first time, it's probably going to require a far deeper and wider cultural shift than you expect. At a bare minimum, look at which barriers you have in place from the get-go. Allow your people the freedom to try without fear of retribution—either explicit retribution or, more likely, implicit.

CHAPTER 6

# AVOID THE UNPLEASANT
# CONSEQUENCES OF FAILURE

Speaking of explicit, this is probably a good place to be explicit about the purpose of this book, which is to help you avoid implementation failure. Since you are reading this, you're probably either considering an agile implementation or have already done so—and it didn't meet your expectations. Either case brings with it very unpleasant consequences, should a failed agile implementation occur.

There are the obvious consequences of wasted time and money. Going agile is an investment. It requires training, additional roles, and consultant fees. There's the opportunity cost of pausing your organization's overall effectiveness while you pivot toward this new cultural mindset. Unless your organization is filled with lucky geniuses, you're unlikely to get it right the first time. So we're obviously trying to minimize the impact of doing things incorrectly, increase the odds that your investment will add value, and prevent a catastrophic loss—at an organizational level.

But I want to take a minute to tell you the other kinds of consequences that people might not talk about so much. The real reason I wrote this book is to *spare you the personal consequences of failure.*

I've been studying agile processes for 25 years. Some of my greatest professional achievements have been implementing agile against all odds. (Or even with good odds—that also feels satisfying.) But I've also failed at agile implementation, and it's without a doubt the lowest I've ever been as a professional. It's worse than getting laid off, or fired, or suffering the embarrassment of blowing a major decision you should have gotten right.

Here's what happened to me and what my personal consequences were.

Early in my software development career, I realized that certain organizational issues required my team to adopt an agile process. We had an ambitious, high-reward project that our culture was limiting. The development team was understaffed, and the requested features needed a core of experience we didn't have. We also needed to become iterative in order to explore new directions without devoting too much time to dead ends.

After a year or two of leaning on the CEO, I was able to convince him. I became the team lead and was allowed to hire two additional people. I also gained permission to retool our process in an agile way.

I'd been involved in a successful agile transformation at a similar organization in the past and had firsthand experience with the effort involved. Plus, I'd earned a master's degree in the management of information technology *and* created the blur box, a stunningly insightful conceptual model about agile development. Out of anyone on the planet, I figured I probably had the highest odds of success at this.

Reality had different plans. Within a year of becoming a team lead and implementing my first agile process, my team imploded, and I left the organization. The irony is that I failed because we initially succeeded. Our first three sprints were so effective, and the approach worked so well, that I became complacent. I took the process for granted. The organization came to expect that same level of success. An irony on top of that irony is that I warned myself of this very danger in my 2002 PMI International Symposium whitepaper under the subheading "Be Strong in the Face of Success:"

Ironically, at the beginning an agile team's greatest danger may be success. At first, it seems like nothing will be delivered and everyone gets nervous. "… Suddenly people realize the whole thing is going to be pulled off and begin to fight for their functionality making the first release. The manager must remain steadfast to promised features, or risk jeopardizing the entire project" (Kruchten, 2000). Another danger of success is the team getting overconfident in their newfound abilities. An agile approach is meant to foster flexibility and good code; it is not a way to cram more stuff into a shorter time period.[27]

The specifics of my failure definitely matter, and I've sprinkled the lessons learned throughout this book. But regarding this point about personal failure, it's less about what happened compared to what the consequences to me were.

Watching my agile implementation collapse in slow motion and seeing the team dissolve were some of the worst personal setbacks of my career. The horror of going from the top of the world to holding nothing led to a serious depression. I went to therapy for two years with a therapist who specialized in business and management clients. We talked through everything that happened and what decisions I made, good and bad. I was numb to everything around me as I tried to recover from the stunned sense of personal loss. It not only affected me but the people I hired and my downstream customers, who now had personal and professional losses of their own to deal with. I lost friends, made enemies, lost faith in myself, and above all, developed an unhealthy fear of ever trying that again.

In the grand scheme of things, mine was a fairly low-impact venture—one small software team with a handful of people and a limited reach. Even

---

27    Lineberger, "The Blur Box Explored." Philippe Kruchten, "From Waterfall to Iterative Development—A Challenging Transition for Project Managers," *The Rational Edge*, 2001, archived April 9, 2001 at https://web.archive.org/web/20010409202130/http://www.umlchina. com/ProjMan/Fromwater.htm.

that "small" failure had grave consequences in several lives. Those two years of depression were a time I'd never want to revisit under any circumstances, not to mention the dissolution of my related start-up and the time and money that went into it. If you scale this up to a medium- or large-scale enterprise with multiple teams, failure becomes exponentially less palatable.

The people championing agile transformations tend to have very high levels of personal attachment. And the more personal investment you have, the more potential that failure has to affect you. It was three years before I stepped up to the plate again to spearhead an agile transformation—this time at an enterprise level. It was and continues to be a huge success, and this is one of my greatest professional accomplishments. But believe me, I was sweating bullets, and I took nothing for granted the second time around.

In a word, I was terrified. Perhaps unreasonably so. What I'd like to do with this book is scare you a little, just enough to keep the thrill of failure on your radar. But mostly I want to give you enough insight so that you are not terrified but empowered and respectful of the challenge—not overconfident so much as appropriately optimistic.

# PART 1:
# DISCOVERING THE BLUR BOX

THIS PART OF THE BOOK INTRODUCES A DETAILED METAPHOR FOR how iterative development works called the blur box. I'm not pushing any particular methodology or consulting ideology. To give you an idea where I'm coming from, I once coauthored an article with John Mendonca called "Methodology as Road Kill: The Decade-Long Assault on Quality Assurance" for the American Society for Quality. This was for *Software Quality*, their spring 2001 newsletter. In that article, we made the point that any methodology that does not account for the hard, uncomfortable truths of software development is a complete waste of time.[28] That article ignited a storm of angry feedback unlike the editors had ever seen. I had to go back and write a rebuttal letter, in which I doubled down on how detrimental methodology can be.

The purpose of the blur box is to provide a memorable visual illustration of why predictive approaches are likely to fail against an iterative process. It is meant to challenge commonly held assumptions about the "right way" to manage software development. Use it first to clarify your own understanding of the problem, and second to convince others why certain approaches are risky and will threaten an agile initiative.

So if I have an agenda, it's this: know what you are getting into, and make no assumptions about what is going to be effective. Be as iterative, adaptive, and responsive as you can get away with. Throw away anything that doesn't help, no matter how necessary it's supposed to be.

## GENERATIVE AI PROMPTS ARE THE PERFECT METAPHOR FOR ITERATION

My editor tells me I used some variation of the word "iterative" over 230 times in this book. We'll get to general definitions later. But this word is important to understand since it is so crucial to the discussion I'm about to unfold.

Using generative AI such as ChatGPT perfectly illustrates the benefits of iteration and discovery that are at the heart of agile. The following metaphor is going to provide a time capsule of the mindset of the waterfall as described in 1976, and then explain the iterative approach suggested in 2000 by the agile movement. Refinements have been made to both approaches since, and this is an oversimplification of the history. Even so, the metaphor below is meant to give you a historical perspective on what

---

28  Rob Lineberger and John Mendonca, "Methodology as Road Kill: The Decade-Long Assault on Quality Assurance," *Software Quality*, American Society for Quality (Spring 2001).

the term "iterative" means and how it differed from the strict, phase-based approaches of the day.

The metaphor is this. Perhaps you have used a generative AI tool such as ChatGPT or copy.ai to help you brainstorm ideas or write drafts of a business document. If so, have you ever had an idea of the text you wished to generate, provided an initial prompt, and gotten back text that absolutely missed the mark of what you were trying to achieve? That represents a failed software project.

What did you do next?

Let's explore two different paths. To make things even more representative of the historical difference between iterative and non-iterative methods at the time, and how the AI prompt metaphor applies to software development, I'm going to add a wrinkle. Let us pretend that the process around using this AI prompt tool costs $60 per hour, and you happen to have exactly $60 to spend to get the best result you can. Let us also admit that the time scale here is not exactly right, because interacting with an AI tool is really faster than this—but maybe the whole thing is heavily regulated so you can't speed it up.

In the 1980s and 1990s, if you followed a pure waterfall-based or other phase-type approach, here is what the above process would have looked like:

1. Minutes 0–10 (cost $10): Analyze the question you want AI to answer.
2. 2) Minutes 10–40 (cost $30): Design a prompt that answers that question as clearly as you can possibly think of. Think of everything, because you really want to get this right. For example: "Please generate a detailed business plan for commercializing software that helps people plan events. Tailor it to an audience of investors who do not have software commercialization experience. Include an overview of what event planning entails, and also explain the benefits and drawbacks of software commercialization. Finally, provide references for further reading."

3. Minutes 40–55 (cost $15): Send that prompt to your friends for feedback on whether it makes sense. Wait for their reply. If you get answers back in time, refine the prompt based on their responses. If not, proceed.

4. Minutes 55–56 ($1): Submit the prompt to the AI program and get back the response.

5. Minutes 56–60 ($4): Double check that you entered the prompt correctly, and copy the result you got back for your records.

6. You are out of time and money. The result you got is the final product. If you do not like it, then you need to either go with it and make the best you can of the situation, or borrow money from your friends to buy more time and submit a new prompt. You need to borrow at least $50 because your process requires you to do steps 2–5 on the new prompt, but you don't have to do step 1 over because you already know what you're trying to ask and that hasn't changed.

The above explains the thinking of a phase-based approach. Now what if you were to follow an iterative process, as popularized by the Agile Manifesto in 2000? It would look like this:

1. 1) Minutes 0–10 (cost $10): Analyze the question you want AI to answer. That's the same as above, because the analysis is pretty much the same.

2. 2) Minutes 11–15 (cost $5): Design an initial prompt that answers the question. Unlike step 2 above, which resulted in a pretty detailed prompt, you don't spend much time here. You just get something that barely asks the question in its most basic form (minimum viable product, or MVP): "Please generate a business plan for commercializing software that helps people plan events." Send that MVP prompt to your friends and ask for feedback.

3. Minutes 16–17 (cost $1): In the meantime, start trying stuff. Submit the MVP prompt to the AI program and get back the response.

4. Minutes 17–20 ($4): Read over the initial result. Do you want to use the first answer you get back? (That's following the original specification.) If so, you are done. You saved $40 of your $60 budget. Or—as is far more likely—do you realize that the results you got back weren't even close, and you need to be more specific with your prompt? That is iteration. Also, let's further say you learned about SaaS vs. open source from the result. That is discovery of new requirements.

5. Minutes 20–25 (cost $5): Design a follow-up prompt that answers the new question, incorporating the new requirements. "Please generate a business plan for subscription software via a SaaS model that helps people plan events." You have now iterated based on uncovering better information.

6. Minutes 26–27 (cost $1): Submit the second prompt (iteration 2).

7. Minutes 27–30 ($4): Read over the second result. Send it to your friends. In the meantime, is the answer you got back good enough? If so, you are done. You saved $30 of your original budget and the answer is arguably more helpful than what you got back in the phase-based example, even if it lacks some of the details. You can decide whether to spend more money to flesh that out, accept what you have, or refine your prompt some more.

8. Minutes 30–35 ($5): Oh good! Your friends got back to you about your initial MVP prompt, and they express how vague it is. It's not just any kind of event, it's weddings. And the reason why they care is because they don't have a lot of money. Thus, your friends present a specific value proposition that you alone had not considered (a.k.a. collaboration): "Please generate a business plan for commercializing software that helps budget-conscious people plan weddings." You merge that with your iteration 2 prompt and get

this: "Please generate a business plan for subscription software via a SaaS model that helps budget-conscious people plan weddings."

9. Repeat steps 6, 7, and 8 as many times as you have remaining funds for, stopping when you reach a point that you and your friends are satisfied with.

10. Whenever you are happy with the result, spend four minutes to double check that you entered the prompt correctly, and copy the result you got back for your records. That is the same as the final step above.

Steps 1–10 above describe an iterative approach.

# CHAPTER 7

# WATERFALL VS. AGILE IS A MYTH

It's traditional for agile enthusiasts (who embrace an iterative, adaptive, light-footed approach to software development) to speak out against monolithic processes such as the very popular waterfall methodology (a carefully controlled, sequential, heavyweight process.) I've heard several common portrayals of this dynamic over the years:

- The waterfall methodology is an inflexible approach to software development that completely fails to take iteration into account but somehow has been written into law.
- Agile proponents think waterfall is an outdated approach, and the people who use it are out-of-touch control freaks.
- Traditional engineering management proponents think the agile movement consists of a bunch of naive hipsters and rebels who have no idea how business works.
- Agile works for any project.
- By the way, no one uses the waterfall anymore.

All of those bullet points are wildly incorrect.

## SETUP FOR THE WATERFALL

First of all, what is the waterfall methodology? It's a widely adopted approach codified in the late '80s that was the foundation for many software development management approaches in use today. In the waterfall, software development is broken down into phases, starting with systems design before moving through analysis, development, and a bunch of other phases. A gut check gatekeeping meeting is held at the end of each phase, then the next one begins. It's like a relay race, where runners pass the baton at each gate, until finally the software development process trickles down into operations.

Ordinarily, this is the part where I would provide the same level of detail about the waterfall methodology as I did about agile in the preceding sections. However, I'm not going to. Instead, I'm going to yank the steering wheel and veer right out of the lane we're in, for two reasons.

First, the term "waterfall" is a political land mine in the field of IT management, and if you are new to the field, you need to understand that first. From my perspective, that understanding is even more critical than the techniques themselves. There was a backlash against the waterfall in the late 1990s, and now there is a resurgent backlash against *that* backlash. Just as agile has heated discussions, debate, and misunderstandings around the term, so too does the term "waterfall." It is less important to go into the phase-driven techniques as it is to go into the cultural minefield that surrounds this term.

Why? Why am I not giving "waterfall" the same level of description as "agile"? Isn't that unbalanced journalism?

## THE WATERFALL NEVER EXISTED

Well, those questions lead me to the second reason for veering away from a thorough description of waterfall, and it is the true purpose of this section: to convince you that the waterfall methodology *never existed at all.*

I'm serious, and not being sensationalistic. The waterfall was a mirage before it even went to press.

A lot of people have positive associations with the waterfall. In fact, I have noticed an increasing resistance to the backlash against the waterfall. There is a spirit of "both sides have their positives" and that we should find some middle ground. A recent comment on LinkedIn by author Shawn Belling, who has earned one of the most rigorous agile certifications (PMI-ACP), phrases the fatigue with "agile vs. waterfall" in a clear way that fairly represents this viewpoint:

> People need to stop thinking and talking about "waterfall versus agile." It's not a contest or a battle, and there is a lot of wasted energy spent on this topic. Experienced and savvy practitioners tailor their approach to projects based on many factors. As a Scrum advocate, trainer, and practitioner, I enjoy using Scrum and find that Scrum and Agile practices work great for many projects and scenarios. "Waterfall" (or whatever one chooses to call phase-based or plan-driven approaches to projects) also works well for many types of projects, as long as the project team is pragmatic about acknowledging that no amount of planning can predict the future.[29]

Conflating "predictive vs. adaptive" with "agile vs. waterfall" is a subtly dangerous point of view because it comes from a standpoint that the waterfall did, in fact, exist. That the waterfall is a real thing we should respect for what it has accomplished, and debate honestly and openly. If everyone expressing a desire for the agile vs. waterfall debate to be put to rest were to rephrase as "predictive and adaptive techniques both have their merits," then I would happily agree.

But this "waterfall never existed" claim is something different, something widely misunderstood and extremely critical to understand.

---

29    Shawn Belling, comment on post by Henrik Mårtensson, LinkedIn, November 19, 2023.
      https://www.linkedin.com/feed/update/urn:li:activity:7130914426941030401.

I'm about to take a very harsh stance on the history of the waterfall and how tragic the consequences of the misinformation has been to our industry. If you appreciate moderation in all things, you could be forgiven for concluding that I am exaggerating things for dramatic effect. Especially if you are wary of agile in the first place, you might interpret what you're about to read as a lack of impartiality. The same tired "agile vs. waterfall" argument that has played out so many times, with agile not giving waterfall its hard-earned due respect.

That's not what this is at all, and that's why I'm bringing the point up now. If you're familiar with this debate already and have one foot out the door at my statement that "the waterfall methodology never existed at all," you are about to do yourself a huge disservice that invalidates the entire driving force behind this book.

Hear me out. If by the time you're done reading this chapter you think I am overattributing our industry's widespread failures to this historical tragedy, then I encourage you to read Henrik Mårtensson's article "Waterfall vs. Agile: Battle of the Dunces or A Race to the Bottom?" I will tease that article by posting a quote here, which is going to sound familiar: "In a recent HBR article, *It's Time to End the Battle Between Waterfall and Agile*, the author sets up a false premise, that there is a war between Waterfall methodology and Agile, that it must end, and that you can combine the approaches to get the best of both worlds. This sounds good, but the article is based on a misunderstanding of both Waterfall and Agile. Also, there is no war between Waterfall methodology and Agile. There can't be, because Waterfall methodology does not exist!"[30]

Henrik's article is an interesting companion to *Inheriting Agile* for three reasons. One, Henrik goes far deeper into the history of IT project management methodologies than I have here. Two, he draws the precise same conclusions that I have based on the history of agile and waterfall. And

---

30    Henrik Mårtensson, "Waterfall vs. Agile: Battle of the Dunces or A Race to the Bottom?," *Kallokain: From the Trenches of Business Management Consulting*, November 16, 2023, https://kallokain.blogspot.com/2023/11/waterfall-vs-agile-battle-of-dunces-or.html.

finally, Henrik's condemnation of this fallout is, if anything, far more harsh than my own.

Various authors have pointed out the historical snafu I'm about to discuss that led to the formation of the waterfall methodology, but somehow it has not been widely realized. Craig Larman and Victor Basili dig into it in their fantastic 2003 article for the Institute of Electrical and Electronics Engineers, titled "Iterative and Incremental Developments: A Brief History."[31] Victor Andreas Zwinkau does an excellent job deconstructing the history of the waterfall. Tobias Pfieffer, a.k.a. PragTob, draws similar conclusions in his article "Why Waterfall Was a Big Misunderstanding from the Beginning."[32]Even though people have been writing about this for 20 years, it somehow flies under the radar.

## THE LAST GASP OF INNOCENCE

So why did the waterfall never exist? In 1970, visionary software engineer Winston Royce published "Managing the Development of Large Software Systems." He lays out his experiences in software development, learned from safely launching the *Pioneer 9* spacecraft. Royce describes that analysis and coding are two widely understood and supported steps that most people know about and accept. He then states,

"An implementation plan to manufacture larger software systems, and keyed only to these steps, however, is doomed to failure. Many additional development steps are required, none contribute as directly to the final product as analysis and coding, and all drive up the development costs. Customer personnel typically would rather not pay for them, and development personnel would rather not implement them. The prime function

---

31   Craig Larman and Victor Basili, "Iterative and Incremental Developments: A Brief History," *Computer* 36, no. 6 (July 2003): 47–56, https://doi.org/10.1109/mc.2003.1204375.

32   Tobias Pfieffer, "Why Waterfall Was a Big Misunderstanding from the Beginning," *Journeys of a Not So Young Anymore Software Engineer* (blog), March 2, 2012, https://pragtob. wordpress.com/2012/03/02/why-waterfall-was-a-big-misunderstanding-from-the-beginning-reading-the-original-paper/.

of management is to sell these concepts to both groups and then enforce compliance on the part of development personnel."[33]

Winston then introduces Figure 2, the diagram that would change software development forever:

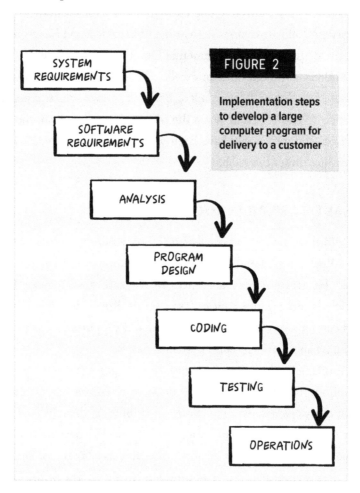

At first glance, it seems as though Royce endorses this new way of approaching software development. He even introduces the diagram as

33  Winston W Royce, "Managing the Development of Large Software Systems" (lecture, Institute of Electrical and Electronics Engineers WESCon, Los Angeles, CA, August 1970), 1–9, https://typeset.io/papers/managing-the-development-of-large-software-systems-zl45s18on/.

such: "A more grandiose approach to software development is illustrated in figure 2."[34]

But on *the very same page*, Royce condemns this approach:

> I believe in this concept, but the implementation described above is risky and invites failure. ... If these phenomena fail to satisfy the various external constraints, then invariably a major redesign is required. A simple octal patch or redo of some isolated code will not fix these kinds of difficulties. The required design changes are likely to be so disruptive that the software requirements upon which the design is based, and which provides the rationale for everything, are violated. Either the requirements must be modified or a substantial change in the design is required. In effect the development process has returned to the origin, and one can expect up to a 100% overrun in schedule and/or costs.[35]

That's not a positive take at all:

"Risky."

"Invites failure."

"Invariably a major redesign is required."

*"So disruptive that the design and rationale for everything are violated."*

In other words, Winston Royce used his figure 2 as a cautionary tale of what *not* to do. Several pages after that diagram, he explicitly said that such a diagram does not take iteration into account and that customer feedback is necessary before moving forward. He went on to introduce improved versions of the diagram above to introduce iteration and frequent customer feedback. Most notably, figure 7, which is eerily prescient of iterative methodologies:[36]

34    Royce, "Managing the Development of Large Software Systems," 2.
35    Royce, "Managing the Development of Large Software Systems," 2.
36    Royce, "Managing the Development of Large Software Systems," 7.

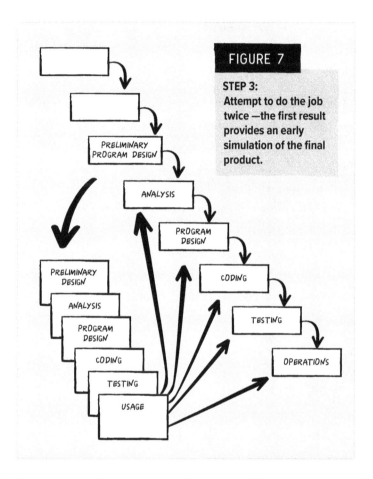

FIGURE 7

STEP 3:
Attempt to do the job twice —the first result provides an early simulation of the final product.

As for contracts, Royce was equally critical: "For some reason what a software design is going to do is subject to wide interpretation even after previous agreement. It is important to involve the customer in a formal way so that he has committed himself at earlier points before final delivery. To give the contractor free rein between requirement definition and operation is inviting trouble."[37]

All of these condemnations come later in the paper, though. Reading just the first page of "Managing the Development of Large Software Systems,"

37    Royce, "Managing the Development of Large Software Systems," 8.

you could be forgiven for thinking Royce is endorsing the monolithic, grandiose process introduced in his figure 2.

Hold on a second. Could you?

Could you be forgiven for thinking Royce is endorsing the monolithic, grandiose process introduced in his figure 2?

Let's find out how forgiving we want to be.

## THE LEVEE BREAKS

Six years after Royce published his visionary paper, T. E. Bell and T. A. Thayer wrote a paper called "Software Requirements: Are They Really a Problem?" for TRW Defense and Space Systems Group. Let's take a look at where the term "waterfall" actually came from:

> The evolution of approaches for the development of software systems has generally paralleled the evolution of ideas for the implementation of code. Over the last ten years more structure and discipline have been adopted, and practitioners have concluded that a top-down approach is superior to the bottom-up approach of the past. The Military Standard set MIL-STD 490/483 recognized this newer approach by specifying a system requirements document, a "design-to" requirements document that is created in response to the system requirements, and then a "code-to" requirements document for each software module in the design. Each of these is at a lower level of detail than the former, so the system developers are led through a top-down process. The same top-down approach to a series of requirements statements is explained, without the specialized military jargon, in an excellent paper by Royce [5]; he introduced the concept of the "*waterfall*" of

development activities. In this approach software is developed in the disciplined sequence of activities shown in Figure I.[38]

This is the first use of the term "waterfall," in reference to Royce's Figure 2. Note that the Bell and Thayer paper *unironically refers to the waterfall as a recommended top-down approach*. They go on to include this troubling diagram introducing a "disciplined sequence of activities." To add insult to injury, they imply that Royce pioneered them:

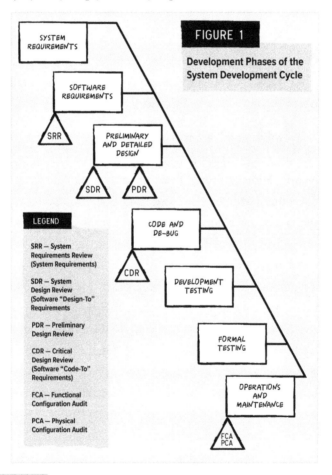

**FIGURE 1**

**Development Phases of the System Development Cycle**

---

38    T. E. Bell and T. A. Thayer, "Software Requirements: Are They Really a Problem?" (proceedings of the second International Conference on Software Engineering, October 1976), https://dl.acm.org/doi/10.5555/800253.807650. Emphasis mine.

Note in particular that Royce's actual suggestions of iteration and tight customer collaboration—doing everything twice in miniature—have been replaced by a series of gatekeeping reviews before moving on to the next waterfall phase:

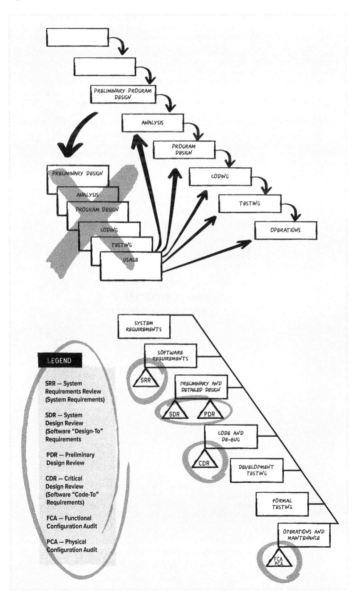

Now let's fast-forward to 1985. The Department of Defense (DOD) wanted a standard operating procedure for software development. Pause and think about that statement for a second: *one* standard procedure for *all* software development, no matter the scale, domain, requirements, team size, etc. That in and of itself is already disturbing.

They implemented DOD-STD-2167, which was widely adopted worldwide as DOD-STD-2167A in 1988, and introduced it with this: "This standard contains requirements for the development of mission-critical computer system software. It establishes a uniform software development process which is applicable throughout the system life cycle."[39]

DOD-STD-2167

4 JUNE 1985

SUPERSEDING
DOD-STD-1679A (NAVY)
22 OCTOBER 1983
MIL-STD-1644B (TD)
2 MARCH 1984

## MILITARY STANDARD

### DEFENSE SYSTEM
### SOFTWARE DEVELOPMENT

AMSC NO. N3806                                    AREA MCCR

DISTRIBUTION STATEMENT A.  Approved for public release; distribution is unlimited.

---

39    "DOD-STD-2167A: Military Standard Defense System Software Development," U.S. Department of Defense, June 4, 1985, iii/iv. https://www.product-lifecycle-management.com/download/DOD-STD-2167A.pdf.

Unfortunately, this new standard, the operating procedure for all DOD software development, was based on the first page of Royce's paper—the part where he describes what *not* to do. The uncredited authors who cribbed "Managing the Development of Large Software Systems" to write DOD-STD-2167 completely ignore or misquote the rest of the paper, which talks about iteration, customer involvement, and other forward-thinking ideas.

It's like a scene from *Raiders of the Lost Ark*. When trying to locate the Ark of the Covenant, the bad guys use a copy of the medallion to find the Well of Souls on the map—except they only use one side of the medallion's runes. Had they read the other side too, they would have used the right approach and located the correct point on the map. Instead, they based their entire archaeological infrastructure on a misinterpretation.

DOD-STD-2167 seems fine at first glance. Royce's ideas are definitely mentioned. For example, this line is quite promising: "This standard is intended to be dynamic and responsive to the rapidly evolving software technology field. As such, this standard should be selectively applied and tailored to fit the unique characteristics of each software acquisition program."[40]

That is, it's promising until you realize how such tailoring needs to take place. To deviate from the approach, one merely needs to send a self-addressed, stamped envelope to the commander of Space and Naval Warfare Systems Command: "Beneficial comments (recommendations, additions, deletions) and any pertinent data which may be of use in improving this document should be addressed to: COMMANDER, Space and Naval Warfare Systems Command, ATTN: SPAWAR 8111, Washington, D.C. 20363-5100, by using the self-addressed Standardization Document Improvement Proposal (DD Form 1426) appearing at the end of this document or by letter."[41]

Even more promising is this mandate: "Software development is usually an iterative process, in which an iteration of the software development life

---

40   "DOD-STD-2167A," U.S. Department of Defense, iii/iv.
41   "DOD-STD-2167A," U.S. Department of Defense, ii.

cycle occurs one or more times during each of the system life cycle phases (Figure 1). Appendix B describes a typical system life cycle, the activities that take place during each iteration of software development, and the documentation which typically exists at the beginning of an iteration in any given system life cycle phase. The requirements of this standard shall be applied to each iteration, as described below."[42]

And then Appendix B introduces the process the world would come to know as the waterfall. See if the diagram on the next page looks familiar.[43]

The rest of Appendix B is a very detailed explanation of how to complete the sequential, monolithic steps Royce explicitly railed against in "Managing the Development of Large Software Systems." There is *no mention* of the iterative process teased in the specification's introduction. Indeed, there is no incorporation of any of Royce's actual recommendations at all.

As Indiana Jones and Sallah would say: "They're digging in the wrong place!"[44]

Now, almost 40 years since DOD-STD-2167A was released, we are left with the aftermath. The aftermath of a visionary systems engineer who set up the waterfall as a grandiose strawman, then advocated for iteration, tight customer collaboration, and adapting to change. He railed against contracts and monolithic processes. He was then misquoted into a U.S. Department of Defense–mandated standard operating procedure that explicitly ignored those concerns and instead mandated a monolithic, inflexible, sequential process with added mandatory overhead at each step.

In the first chapter of his book *Real-World Maintainable Software* (appropriately titled "How Did We Get into This Mess?") Abraham Marín-Pérez comes to similar conclusions:

---

42    "DOD-STD-2167A," U.S. Department of Defense, 1.
43    "DOD-STD-2167A," U.S. Department of Defense, 2.
44    *Raiders of the Lost Ark*, directed by Steven Spielberg (1981; Hollywood, CA: Paramount Pictures).

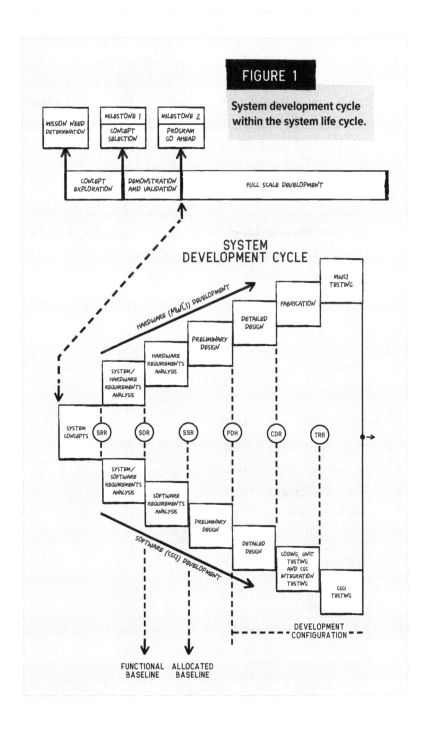

FIGURE 1

System development cycle within the system life cycle.

However, in what may be a prophecy of the hunger for quick wins that would come to plague the software development industry, the early adopters of the Waterfall Model failed to properly read Royce's paper. Even though he described the Waterfall Model as the ideal way to build software, he also said that "the implementation described above is risky and invites failure." He then went on for several pages explaining the risks and downsides of his model, concluding that the only way to make it work is to run the same project at least twice so that subsequent implementations can learn from the mistakes of the previous ones. And so it happened that software projects across the board consistently failed to meet expectations for decades.[45]

You might be thinking, so what? So what if the DOD spec was erroneously based? These kinds of things sort themselves out ... right?

Well, software development was in its infancy in 1983. None of the following existed:

- Microsoft Windows, MacOS, or Linux
- Python, Java, Visual Basic, R, Perl, Ruby, or JavaScript
- Structured Query Language (SQL)
- Cisco, SAS, Amazon, Accenture, Salesforce, Adobe, VM-Ware, or Intuit
- The internet
- Cell phones
- Mobile apps
- Cryptocurrency
- Artificial intelligence (except for very specialized applications)

---

45  Abraham Márin-Pérez, *Real-World Maintainable Software* (O'Reilly Media, Inc., 2016), https://www.oreilly.com/library/view/real-world-maintainable-software/9781492042853/ch01.html.

Forty years in the lifetime of one person is a long stretch of time. But forty years across the entire discipline of computer engineering is logarithmically more influential. Millions upon millions of people have learned and shared knowledge over four decades, as the young discipline of software development matured into the AI-driven, networked, global juggernaut it is today.

When the DOD dropped the mic with DOD-STD-2167A, it had immense impact. Every military software project used it. So every government contractor did as well. Every private industry that used any people who'd touched DOD-STD-2167A adopted it too, either explicitly or through implication. The talent pool was smaller then, so crossover was a high probability. The waterfall was taught at every university—even in high schools and middle schools. I can personally attest that even some elementary schools taught these basic steps with the advent of the LOGO programming language aimed at fourth graders. Every book, magazine, or computer user group assumed you knew what the waterfall was. By the mid-1990s, the next generation of project managers and programmers grew up learning a process they had no way to know was based on a grandiose strawman.

## AGILE DIDN'T DO ITSELF ANY FAVORS EITHER

Given the intensity of the ever-changing software development landscape in the late '80s and early '90s, that DOD standard carved into stone a misguided approach that trickled down from the military into the private sector, consulting, and college textbooks, dominating the conversation for decades thereafter. And why not? Breaking the software development systems' life cycle down into distinct phases seems logical enough on the surface.

But something deeply broken lurked in the depths of DOD-STD-2167A. People spent years putting all kinds of scaffolding in place to make it work better. That scaffolding rarely incorporated iterative processes. It usually included some form of tighter and more rigid prediction or scheduling of each step to give it the best chance of success moving forward.

In the meantime, four groups emerged:

- People who adopted the waterfall whole hog (the majority)
- People who adopted it but realized it wasn't quite right and tried to change it
- People who realized it was completely wrong and did something else
- People who have used the chaos to push their own agendas

Few of those people trusted the other people, and thought their own approach was correct.

Well, three of those types of people were involved in forming the agile movement. Somewhere around the year 2000, tensions against the waterfall methodology came to a head. A small minority of people, myself included, had been meeting in chat rooms and starting to voice an ever more coherent objection to traditional management processes. For my part, I met online with Scott Ambler, Kent Beck, and Ron Jeffries to talk about ideas. I read a lot of Martin Fowler's work, as well as Grady Booch's and Jim Highsmith's. They influenced the conceptual model I developed as part of my master's thesis work, which was the precursor to this book. I went around the country presenting that model to PMI chapters.

There was fervent disagreement among the different groups of "light-weight practitioners," as we called ourselves then, and we were deeply misunderstood by our management. In his book *Wild West to Agile*, Jim Highsmith names this the Rogue Teams period of 2001–2004.[46] (Although I'm proud to say my team was doing this in 1997, so I hope that makes us part of Rogue Team One?) Various lightweight practitioners tried to meet, but due to clashing personalities or lack of alignment, nothing much happened.

---

46   Jim Highsmith, *Wild West to Agile: Adventures in Software Development Evolution and Revolution* (Addison-Wesley Professional, 2003), 149.

Then in 2001, 17 people met at a ski resort to talk about the problem at a deeper level. As the gathering proceeded, the attendees started organically writing down their areas of core agreement. By the end, they realized they had drafted the "Manifesto for Agile Software Development." I asked Jon Kern about it and he put it like this: "I do not recall any explicit tasking of ourselves to come out with something tangible. I have heard Uncle Bob may have thought we could produce a manifesto of sorts, but I am not sure. I would consider it a nice outcome that we came up with some common values across our collective selves. Putting it on the nascent web was almost an afterthought."[47]

Afterthought or no, the ideas in that document caught on like wildfire. The concepts are truly foundational—but infinitely flexible. And they didn't form a cohesive, implementable methodology. The people in that room preferred to set the stage and let the software teams decide for themselves what to do.

You know what is a cohesive, implementable methodology? Scrum. A scrum is a group of burly, aggressive people charging down a rugby field and trampling anything in their wake. And that's just what scrum did.

I love scrum and still use many of its ideas. But there is no arguing that scrum has a distinct, prescriptive approach that didn't rub everyone the right way. It became the de facto face of agile—arguably not the most representative face. For better or worse, Jeff Sutherland found himself in the center of a lot of crosshairs. Today, scrum continues to be highly divisive in terms of its agility or lack thereof.

As someone who was involved back then, and looking back on things now, I believe there is a hidden factor that set agile back even further from the starting gate, which is the grandiose "strawman-to-DOD-STD-2167" snafu I described in the previous chapter. The manifesto authors were working within the confines of that misattribution, as we all were, which Jim describes in his book *Wild West to Agile*: "A 1970 paper by Winston

47    Jon Kern, personal communication, October 22, 2023.

Royce was credited with starting the 'waterfall' trend. In fact, Royce was an advocate of iterative development for anything more than simple projects. Royce recommended a type of iterative model but given the serial 'hardware' mindset of the time, it's easy to see how his serial waterfall diagram took hold even though he explained its dangers in the text."[48]

I asked Jim Highsmith recently if Royce's intended recommendations were incorporated into the Agile Manifesto. He replied:

> I knew about the Royce paper and that it was one of the threads resulting in the waterfall approach, but I don't think his paper had much influence. ...
>
> As Larry Constantine commented—"Ed [Yourdon] and I conceived that model as a form of 'training wheels' but it took off with management." I queried Larry about the concurrent thinking about waterfall lifecycles, but he was not aware of Royce's paper. Since waterfall-like stages were becoming widely used in management practices at the time, their growing use in software development wasn't surprising. It's also interesting that Larry and Ed considered waterfall "training wheels" for budding software developers and not for use in serious projects.[49]

In other words, at least according to Jim's recollection above, Royce was on the radar as someone being attributed to the waterfall but not as a primary source. Jon Kern supported that sentiment as well, confirming that he learned of the actual origins of the waterfall later: "I learned about the IEE paper when [Winston Royce's son Walker Royce] asked me to review his book. And when I read it I was stunned. Feedback loops (eddy currents?) were written about."[50]

---

48   Jim Highsmith, *Wild West to Agile*, 72.
49   Jim Highsmith, personal communication, March 8, 2023.
50   Jon Kern, personal communication, October 22, 2023.

The manifesto authors definitely were reacting to the waterfall, however. Jon Kern explicitly says as much in "Ten Years of Agile: An Interview with Jon Kern": "My recollection was that heavy-weight processes—like RUP and MIL-STD 2167—were more commonplace than I liked. The massive rigor of RUP especially rubbed me the wrong way—and, at TogetherSoft, we were always going head-to-head (and frequently winning) against Rational. But Rational was a huge marketing machine, and people were fawning all over the heavyweight process CDs. UGH."[51]

If you want to read a takedown of the failings of agile, try "The Age of Agile Must End" by Michael Burnett.[52] I don't agree with everything in that article, but it's a rebuttal of the agile movement that is a representative example of the common accusations levied against the approach.

Meanwhile, the vacuum of "Hey, wait a minute—there's no methodology in this here manifesto" started being filled by consultants who had nothing to do with the Agile Manifesto. Pseudoframeworks and certifications took prominence. Few of them actually helped organizations become agile. Some did.

Recently, pseudoframeworks and certifications have devolved even further into a parody of hand-waving and cursory three-hour tours, with graduates proclaiming themselves experts by the time their coconut daiquiris reach room temperature. It has become truly comical. But this parody is sad as well, because good ideas are being cheapened.

## WE ARE IN AN ALTERNATE TIMELINE

As of the writing of this book, everyone from agile detractors to manifesto authors are recognizing that agile hasn't had the saturation it needs to truly transform processes. There's a perception among some that the emperor

---

51    Jon Kern, "Ten Years of Agile: An Interview with Jon Kern," informIT, August 3, 2011, https://www.informit.com/articles/article.aspx?p=1739476.

52    Michael Burnett, "The Age of Agile Must End," UX Collective (blog), February 12, 2023, https://uxdesign.cc/the-age-of-agile-must-end-bc89c0f084b7.

has no clothes.

There's also the tragic irony that agile could be interpreted as railing against a monolithic, predictive process that never should have existed in the first place. The entire debate is a sideshow.

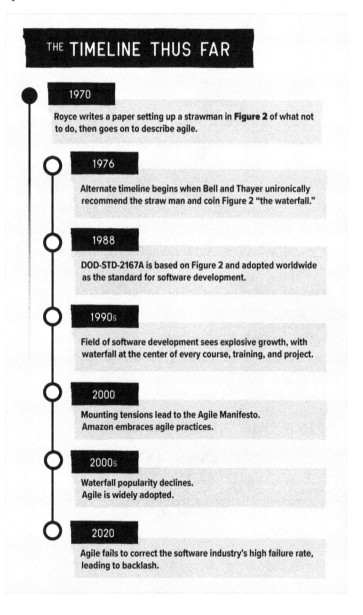

THE **TIMELINE THUS FAR**

**1970**
Royce writes a paper setting up a strawman in **Figure 2** of what not to do, then goes on to describe agile.

**1976**
Alternate timeline begins when Bell and Thayer unironically recommend the straw man and coin Figure 2 "the waterfall."

**1988**
DOD-STD-2167A is based on Figure 2 and adopted worldwide as the standard for software development.

**1990s**
Field of software development sees explosive growth, with waterfall at the center of every course, training, and project.

**2000**
Mounting tensions lead to the Agile Manifesto.
Amazon embraces agile practices.

**2000s**
Waterfall popularity declines.
Agile is widely adopted.

**2020**
Agile fails to correct the software industry's high failure rate, leading to backlash.

And now here we are. We don't know what our present situation would have been had Royce's actual recommendations been incorporated from the beginning by the DOD spec. There are processes, attitudes, and protocols that have been erroneously baked into software development since its infancy, for four decades, which color every aspect of our profession. We don't even know what we don't know. We can't see how far-reaching these misunderstandings have gone. We lack perspective because we are right in the middle of the bear trap.

We need to fix this, starting right now. And we can. It's freeing to realize that we need to reframe our entire approach to iterative development.

## THE BUZZ IS OUT OF HAND…LET'S GET OUR TERMS STRAIGHT

Part of the reason I wrote this book is because there's so much methodological terminology out there, so many agendas and misconceptions, that it's hard to keep it all straight. So let's take a moment to establish some terms.

The first, and probably most important, term to define is "agile."

Agile is a philosophy that was codified in the Agile Manifesto. It's a set of core values and practices that will lead an organization toward being iterative and light on its feet. Agile is not a framework, a methodology, or even a unified approach. So there is a lot of leeway for frameworks, methodologies, or approaches to label themselves as agile—perhaps in an attempt to lure your dollars.

A methodology is a suite of defined practices, steps, tools, inputs, and outputs. A methodology tells you what to do. It's very opinionated. It can be self-created or learned from others.

A framework is a published, endorsed methodology that has been widely disseminated to the field as a whole, with one key difference: a framework is meant to be modified to suit your specific use case. Scrum and SAFe™ are examples. You can pick up a book about scrum, and by the end, you will have more or less the same understanding of scrum as someone across the world will.

But scrum is highly structured, so some people argue it is not a true framework, but a methodology. You might be asking yourself, Why are those distinctions critical? Who cares?

Those terms are important to me, but not nearly as important as the illusion of authority that often accompanies them. If someone tells you XYZ is "the way to do agile," then there's already a big problem. No one but you can tell you the way to do agile. "Agility" by definition "involves flexible processes, rapid decision-making and a culture that embraces change and innovation."[53] An organization with a mature agile implementation most likely has a custom *methodology* loosely based on a *framework* that takes an *agile approach*.

So much for agile. What about traditional? I will often refer to the waterfall in this book. I'll also mention predictive approaches or traditional engineering practices. Those terms are all shorthand for processes ingrained into management culture, possibly erroneously, that you should back far away from and take a hard look at. It's definitely an oversimplification. There are many nonagile approaches that have nothing to do with the waterfall, just as there are many nonwaterfall approaches that have nothing to do with agile.

Based on the widespread permeation of the term "waterfall," I think that the better distinction is *adaptive vs. predictive*. However, the methodology did proceed under the title "waterfall." The term itself is widely used and understood, for better or worse. Moving forward, whenever I reference the waterfall, please keep in mind its mythical origins.

Ultimately, the label attached to your process doesn't matter. What matters in this book is figuring out how iterative development projects behave and whether your process accounts for it.

---

53    Oliver Kuttruff, "The Definition of Business Agility and How to Put It into Practice," *Workpath Magazine*, November 16, 2023, https://www.workpath.com/magazine/agility-definition.

This book often uses the term "project manager." Some agile frameworks have no project manager. Those activities fall partially under a scrum master or product owner, or they may even be completely undefined. In my experience, practically speaking, there is someone on the team who would identify themselves as a project manager. If that term does not fit your team, then replace it with anyone who has some autonomy for directing the project and needs to communicate status/requirements/priorities back and forth from the project team to the rest of the enterprise.

That said, allow me to tell you ...

# CHAPTER 8

# A TALE OF TWO PROJECTS

Imagine you are an executive overseeing two projects with equal staff and equal budgets. The goals of the projects are identical. The customer is in-house. You trust your development staff because they have proven reliable in the past, but the problem this time is one that your company hasn't faced before. The business requirements are somewhat clear, and you know on which platform you will implement.

The project manager of the first project has done much preparation. He has provided you with detailed road maps for each phase of the project and allocated his resources accordingly. There is a solid timeline with phases broken down into weeklong time boxes. The developers follow a clearly defined methodology:

- Perform analysis and document the findings
- Design the system into specs
- Code the system
- Test the system
- Implement the system before the delivery date

There is a teamwide meeting and a status report generated before each phase begins so that everyone is on the same page. When customers need to be consulted, meetings are scheduled in advance and agendas drawn up so that the customer knows what will be covered. The first week of the project, the team has already produced a software specification.

The project manager of the second project has a pretty good idea of what her team will be doing in the next couple weeks but is vague about anything thereafter. You have asked for some indication of scheduling or resource allocation, but she says she has no idea what her team members are doing at any given time. Furthermore, she requests you stop asking her for schedule updates because it's getting annoying. The team is one-third of the way into the project and hasn't produced a single working piece of software. When customers need to be consulted, developers call up at the last minute and ask if they can meet that afternoon because they still need to analyze part of the system. Your customers are calling you in a panic wondering why such simple questions are only now coming up. There is no clear documentation of how the team plans to develop the software, just a partial list of features they plan to implement. You get concerned and call a meeting to discuss the status of the project, only to find that there is no work breakdown structure, resource allocation chart, or project timeline.

Which one is the better project? These are admittedly arbitrary examples, but according to the blur box conceptual model, the second project is on the right track—by a landslide.

One possible subtitle for the blur box model is "why we need a new business culture." This model is an attempt to describe why it's impossible to apply traditionally successful management strategies to iterative projects.

Iteration occurs any time a team revisits a design or plan in light of new information. The essence of the blur box model is this: the development process is inherently iterative and therefore changes rapidly. It looks like chaos or anarchy, and the very act of measuring it slows it down. But it's not chaos, and if you know how things work, you can better manage it.

The problem is that your instincts and training are working against you.

# CHAPTER 9

# WHAT IS THE BLUR BOX, AND WHY SHOULD YOU CARE?

As you've seen above, both waterfall and agile, the two most popular approaches to software development, were influenced by a horrible misinterpretation in 1976. It led us to where we are: a cultural and political environment within information technology that considers predictive methods to be not only wise and effective, but necessary—and mandatory. Some-

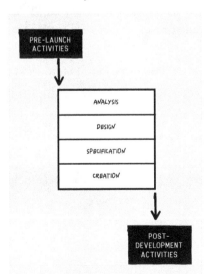

times, that is the case. Sometimes, it is not. The problem is, the expectation that prediction and control are "right" is so deeply ingrained that most people don't even question it. Very few managers, for example, will agree that their project failed because they insisted on setting deadlines in advance. People just don't question those sorts of things.

They really, *really* should.

So the blur box model was created as an explicit takedown of why predictive methods often fail against an iterative process. This model is meant to highlight common cultural assumptions, put them in the context of an agile approach, and reveal the poor outcomes that might ensue. It is my best effort to tear down a predictive mentality as thoroughly as possible. I hope to convince you that every assumption you've ever been taught is either highly situational, inherently flawed, or at the very least up for discussion. Nothing is off the table. Neither time, space, schedule, reporting, team structure, nor anything else your organization assumes is necessary. Any of it can be questioned—and *should* be questioned.

By the end of learning this model, you very well might decide to retain some predictive techniques in your software development process. But I will have thoroughly failed if you don't recognize that each predictive effort you make has a cost, sometimes a significant cost, that demands a conscious trade-off. I will have failed if, by the end of learning about the blur box, you are unwilling to cast the blame for failure just as squarely on work breakdown structures as you are for implementing "risky" lean methods such as work-in-progress limits.

If you walk away from the blur box as convinced as ever that up-front effort like making road maps is more valuable than adapting to new information as it arises, then I have utterly failed to make a critical point that your success hinges on.

If you walk away believing that there is anything sacred in your development process that cannot be examined, iterated, tweaked, or disposed of—no matter how fundamental you assumed it was before I discussed the blur box—then I fear you will be walking into a failed software development process.

This diagram depicts the basic structure of the blur box. The prelaunch phase contains all of the pretechnical elements, such as these:

- Requirements gathering
- Delimiting the scope

- Budgeting
- Hiring personnel
- Defining roles and responsibilities

Those tasks are not inherently iterative, and traditional management practices can manage them perfectly well. The same goes for postdevelopment tasks, like these:

- System testing
- User acceptance testing
- Implementation

I have to draw a box somewhere for the purposes of discussion. I've picked what I feel is the most inherently iterative part of the software development life cycle. Neither prelaunch nor postdevelopment activities are the focus of this model. This delineation is a simple representation of a complex organizational phenomenon known as hybrid agile. It's too early to go into this now since I haven't even discussed the model yet. I'll say more in part 2 in the section "Know Where to Draw the Line." For now, I wanted you to be aware of the term "hybrid agile" and recognize that there are different approaches for where to distinguish between predictive and agile approaches within your organization.

That leaves the middle part, which has four phases that are vague remnants of the waterfall methodology. I am going to describe these phases below, but their exact definition is not important. What is important is for you to determine which types of effort fall inside of the blur box and which types don't.

**Analysis:** communication with the customers about the system and their needs. This is when you ask questions, rule out exceptions, teach, learn, and listen until you understand the problem and potential solutions.

**Design:** nontechnical design about how the system will function. This could be as simple as squiggles on a whiteboard or as complicated as a fully functional simulated environment. Mock-ups, wireframes, and other artifacts are usually created in the design phase.

**Specification:** conversion of the general design into something technical that a programmer can use to write the code. This could look like user stories, technical specifications, pseudocode, or whatever the dev team needs to do to adequately explain to themselves the agreed-upon technical solution.

**Creation:** Actual work on the system. In this book I'm primarily discussing iterative software development, so "creation" means programmers writing code to produce software. I may often refer to "creation" as "development" because that's mostly what this book is about. But creation can also apply to nonsoftware efforts. For example, if we were discussing business process redesign, creation could refer to the creation of new business practices. If we were discussing a data integration process improvement, creation could refer to the creation of new database schemas, query optimizations, etc. I'm making this point now because there will be a time coming up when it's important to recognize that software development often exists next to processes like devops and business process redesign.

Those four phases mostly follow a temporal timeline. You can't create something before you've learned what you're supposed to create. You can't write a specification if there is no design in hand. So, *generally speaking*, there is a time flow through the model that looks like this:

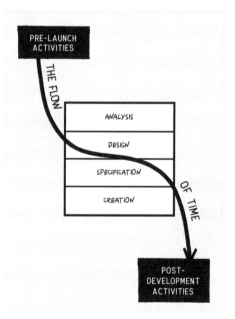

CHAPTER 10

# "EXCEPT": THE WORD
# THAT SHATTERS YOUR WORLD

I just italicized something important a second ago: *generally speaking*. We all know that things don't always follow neat patterns, and there's an exception for everything.

In programming, there's a term called exception handling. It's where the normal code bumps into an error or unexpected input—a.k.a., exception—which must be handled. Otherwise, the computer will just stare at you and sit there like a crystallized lump of sand—because that's what a computer is.

Coding for error handling and testing for these unexpected results takes a lot of time. We developers prefer not to be surprised by exceptions. We prefer to develop systems that are flexible enough to account for them.

Let's say you've asked the software team to build a coffee mug. This coffee mug metaphor I'm about to spin isn't amazing, but I need a visual of something with a handle to represent exception handling. And hey! Coffee.

Whenever we're in requirements-gathering sessions with the customers, we listen for danger words such as "always," "never," and "except," like in this example:

"We *always* get the data from Stan on Tuesday and pour it into the coffee mug. His hands are medium size. So we only need a medium-size handle. We *never* enter data on Wednesday because it would throw off the numbers. And the Wednesday guy's hands are too big to fit the coffee mug handle."

Now as a developer, my BS radar is beeping hard. What if Stan is sick? What if it's a holiday week? What if the tracking system goes down? Who is "the Wednesday guy?" So my team and I will do our best to shake this flimsy story and get to the real facts.

But eventually, once we've exhausted our best good cop/bad cop routines and used up our spotlight-in-the-eyeball trick, and the customer sticks to their alibi, we have no choice but to code to those parameters and make a coffee mug with one medium sized handle.

It's bad software design to code an inflexible system. But it's bad resource management to code a superflexible system when 10 out of 10 customers swear it will only be used on Tuesday by one guy. We have to make a call. And as much as we distrust this situation, we have no hard evidence, so we code for the medium-handle coffee mug.

A month later, we're in another meeting. But this time Brenda Sue, who was on vacation when we did requirements gathering, perks up in the back.

"Yeah, we always get the data from Stan on Tuesday. *Except* at the end of the quarter, when it comes on Wednesday."

EXCEPT.

*Except.*

Now we have an exception to handle.

But I'm not talking about exception handling like programmers do—although that will almost certainly be involved. I'm talking about something far worse.

You managers and customers thought we developers were building a coffee mug for you. In the course of our meetings, you've given us the basic size and shape of that coffee mug. And it's almost done. We fired up the kiln, and the ceramic is baking in there. You've even started cheating a little bit. Somewhere down the line, water is already heating up, and someone is grinding coffee. Own up to it, now. You know you told the coffee-brewing people that the developers almost have the mug ready.

With this new information that has come to light, you probably think we'll need to make the handle a little bigger to accommodate Stan's and the Wednesday guy's hands. Just a little tweak to make the handle a little bigger—it's the same basic idea as before, right?

But we developers have already picked up that coffee mug we were building and smashed it against the wall. There's broken pottery and coffee everywhere.

The existence of multiple data entry days now means a calendaring system. The existence of multiple people, Stan and the Wednesday guy, means a user login and tracking system. We need a Handle Resizer 3000 app. We need the concept of a weekly "normal" case and a quarterly case. That almost certainly suggests annual exceptions as well, which we have yet to discover.

Now we have to design normal coffee mugs and end-of-quarter coffee urns. We need a commercial kitchen instead of a breakfast nook because of universal building code ordinance 321 subsection 42. We need to account for quarterly coffee streams that you never see, that have only been revealed by your offhand comment, "except." We have to write two front ends and merge them together into the illusion of one coffee mug—with one dynamically shaped handle on it.

And now you're looking at us developers as if we're fools because we're telling you this project is now 18 months behind and we're going to need two additional developers, food service hair nets, and a city building inspector.

That's an exception handle. It's an alteration, seemingly minor, that actually reveals a monumental shift in the entire bedrock of the project. Now you know what I mean when I say:

 # EXCEPT...

The blur box has *a lot* of exceptions.

OK, where are we now? We have our two hypothetical projects equally staffed. One is following a predictive engineering management approach, and one is an agile, adaptive process. We have the basic outline of a blur box conceptual model with prelaunch and postdevelopment efforts that are not the focus of this model. And finally we have four phases of effort that we generally expect to go in order but with some exceptions along the way.

That brings us to the final key concept before we kick off the fun.

# CHAPTER 11

# THREADS OF WORK:
# THE STUFF YOU ARE PROBABLY
# MANAGING RIGHT NOW

A thread of work is a concerted effort by multiple people that is somewhat autonomous from the rest of the enterprise.[54] The simplest example is software development. Other examples are business process redesign, devops, or operational data storage. All of those things are related to each other but are generally independent. You can do devops work even if the operational data storage is not yet complete. Business process redesign can occur even if the software is not written yet.

A thread of work is not a task: Threads of work have tasks. A thread also differs from a subproject in that it does not imply dedicated resources. Anyone on the team may hop over as needed from developing software to redesigning business processes or devops. (This is assuming you have cross-functional teams, which is one of the prerequisites of iterative development.)

---

54 Gary Yates, personal communication, 1997.

The image below depicts several threads moving through the project: business process redesign, software development, and devops. According to this model, all three of these processes are threads because they move back and forth between analysis, design, specification, and creation on their way to postdevelopment activities. Each of these threads has different tasks to be accomplished by different people, who may or may not be involved with another thread.

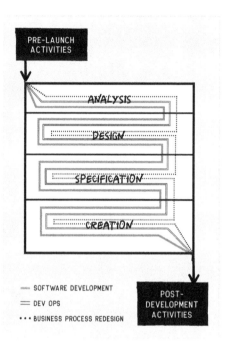

OK, who's ready for our first "except"?

Except…phases don't really work that way. You don't do 100% of the analysis up front, and end up with 100% of the creation at the end. So let's tilt those phases a bit.[55]

One of the biggest criticisms of the waterfall methodology is that you cannot realistically analyze and specify a system at the beginning, then assume that the software team can just work in a vacuum against that specification. You can't expect the specification to be adequate. There will be questions and revisited designs, which change the spec. So a waterfall-y way

---

55    Gary Yates, personal communication, 1997.

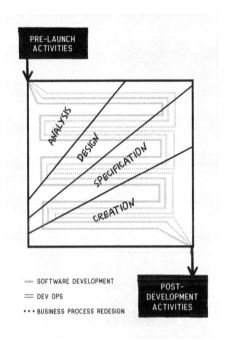

to handle that is maybe business analysts who go ask customers more questions. Or you could track revisions to the specs.

Waterfall-y ... hmm ... water folly? Perfect.

The blur box phases are now skewed. How does that change our thread of work? Well, we no longer spend the first third of the project timeline locked in analysis and design, the middle third in specification, and the final third in creation. Instead, there's a little of each phase all throughout the project.

As a thread moves through the project timeline, the time spent in analysis decreases while the time spent in creation increases. The model depicts this with the wedge shapes of the phases.

This next image breaks the blur box down into thirds to depict the rough proportions of time spent in each phase as the project moves along. There is not a direct time correlation, but the top third reveals that there is very little time spent in development. The middle third has all four phases in roughly equivalent portions. Development dominates the bottom third, although some analysis can still occur even at this late stage; at any time a person or group of people can revisit design or analysis if it makes sense to do so for their part of the thread.

Let's pretend your overall timeline is one year. This image more realistically depicts the breakdown of time spent in each phase. Obviously the numbers are not exact. It's just a more realistic distribution of effort than 100% → 100% → 100% → 100% → boom! The project is done.

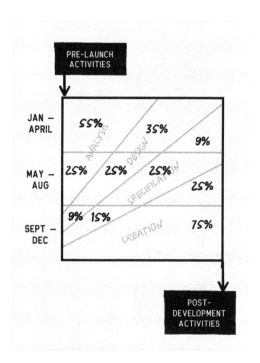

 **EXCEPT...**

Except…tracking what percentage of time anybody spent in any phase is a trap. That's the same kind of thinking that leads to resource optimization or utilization.

It really seems as if resource utilization improvement is a good idea. I am 100% with you. If you interviewed a thousand people, probably 999 of them would say, as a manager, it's a good idea to figure out what your people are doing and try to optimize that effort. It just makes sense.

But in an iterative process, if you are trying to think of ways to optimize how your people are spending their time, there is a high probability that those ways will backfire. And when I say "backfire," I mean "possibly spring the bear trap and kill the entire project."

Don't believe me? Then you likely haven't heard of Tim Mackinnon, who Dan North calls out as "The Worst Programmer I Know."[56] This post is only a couple months old as of the time of this writing. But I hope it blows up and becomes a legend whispered in the hallowed halls of every training venue from now until the distant future, when the idea of evaluating individual efforts vs. team efforts dies in the illuminating flames of enlightenment.

I don't want to steal too much of Dan's spotlight on this; you simply must take four minutes out of your life and read the entire post. I'll just say that measuring individual developer productivity is a surefire way to capsize your improvement efforts, while giving Wally the means to write himself a new minivan:

> Instead we would measure stories delivered, or it may have been story points (it turns out it doesn't matter), because these represented business value. We were using something like Jira, and people would put their name against stories, which made it super easy to generate these productivity metrics.
>
> Which brings me to Tim. Tim's score was consistently zero. Zero! Not just low, or trending downwards, but literally zero. Week after week, iteration after iteration. Zero points for Tim.
>
> Well Tim clearly had to go. This was the manager's conclusion, and he asked me to make the necessary arrangements to have Tim removed and replaced by someone who actually delivered, you know, stories.
>
> And I flatly refused. It wasn't even a hard decision for me, I just said no.

---

56  Dan North, "The Worst Programmer I Know," Dan North & Associates Limited, September 2, 2023, https://dannorth.net/the-worst-programmer/.

You see, the reason that Tim's productivity score was zero, was that **he never signed up for any stories**. Instead he would spend his day pairing with different teammates. With less experienced developers he would patiently let them drive whilst nudging them towards a solution. He would not crowd them or railroad them, but let them take the time to learn whilst carefully crafting moments of insight and learning, often as Socratic questions, what ifs, how elses.[57]

The good news is, there are definitely management strategies to improve the output of the team, which I'll cover in parts 2 and 3.

Now our threads of work are moving through the timeline in a more realistic way, like so:

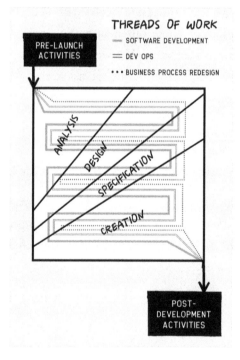

OK, *now* we're getting somewhere.

---

57    Dan North, "The Worst Programmer I Know."

# EXCEPT...

Except…threads of work don't work like that. Don't get too attached to the notion that threads follow a noticeable pattern. Threads do wildly unpredictable things.

Much like it's vaguely ridiculous to write a software spec when no design exists yet, it's also vaguely ridiculous to write software against a business process that has not yet been designed. Starting devops when you don't know what the operational data store is going to look like is vaguely ridiculous. In other words, threads are dependent upon one another. And if threads of work have dependencies, that nice, neat picture up there just isn't realistic. It's going to look more like this:

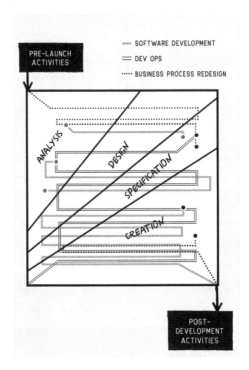

Based on that reality, there are a couple timeline points that become very important: thread divergence and thread convergence.

**Thread divergence:** Threads occur simultaneously, but none of them can start before the prelaunch tasks are "finished." There is a point where the prelaunch arrow meets the beginning points for all of the threads. This point is the divergence point. The ride is about to begin. After this, the controlled chaos of multiple, simultaneous threads ensues. The divergence point is an important time because it's the last traditionally manageable point. It's a good time to schedule one last team meeting.

**Thread convergence:** At some point these various threads must come together so that a logical analysis of the entire system can occur and testing can begin; don't trade analysis paralysis for unending developing.

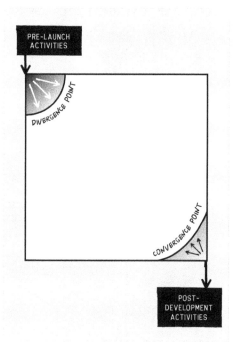

Specifying a convergence point lets all threads know when they must be finished. What does the convergence point mean for our hypothetical three threads? In the case of business process redesign (BPR), all redesign should be complete, taking into account the coding that has been done and the best possible business solutions. System development should have produced all code for the expected functionality and done unit testing on the code. The devops infrastructure should reflect the changes the coders made and account for the new business practices detailed by the BPR thread. Because of the complexity of thread convergence, it's not really a single point in time but rather a date to begin unification. It's only at thread convergence that the team truly can sit back and see what it has.

The take-home message from a management perspective is that the closer a thread is to the divergence or convergence point, the more accurately you'll know what is going on in that thread. Think of the threads as ribbons, each with a single pushpin through the end. That pin is the divergence point. It looks something like this:

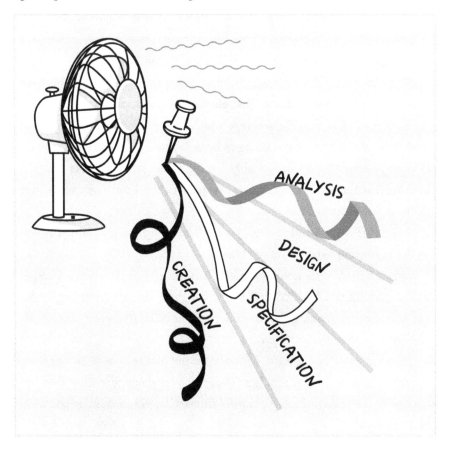

So the divergence point is your best chance to get a handle on where each thread is going.

 # EXCEPT...

Except ... getting a handle on where each thread is going is *antithetical to successfully managing an iterative process.*

Probably, most of your threads of work will begin in the analysis phase. *Probably.* But shortly thereafter, your crystal ball will go dark. The system development thread might say, "Oh, we've seen this type of problem already, so we can do a quick prototype." Boom, that thread of work is now in creation. Devops is looking on and says, "Ooh, interesting. That means I need to go think about stuff." Boom, devops is now in analysis.

And now that fan is blowing and those ribbons are flapping all over the place. Those beautiful ribbons. That glorious unpredictability.

Any game plan you are writing, which makes any assumption about what type of work anyone is going to be doing at any given point in time, is wrong—immediately, irrevocably wrong. That goes for plans over the long-term scope of the project (road maps) or even short-term plans over the next few months or so.

Any effort you expend saying, "Jack will be doing analysis, and Sally will be doing specification," is wasted effort.

In fact it's worse than wasted effort. It is misleading. It sends a message that you think you have control over what these threads are going to do. Or worse, you're sending the message that *you think it's a good idea for you to exert some control over the process.*

It's not a good idea to exert control over the process—at least, not from a predictive management mindset. Those are very dangerous ideas that run counter to the reality of those beautiful threads flapping around in the wind of iteration.

You will not be able to predict or control the process. It's impossible to do so. You might be able to concentrate on one thread and guess where it will go, but then you'll lose comprehension of the other threads.

I urge you, as a fellow human who values your sanity, do not try.

I urge you, as a fellow human who values the sanity of any software developer you are going to foist these ill-advised plans onto, do not try.

Do not make a schedule. Schedule, bad.

. . .call me suspicious, but I detect some incredulity. I think you think there is a way to predict or control (a.k.a., manage) this. I think you think I'm overlooking some vital point or that I'm opening you up to some horrible risk.

I think you think that the point I just made about the fan and the threads flapping all over the place, uncontrolled and unmanageable, and not having a schedule is ridiculous.

So let's dig a little deeper and see if I'm spouting nonsense.

CHAPTER 12

# UNDERSTANDING THREAD DYNAMICS

At this point you may still have the idea that you can track where the team is going and roughly when they will get there. But there is still a little more reality to contend with.

A thread is a concerted effort that is somewhat autonomous. Remember that we don't call it a "subproject" because that would imply dedicated resources.[58] What is actually happening with resources, and how does it make the thread look?

A thread has a collection of resources, such as customers, database administrators, managers, developers, and analysts, all working toward a goal. However, all of the resources available to a given thread will not work on that thread simultaneously. Perhaps everyone will follow the same path at the beginning, then break off to pursue other tasks. There are also other threads, which means at times no one will work on a particular thread. A thread actually looks more like this:

---

58   Gary Yates, personal communication, 1997.

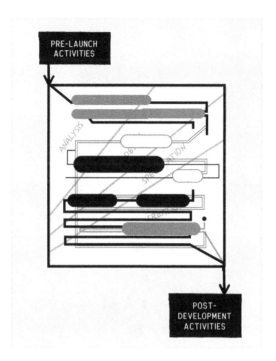

The thread is thicker when more people are working on it, then it frays as people move to thread-specific tasks or to other threads. There may be large gaps as people leave a thread or large clumps as many people join a thread. You simply cannot tell where a thread is going with any real clarity.

Multiple threads of work actually cloud the picture even more. If someone leaves a thread and works on another for a brief amount of time, it affects two threads. If you were to stop and ask for a status report, you might find that the report is almost a complete reversal from the last report. Last week John was analyzing for the business process redesign thread, but this week he is creating scripts for devops.

CHAPTER *13*

# TELEPORTATION WREAKS HAVOC

Just to drive the point home, even thinking of a thread as having an observable direction is misleading. This image shows a possible path for system development. Once finished with a round of design (point 2), the team

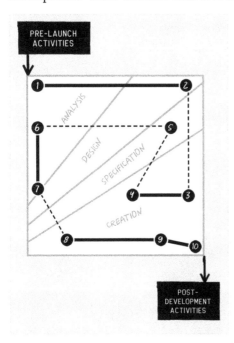

may decide to skip to creation (point 3) for rapid prototyping. When the prototyping has progressed awhile (point 4), they may need a more specific design (point 5), which immediately causes them to realize they need to hop over to analysis for more customer input (point 6). With that input comes clarification, (point 7), so the team jumps right back into development, bypassing the specification they jump-started (point 8).

The team does not actually pass through the phases as depicted by the dotted lines. They jump directly to the required phase. As illustrated by point 5, the team may not actually remain in a phase for very long.

It's important to note that this skipping around is not the result of poor design or analysis in the previous phases. It's iteration brought on by learning new things or facing unknowns. This model embraces the concept that the team doesn't know where it will go; sometimes the team doesn't even know what it needs to know.

# CHAPTER 14

# THE UNCERTAINTY PRINCIPLE LIMITS YOUR OPTIONS

In physics there is Heisenberg's uncertainty principle. In simple terms, you can know the speed or location of a particle but not both at the same time.[59] This is how the blur box model treats human resources. You can know in what general direction a person or team is going but not exactly where they are in the process.

You *could* know if you stopped the process and had everyone analyze where they are. It's like freeze tag, where everyone runs around, but when someone calls "freeze," everyone stops in place. If you wanted to, you could stop the process of iteration and figure out who is doing what. But is that productive?

It depends on the frequency and duration of the iterations. At the beginning of a thread, most people are working on the same thing in the same phase, and stopping time would allow you to get a good idea of where everyone is. But the most productive iterations also tend to be the fastest. If a team is in the heat of iteration, one person could teleport between phases

---

59   W Heisenberg, "Über den anschaulichen Inhalt der quantentheoretischen Kinematik und Mechanik." *Zeitschrift für Physik* 43, no. 3 (1927): 172–198.

almost hourly. If you were to stop time and ask where everyone is in the process, it might take longer for them to deconstruct where they are and how they got there than the actual iteration would take. This status check would also disrupt the process, probably slowing it.

How is this reflected in the model?

The figures so far have depicted a line, let's say BPR, moving back and forth through the stages. What that line represents is the general direction of the team working on BPR. The line is actually a team of people all doing different things that take the thread in a general direction. It's not clear exactly when the team is in design as opposed to analysis, because they could hop back and forth between design and analysis several times within the same day. So the line is just an impression of the general direction the team is moving. And the pictures in this book haven't been moving. If they'd been moving, it would more realistically look the image pictured here.

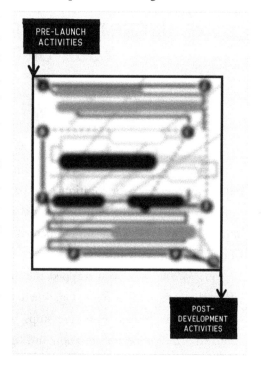

That is the fuzzy blur of iteration.

All of the above concepts are meant to illustrate how iteration looks and how it can be conceptually irritating. Needless to say, many traditional management practices that depend on predicting resource utilization are ineffective when applied to such a project.

# CHAPTER 15

# TAPESTRY ON A LOOM

You could think of the process like weaving a tapestry. You have a handful of threads, and you want to weave a tapestry. You could opt for a manual loom. You would have control over each thread, dictating when each thread starts or stops. You would know where everything is and can explain to others where each thread will go next. You can even control exactly how the tapestry looks. But it would take a long time and your fingers would get very tired. It would be slow—awkwardly slow. This is a metaphor for large-scale implementations with a lot of moving parts. You give up speed and flexibility for control and predictability.

If you used an automated loom, you would select your threads and position them. You would tell the loom how you want the tapestry to look. Then you would start the loom and watch the threads dance. You could try to follow the threads' movements, but you might get dizzy. You could explain to someone where a particular thread is going, but by the time you had explained it, the thread would be going somewhere else. As the process went along, you wouldn't know precisely how the tapestry was shaping up until the automated loom had stopped and you'd clipped the threads. You would lose control over the details of how the threads went together, but the finished tapestry would look similar to what you had envisioned. The process was much faster, with much less hands-on effort from you.

# CHAPTER 16

# THE THIRD DIMENSION

OK, just in case you still think there is some hope of efficiently predicting who is going to be doing what with any clarity, here is the last straw.

EXCEPT...

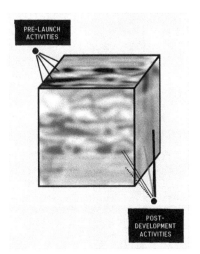

PRE-LAUNCH
ACTIVITIES

POST-
DEVELOPMENT
ACTIVITIES

Except…this isn't a two-dimensional process as we've been looking at it. It's more like the image pictured here.

Unless you have a very constrained set of parameters you're dealing with, this whole mess is going to be three-dimensional. The minute you introduce any of the following, your complexity has just quadrupled:

- Different physical locations
- Physical products

- Time zones
- Multiple projects in a portfolio management scenario
- Heterogeneous team structures
- Bitcoin

And that is the blur box—a completely unpredictable vortex of people and resources hopping around among different threads of work, in different phases, in lengths of time so minuscule that they're obsolete the minute you attempt to track them.

My advice to you is, don't. Don't attempt to track them. Whatever you do, don't try to predict them. And if you do try to predict them, whatever you do, don't try to control the process to meet your predictions. Best to just turn on that fan and watch those beautiful ribbons flap around.

What does that mean, practically speaking?

# PART 2:
# WELCOME TO THE AGILE CIRCUS

PART 1 WAS KIND OF A WHIRLWIND, WASN'T IT? I SHOWED YOU THAT most modern IT project management is based on a grandiose strawman. We're on an alternate timeline where we don't know what is solid advice and what isn't when it comes to building software. Many of us have internalized the ideas that prediction and control are good and that unpredictability and chaos are bad. The blur box model described the realities of iterative creation and illustrated that unpredictability and chaos are neither good nor bad but simple reality.

It is clear that the current strategies of application development rarely work. That's not to say there aren't successes, but IT hasn't achieved repeatable standards for project management success. In an age of e-commerce when delaying an implementation by a month can mean complete failure, IT needs to reassess which management tools are necessary and which are merely artifacts of the need to feel control over a project. We must manage projects, but the key question is "how?"

It's up to each organization to consider how an iterative process affects them. With that understanding, managers can build a management strategy that will help avoid disaster and increase the likelihood of project success.

I have elucidated the problem as clearly as I know how. In part 2 I'll walk through some loosely related talking points that use the blur box as a jumping-off point for exploring iterative software development. This is more conversational, with advice, venting, and observations. Pointing out what not to do is easier, so expect a fair amount of that. Saying what you should do is more challenging, and you can look forward to a little bit of that.

Welcome to the agile circus!

# CHAPTER 18

# GOOD NEWS:
# YOU ARE NOT ALONE!

The first thing you should know as a recent beneficiary of agile is that you are not alone. There are thousands of people out there who want to help you. You have a wealth of resources at your disposal, a vibrant community of passionate practitioners who want to help, and some very promising movements currently in the works.

## AGILE ALLIANCE

The Agile Alliance has been around a long time—almost as long as agile itself—and is highly respected. It has many free resources, and lots more for $49 (as of the time of this writing.) Their newsletter is informative, their events are well organized, and the breadth of information cannot be beat.

## REIMAGINING AGILE

It might be a little early to endorse this initiative since, at the time of this writing, it is only one shared post of a call to action from four people.[60]

---

60    Musser et al. "Reimagine Agile."

However, everything I know, and everything my intuition tells me, is that this is a promising place to learn about agile and contribute to its reinvention. Current me certainly plans to get involved. I hope to see you there too.

## BOOKS

Related to the above, my passion is agile, and you have my book in your hands or on your screen right now. Thanks for that. There are tons of other books on almost every topic related to agile or iterative software development. I have tried to highlight my favorites in this book, and you can find them in the appendix under recommended reading and in the references section.

## THE R/AGILE SUBREDDIT

Maybe you love reddit, maybe you hate it, but there's one thing I can tell you for sure: if you post a question to the r/agile subreddit and it's clear you have done your own research, you are likely to get quality responses from people who have lived agile from the trenches. You'll notice some of my solicitations for reddit war stories peppered throughout this book. Ephemeral as reddit is, most of these discussions no longer exist and the posters are anonymous and usually decline to be credited. But the intel is solid. For example, I recently asked someone to point me to original sources for work-in-progress limits, and I got a slew of thoughtful responses that taught me things I had no idea about, such as WIP's origins in kaizen-driven auto factories—and I started working in a just-in-time manufacturing plant, Subaru, back in 1996. So you can glean a lot of experienced insight there.

## LINKEDIN'S AGILE ECOSYSTEM

Compared to r/agile, you need to be especially careful on LinkedIn. There are tons of trolls, charlatans, and snake oil salesmen. In particular, the volume needed to be heard there drives people to post dramatic proclamations of some controversial viewpoint or another. So you need to look where the real action is: in the comments sections. We agilists are quick to hop onto snake oil grenades.

Caveats aside, LinkedIn is the front page of the agile newspaper in a lot of ways. For example, I did not learn about Reimagining Agile from its homepage on the Agile alliance website, but from LinkedIn.

## PMI'S AGILE RESOURCES

If you happen to already be a member of the Project Management Institute, they've put a lot of work into their agile offerings lately. Two people I have seen speak in person that I'm impressed with, Scott Ambler and Mike Griffiths, in particular have contributed a lot of great information.

There's a toolkit I've already discussed in this book called Disciplined Agile, described thusly on the PMI website: "The Disciplined Agile (DA™) tool kit supplies straightforward guidance to help you, your team, and your enterprise increase effectiveness. Apply and evolve your way of working (WoW) in a context-sensitive manner with this people-first, learning-oriented hybrid agile approach."[61]

There's also the PMI Agile Certified Practitioner (ACP) certification, which Mike Griffiths spearheaded. As long as you take into account that PMI tends to take a conservative and broad approach to agile, and thus might not be as streamlined as other sources, you can glean a lot of good information from those two resources. Also, the basic PMP certification itself has much more agile practices included than it used to, so even the PMP will give you a decent foundation.

I would not necessarily recommend seeking out ACP training if you are not already a member with easier access to the information via your em-

---

61    "The Disciplined Agile® (DA™) Tool Kit," Project Management Institute, December 2021, https://www.pmi.org/disciplined-agile/toolkit.

ployer fronting the costs or some other access. There are other ways to get the information. But if the PMI ecosystem is already part of your life, check them out. And the ACP is much more rigorous than other certifications on the market, and therefore more valuable to some employers.

## INHERITING AGILE

All of the above leads me to a plug for my own initiative, Inheriting Agile. In both a YouTube channel[62] and a LinkedIn group,[63] my cohost Chris Vestal and I do our best to discuss the hot topics of the day and provide balanced commentary. Between us we have fifty years of experience with agile and know some of the key people personally, so I feel OK asking you to trust our opinions. We'll do our best to cover the basics of agile practice as well as some of the deeper topics that help inform other online resources.

62    Rob Lineberger and Chris Vestal, Inheriting Agile channel, YouTube, https://www.youtube.com/@InheritingAgile.

63    Chris Vestal and Rob Lineberger, Inheriting Agile, LinkedIn group, https://www.linkedin.com/groups/14330207/.

CHAPTER 19

# BAD NEWS:
# YOU ARE NOT ALONE!

I told you all about those positive, encouraging resources above, but I want to get a few things out of the way before we get too deep into things. Inheriting agile is not all roses and sunshine, and it would be disingenuous of me to pretend that it is.

## SNAKE OIL ABOUNDS

The first trap to look out for is that some of the people who agree to help you will eventually ask for money—particularly if you're getting into a deeper consulting or coaching scenario. That's to be expected, and it is not in and of itself a bad sign. The ethical ones will help get you oriented out of the goodness of their hearts, point you to resources for you to learn on your own, and only pursue a professional relationship when they are certain you're a good fit for their services.

I only bring this up because, much like a tourist stepping off of a cruise ship into a crowded port, you're likely to encounter lots of sales pitches as you explore the world of agile. Many of those are perfectly legitimate.

Many are not. And you probably won't know the difference when you're just starting out.

But much like tourist-trappy sales pitches, you can gauge the legitimacy of an offer by how aggressive it is, how much fear it tries to instill, and how much flattery is involved. Legitimate offers for services are not aggressive, are based on collaboration rather than fear, and will not try to flatter you. Legitimate certifications are not easily earned and will require lots of study and professional practice.

Above all, if anyone tries to tell you their way is the one true and only way to be agile, you can safely bet that they're more interested in your dollars than your company's success. There are as many ways to be agile as there are development teams. It's why the manifesto authors were conscientious about not endorsing any specific frameworks or methodologies.

## CONFLICT ABOUNDS

If you talk about agile for more than thirty seconds, you're going to encounter conflict. One framework vs. another. Different definitions of terms. Disingenuous posing of non-agile approaches as agile. Flame wars. Longstanding grudges. It's all out there, and more.

In fact, my recommendations you're about to read in part 3? I give it two minutes before vehement disagreement is expressed by someone espousing the exact opposite opinion. (If that hasn't already happened by now, which it likely has.)

Your overriding mantra should be this: there is room for almost any approach in the right circumstances and context. Anyone who tells you something can't be done, must be done, is agile, or is not agile? Learn to dig deeper. Ask them what assumptions and context they're working within. Assess whether that context is a good fit for your situation. Many of the contentious agile discussions can be quickly defused with a little healthy questioning of assumptions and a healthy respect for counterpoints and alternate viewpoints.

## SOFTWARE DEVELOPMENT IS HARD

Let me give you a sneak peek into my development team's documented development process and requirements-gathering approach. Our three-step development process was articulated by College Humor in a post titled "Realistic Gym Workout Diagrams," which isn't freely available online anymore. But you can find out more at Know Your Meme.[64]

As for our requirements-gathering process, it comes courtesy of K.C. Green's Gunshow comic #648, "The Pills Are Working," which depicts a dog sitting in a cafe that is on fire, saying "this is fine."[65]

OK, I realize that this might not be the most promising kickoff to the advice section of this book. I'm not trying to discourage you, but rather to acknowledge that *software development is hard*—no matter how much experience you have. Agile is not going to swoop in and fix all of your development challenges. Agile is not going to download a lifetime of experience into your brain. Agile is not going to provide you with any shortcuts to learning the tricky parts of software development nor managing software development.

You need to learn to distinguish between what is an agile-related consideration and what is simply a general software development challenge. So many inexperienced developers and managers get frustrated or blame agile for things that really have nothing inherent to do with agile. There's mastering agile software development and mastering general professional skills, and they are not the same thing. Related, perhaps, but distinct.

---

64    Midnight Sparkle, "Lie Down / Try Not To Cry / Cry A Lot," Know Your Meme, 2013, updated 2019. https://knowyourmeme.com/memes/lie-down-try-not-to-cry-cry-a-lot. Original post by Alex Watt, "Realistic Gym Workout Diagrams," College Humor, September 10, 2010, archived March 22, 2014 at the Wayback Machine, https://web.archive.org/web/20140322074435/http://www.collegehumor.com/post/6283767/realistic-gym-workout-diagrams.

65    K.C Green, "The Pills Are Working," *Gunshow* #648, January 9th, 2013, https://gunshowcomic.com/648.

# CHAPTER 20

# STEP OUT OF THE COMFORT ZONE

The blur box thwarts many of the comforts we've come to rely on. Its dizzying pace and unpredictability invalidate our traditional roles, responsibilities, tools, and techniques. If I were to summarize your best defense against the blur box in one phrase, it would be this: step out of your comfort zone.

Everyone needs to do this, from customer to CEO. No one is immune. No one is above or below the necessity of taking on (or letting go of) roles, responsibilities, tools, and techniques that are outside of their comfort zone—even ones that fly in the face of what they've been taught, what they believe, or even what they prefer. The blur box does not care what you were taught. It doesn't care what you believe. It definitely does not care what you prefer.

## STEPPING OUT: IT'S COMPLICATED

The first thing you should know about the process of stepping out of one's comfort zone is that *it's a process*. There is a concept known as comfort vs. growth zone, brilliantly illustrated by Larry Kim and posted to

Medium.com:[66]

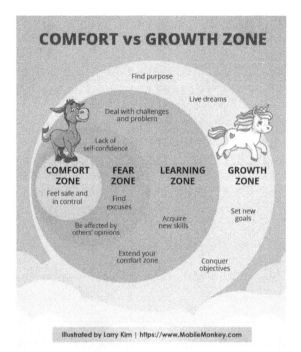

Maury Rogow discusses the process of breaking out of comfort zones this way in a LinkedIn post from August 2023:

> It is important to be aware of the different types of zones that can affect learning. Each of these zones has its own benefits and drawbacks. The comfort zone can lead to complacency, while the learning zone can lead to growth. The fear zone can lead to anxiety and stress, but it can also be a source of motivation. It is important to find the right balance between these three zones in order to optimize learning.[67]

---

66   Larry Kim, "Comfort vs Growth Zone," Medium, April 16, 2019, https://medium.com/marketing-and-entrepreneurship/comfort-vs-growth-zone-3f0b4f9e5638.

67   Maury Rogow, "Growth Zone," LinkedIn, August 2023, https://www.linkedin.com/posts/mauryrogow_growthzone-growth-weeklymarketingtips-activity-7094742938831736832-MbMM/.

The goal is to acknowledge that fear and uncertainty. Reassure everyone that these shifting roles will come with setbacks, and that is OK. Turn their discomfort into motivation. If your organization handles this transition gracefully, you'll wind up in a phase of learning and, ideally, growth.

From a practical standpoint, stepping out of your comfort zone might look something like the four subsections below from the point of view of various stakeholders. Each describes the status quo and how that needs to change. There are hypothetical internal monologues that I have surmised after dozens of enterprise-level implementations and speaking with hundreds of stakeholders. Let's see what might be in store for your customers, developers, managers, and project managers.

## CUSTOMER COMFORT ZONE

The customers need to become proactive rather than passive. That's a pretty bland way of describing what might be a monumental shift for your organization. "Proactive" means that the customer suddenly has new responsibilities. Depending on the level of integration you are aiming for, that's possibly a lot of new responsibilities. The Agile Manifesto lays down this mandate: "Business people and developers must work together daily throughout the project."[68] If you buy that, it suggests a fairly large impact on the customer. Do business people typically attend your daily standup? Do they routinely log into your project management software and update priorities? Perform daily feature reviews?

The customer can no longer hide behind the curtain of the contract. They can no longer sit around and wait for working software to fall out of the sky into their laps.

They can no longer claim to be surprised on demo day.

No. The customer now is your organization's leading expert on what is happening … if you adhere to the Agile Manifesto.

---

68    "Manifesto for Agile Software Development."

The further you stray from that, the more you are risking your projects. I have worked in enterprise projects with daily customer interaction, bi-weekly interaction, and end-of-life cycle interaction. They were successful in about the same order. Daily interaction ensured success, while "Surprise! Here's your software," practically guaranteed failure.

The customer is not going to like this. They might make a resource-based argument. They might protest on social grounds. Maybe both:

> "But … but … we are already understaffed! I can barely keep my widgets moving out the door as it is! And I don't know a darn thing about software development—that's your department. Count me out."

I can almost guarantee you they will not say:

> "Oh, wonderful! I've always wanted to learn how to update issue-tracking software, and I'm looking forward to attending more meetings!"

Customers don't want to step out of their comfort zone, the zone where they tell you some vague wish list items and you convert their wishes into software. The customer must understand that their involvement is about to increase—not for a day or a week but for the *rest of your days together.*

## DEVELOPER COMFORT ZONE

The development team needs to embrace soft skills that they stereotypically abhor. Developers tend to be introverts and tend to put more stock in the intellectual rather than the emotional. That's a huge generalization, of course, but in my experience software developers spend significantly more of their time and mental effort on building technical skills than soft skills. They learn new languages and talk about code or technology. Most developers don't spend their day thinking:

"Have I reached out to enough people today? How is the truck driver/ CEO/sales guy thinking about our upcoming launch? Are they concerned? Intrigued? I should really check in on them. I really wish someone would schedule me for a meeting with more people so I can stop writing all this code and just talk about business stuff."

That's exactly what your dev team needs to do. They need to engage with stakeholders more, so much more that it's no longer weird for anyone.

This soft-skills thing is far more than asking about the weather or Sally's dog. It segues into an ongoing analysis session or a daily requirements-gathering touchstone. It's a domain knowledge by osmosis that no consultant's fee can buy—a domain knowledge via repetition that cutting corners cannot earn. By the time you're done, the dev team will be experts on your customer's problems and needs. They'll be finishing each other's sentences.

That's when business value really starts compounding. The best software is the software that was never written. It's code that never saw the light of day because your developers were shrewd enough to sidestep it. How can your developers dodge a thorny mess of code when they have no clue where your customer is coming from? In that case, they're forced to rely on business analysis reports or periodic meetings for guidance. That's a poor substitute for an organic personal relationship with the customer.

## MANAGEMENT COMFORT ZONE

What do managers do? They manage stuff. They predict. They control. They maximize value. How? Probably through some combination of personal strengths, formal business education, cultural expectations, schedules, top-down mandates, or deadlines. They might hire consultants. They might attend management conferences and learn what the next big thing is.

Good managers are always striving to learn, to improve the organization. They're always looking for ways to do things more effectively and to lead the team toward that end. In other words, *managers are biased toward taking action*—steering the ship, driving the bus, watching for pitfalls, and trimming waste. They're biased toward making plans, gauging the success of those plans, and making decisions based on the data.

The blur box does not care what the next big thing is. It doesn't care what plans you made. It doesn't care what deadline you set. It doesn't care where you went to get your MBA or what the consultant you hired just told you.

To succeed in an iterative environment, management must embrace nonintuitive behaviors. For example, the best thing in some cases might be to have no plans, no deadlines, and no top-down mandates.

*No predictions. No control.*

I can't speak for all managers, but in my experience, most managers wouldn't like to hear that. They might laugh at the absurdity or get mad. They definitely won't think:

> "You know what? That makes sense! I should let the team lead itself. I should rip up my road maps and just be responsive to what is produced. Gently shape it from afar. No need to optimize things; it'll all just shake out."

I'm certainly not suggesting that management is off the hook. They need to make perhaps the biggest cultural shift of anyone in the process. They need to lead from behind. Be humble and observant. Use their formidable business acumen not to lead the team, but to clear its way. They need to tell the CEO to back off. They need to make those pesky deadlines go away. They need to provide the dev team with the training, freedom, responsibility, and autonomy they need to be effective.

The best upper managers I've seen managing an agile process have done some of these things:

- Joined the dev team in the basement during crunch time and figured out what needed to happen to make everyone comfortable. They ordered food, drove someone's partner to the airport, or made hard calls about which beloved feature to leave off. They just sat in the room as a team player to help out, even though they couldn't code. They weren't there as a watchdog but as a fellow team member.

- Passed around a copy of *Office Space* for everyone to watch in secret and laugh at.
- Gone into a meeting full of angry hornet customers and defused things by saying, "The setback is my fault. If you want to blame anyone, blame me because I didn't execute this last release properly. Now what can we do to get past this and improve it for next time?"
- Walked around to everyone's office once or twice a week and sat for a few minutes to ask how things were going and what could they do to make the next release a success?
- Told the dev team to stop working on feature XYZ immediately because it no longer made sense, then sat there and took the backlash for making an unpopular decision without responding in kind.

In short, the best managers I've seen involved in an iterative process are inquisitive, protective, humble, involved, and not adverse to taking blame. They listen, watch, refine, shape, and guide. They become people the dev team would stand behind in solidarity through shared respect and earned trust, which goes both ways: they trust the dev team, and the dev team trusts them.

## PROJECT MANAGER COMFORT ZONE

Project managers already know they operate in the tiny space between the rock and the hard place. Project managers become more crucial than ever in an iterative process—but not in the way they think. Or even hope.

Most project managers I know have a tool set they earned through years of training. That tool kit usually contains some combination of scheduling, estimation, structured communication tools, road maps, Gantt charts, work breakdown structures, defect management, etc. The first thing a new project manager asks when they work with one of my teams is some form of "What are the deliverables? What's the timeline?" Project managers have very comprehensive—but biased—training.

They are biased toward scheduling and resource management. Unfortunately, that is exactly the kind of thing that the blur box chews up and spits out. The blur box will laugh at your schedule as it deftly sidesteps all of your detailed plans.

So what does a project manager do in an iterative process? Lots. Their role shifts to protecting and curating the process.

The project manager (perhaps called some other name, depending on your process) is the hub—the focal point for customers, managers, and the dev team. The project managers are the ones who have the unenviable job of making sure no one is in their comfort zones. They tell management to stop predicting and start adapting. They make sure the developers are reaching out to the customers. Project managers are the ones who remind the customers that they're no longer idle passengers in the hang glider but the ones 2,000 feet in the air, who better grab that hang strap and start steering or else fall out of the sky.

The project managers need to take a hard look at the tools they have accumulated over the years, put 80% of those tools on a dusty shelf, and step into the streaking lights of the blur box. I seriously doubt many project managers out there are thinking:

> "OK, I finally did it. After years of studying and late nights I got my project management professional certification. I got that dream job at Big Deal Software Company. I can't wait to toss aside everything I know and love. I look forward to telling everyone from the president to the lunch lady that they need to do exactly what they don't want to do so we can pull this thing off."

The project managers need to become the least comfortable people in the entire organization and relinquish anything that doesn't help. They need to become experts on the shifting sands of the development process—both so they can prevent wasted effort and explain what the heck is happening behind the scenes to other people.

The project manager should become a communication whiz with SPF 5,000 sunblock to stay safe from all the speeding lights. They need to have the confidence to tell the managers things are going well or poorly and the confidence to tell the dev team when they are running out of the end zone and need to stop to focus on the new top priority.

The good news is that many of the tools project managers know are very useful and will serve the team well. It's a matter of picking which ones.

CHAPTER 21

# IMMEDIATE CONCLUSIONS

The main point of the blur box is that effort is going to be unpredictable. Given the futility of leading the team down a prescribed path, an alternate approach is shifting your focus to giving the team its best chance of success. I'll cover each of these topics in more depth later, but let's summarize some immediate takeaways that will help you succeed:

- Build a cross-functional team with a core of experience.
- Let them do what you hired them to do (self-managing teams).
- Aim for a modular, loosely coupled software architecture that can easily adapt to changes in requirements and plans.
- Run interference for your team. Give them white space to accomplish their tasks.
- Break down the icebergs in the water. Reduce the scope of projects; have the managers/customers/users request fewer features at a time.
- Communicate with the stakeholders up and down the chain.
- Refine your focus with each iteration.

And definitely keep a very close eye on the software development process—but as a collaborator who is an expert on what should be built, not as someone whose job is to tell the team how to build it.

I am not saying to overlook an unmotivated dev team. If your gut is telling you there is a problem, listen to it. I am saying that if you hire good people, and you give them autonomy, they'll want to do a good job. They'll want your approval and the customer's approval, and they'll work hard to get it.

Put most of your effort in up front by attracting the best people you possibly can, turning on the fan, then stepping out of the way of the flapping ribbons.

In the loom analogy, your dev team is the automated loom. You need to make sure you bought the right loom (i.e., staffing, team building) and that you gave the loom the correct image you wanted it to make (i.e., requirements gathering). This analogy only goes so far because a loom is very linear. Your team will be refining the whole picture bit by bit as things move forward. Even so, your job as a manager becomes putting together the best team, then letting it do its thing—while maintaining the best possible environment for the fuzzy blur to occur. Then iterate your approach just as the dev team is iterating theirs.

At that point, management's role shifts to facilitating the prioritization of features, ensuring close customer integration, and verifying that the produced software is meeting the needs of the stakeholders. Sometimes we call this style of management "Lead from Behind." It's an excellent fit for agile development. And it's an ancient concept. Lao Tzu described it in 500 BCE in verse 17 of the *Tao Te Ching*:

> *The Master doesn't talk, he acts.*
> *When his work is done,*
> *the people say, "Amazing:*
> *we did it, all by ourselves!"*[69]

---

69    Lao Tzu, *Tao Te Ching: A New English Version*, trans. Stephen Mitchell (Harper Collins, 2009).

# CHAPTER 22

# AVOID COMMON AGILE PITFALLS

You now have some idea of what *to* do. Now let's talk about what *not to* do. There are many common traps, fallacies, and assumptions related to agile that can trip you up if you are not careful.

## AGILE ≠ SPEED

Agile does not inherently speed up your development processes. If you find some other way to accelerate pace while you are becoming agile, there might be some synergy. You might get a bit of a speed boost greater than the accelerant itself adds alone. For example, adding people to the team, using AI tools to streamline code generation, or iterating your own process to eliminate inefficiencies. But if I hear one more person claim that going agile will speed up the development process, I will scream.

*checks LinkedIn*

*screams*

Also, if I hear one more person bash agile because not only did it not speed up development, it *slowed* development? I will cry. And nobody wants to see that. It's ugly.

*checks reddit*

*cries*

Of *course* implementing agile slowed your development process! You were learning an entirely different mindset while still working on your current responsibilities. It has nothing to do with agile itself.

Agile cannot make your software developers instantly become better programmers. A side benefit of some agile practices, such as eXtreme Programming, typically does provide such a benefit over time. And that's a nice bonus. What agile methods are good at, which in a way seems like a speed boost, is they stop you from wasting effort. You aren't coding any faster, but you are coding the right things, and you are often getting to value in a straighter path than you would otherwise. So agile can lead to time savings. That's not the same thing as going faster. Your programmers are going to type as fast as they always have.

## CERTIFICATION ≠ EXPERTISE

You can't take a certification class and become an expert—especially not a certification class that lasts less than a week. You can be exposed to great ideas that way. But nothing is going to give you expertise besides lots of study and experience.

This is not a slight against certifications. Getting one shows that you have interest and initiative. But if you expect to get a certification and then be considered an authority, you should reconsider. If you hire someone with a certification but not much experience, do not consider them an authority. Give them the same training and room to make mistakes as you would any other inexperienced hire.

## DOING AGILE ≠ BEING AGILE

We have a saying in the agile world that "doing" agile is not the same thing as being agile.[70] "Doing agile" means implementing the scaffolding and ceremonies of an agile process without understanding why: sprinting, pair programming, retrospectives, daily standup, or whatever other processes and tools your chosen agile methodology demands. "Zombie Scrum" is another popular term for it.[71]

The act of implementing those processes and ceremonies in and of itself is not enough. You must know why you are doing so, evaluate how it is going, make refinements, double check that you're gaining value, and otherwise be engaged in the mindset as a whole. Following rote steps *just because* is not going to get you very far. Evaluating your organization's unique challenges and opportunities, and finding an agile way to overcome them, is where the benefit lies.

*Esse Quam Videri*, as the motto of my home of North Carolina urges us: to be rather than to seem.

## AGILE CANNOT FIX YOUR ORGANIZATION'S CULTURE BY ITSELF

Your culture might be a very poor fit for agile no matter what you do, or want it to be. You need to be honest with yourself and your stakeholders about how good a fit agile will be for your current culture and ways of working. For example, if you have a huge, distributed company with large teams who work on mission-critical projects, requiring highly specialized and siloed skill sets, with detailed contractual constraints, and your management team's experience is proudly in predictive methods, you have a massive cultural challenge to organizational agility.

---

70    Rash Khan, "Being Agile vs Doing Agile, Why is it important to differentiate!?," LinkedIn. December 5, 2015, https://www.linkedin.com/pulse/being-agile-vs-doing-why-important-differentiate-rash-khan/.

71    ChristiaanVerwijs, "The Rise Of Zombie Scrum," The Liberators, Medium, March 29, 2017, https://medium.com/the-liberators/the-rise-of-zombie-scrum-cd98741015d5.

Any one of those things can be overcome with an agile approach. Arguably, all of them. But you're rowing against the current. If you think that implementing an agile approach in such environment in and of itself will lead to agility, I have bad news for you: the real work lies in addressing deeper cultural issues of trust, autonomy, flexibility, etc. Agile can't do that alone.

The good news is, there are ways to chip away at that organizational challenge. In fact, I'll discuss that in the next section.

# CHAPTER 23

# KNOW WHERE TO DRAW THE LINE

Although it can and has happened, organizations rarely become agile across the board at once. They pick and choose where agile fits best and will provide the most value. Then they section off that area and make changes within it, but still use non-agile methods, too. If all goes well, perhaps they move the goalposts a bit and widen the agile containment area. This is known as hybrid agile.

There's a good introduction to this concept at Agile Alliance called "What is Hybrid Agile, Anyway?" Regarding the line drawing that I'm discussing in this section, which Agile Alliance labels "Hybrid as Transition-to-Agile," they summarize it as: "Many teams are not able to make the switch to Agile ways of working overnight. The larger the organization, the more moving parts, the longer it will take to shift. If you've lived in a plan-driven world for several years, then Agile methods will look and feel very different. As a result, your initial foray into the Agile world will be a messy amalgamation of both. That's okay. You're using specific techniques to move in the direction that you want to go to."[72]

---

72    Johanna Rothman et al., "What is Hybrid Agile, Anyway?," Agile Alliance, January 4, 2017, https://www.agilealliance.org/what-is-hybrid-agile-anyway/.

One of the authors of that article, Mike Griffiths, has a lot to say on this topic. His work highlights the many organizational configurations that combine predictive methods (which he calls the Ordinary World) with agile and hybrid methods (which he calls the Special World.) For example, in Mike's presentation at the PMI Global Summit 2023, "Implementing Agile Practices in an Un-Agile Organization," he describes the barriers and interfaces between the predictive and agile parts of your organization. Various hybrid models exist (such as switchover, sandwich, and encapsulation) that have different structures for combining predictive and adaptive methods.[73]

For example, the blur box model is an example of the sandwich model. There is the pre-launch period, where traditional approaches are used. Then the four iterative phases (analysis, design, specification, creation). Finally, there is a post-launch period that reverts to traditional management approaches.

CTO Tim Dragen highlighted this issue by saying "It seems like what happens within the blur box is too chaotic to model. *But*, it feels like where the blur hits up against established (non-development) process is where the interesting parts lie. That is, how can other teams enable the blur box model? e.g., if the dev team needs Design input, how can the 'Design Desk' be structured so that devs can get answers in near real time?"[74]

The take-home message for your success using agile is to critically evaluate your organization's agile readiness, identify good fits for agile within your structure, and focus your initial efforts there.

---

73    Mike Griffiths, "Implementing Agile Practices in an Un-Agile Organization," PMI Global Summit 2023. October 26, 2023, https://pmiglobalsummit.gcs-web.com/program/agenda#sess55107818.
74    Tim Dragen, personal communication, November 26, 2023.

# CHAPTER 24

# THE DANGERS OF ITERATIVE DEVELOPMENT

I've talked a lot about the benefits of agile. It has some significant drawbacks as well in some cases. There are dangers inherent in iterative development.

## FEATURE ABANDONMENT

A customer's desired feature often gets abandoned in an iterative approach. It happens all the time. This is ironic, because agile is supposed to get the customer's top value tickets done.

The setup is this: an agile team meets with the customers to figure out what the team needs to build. The dev team maybe gives their verbal agreement: "Oh, we'll definitely do that." Or the customer infers, "Well, we talked about my feature a lot. I guess they're going to do it." Either way, the customer has an expectation that the team is going to work on feature X.

Then the team interviews more customers, the product owner reprioritizes features, and feature X drops off the face of the earth.

The customer is not happy about this.

Next cycle, the dev team comes back to the customer and says, "OK, we need to ask you about feature Y." But the customer cancels all the meetings and refuses to talk with the dev team. The customer has lost confidence. They do not trust the dev team at all because the team wasted the customer's time and got their hopes up, then failed to deliver.

As a manager, it's up to you to manage customer expectations, mend fences, play hardball—whatever is in your toolbox. The dev team isn't trying to tick off the customer. But as iterations reveal new priorities, what seemed like a good idea at the time is no longer a good idea.

A guideline I follow is "underpromise, but overdeliver." I take that to heart. I never promise anything unless I am absolutely forced to—not to dodge responsibility, but to protect the customer from disappointment.

Sometimes I wish my manager would be the bad guy and say, "We had to pivot away from feature X because of reasons," then get the customer in the mood to answer my questions again.

## UNPREDICTABILITY

Another shortcoming of agile is unpredictability. This is really a catch-22. You're doing agile because the problem you're trying to solve is unpredictable. But in the real world, people need to know when a feature is coming down the pike. There's a whole chain of marketing and sales and support that is waiting to know: when is feature Y going to be ready?

If a specific feature and date are critical to you, you need to pause the automated loom. Take your foot off the gas. Recognize that you are about to halt a fuzzy blur that is moving at speed. Do the freeze tag thing and say, "Freeze! We've got to get feature Y out by next month."

Everyone will groan and moan. But you will have their attention. You are reprioritizing the whole project—at the expense of efficiency. Whatever features the team was working on, you are relegating to oblivion. And you will need to mend fences with other people.

You don't have to iterate and be agile 100% of the time, but be fore-warned: braking and switching gears come with huge penalties.

## COST ESTIMATION

Agile is also different in the way you estimate costs.

You need to figure out, in any software development project, whether the result will be worth the cost. Some people overestimate how good the traditional approach is at getting to that answer, but the process is definitely easier and more straightforward.

Agile development teams will often tell you "Whatever, dude," and keep working. So how do you estimate costs?

I have good news and bad news.

The bad news is, at the beginning, an iterative process is going to give you horrible cost estimates.

The team doesn't know what it doesn't know. Code frameworks don't exist yet. The team has not yet hit its stride. The first third of any iterative development project timeline is a huge leap of faith for everyone. (I'll talk about that in the next section.) You are lucky to get scientific wild-ass guess-es that are even in the ballpark.

The good news is that iterative software development has built-in course correction and built-in improvement. That middle third is pretty nice. Code sprints move features from the backlog to done, and possibly a burndown chart tells you how accurate the estimates were for what would be delivered.

In my experience, these estimates get more and more accurate. The team isn't even thinking in terms of money. They're thinking in terms of improving software, which matters a great deal to them. Part 3 has much more to say on this point.

You can use that code estimation to get a pretty good idea of what the team will deliver in the near future. If you can attach a dollar figure to that, you have your answers.

By the last third, code sprints are humming along. Features are piling up as the team knocks them out. You really get a huge return on investment if you power through to the mature stages of the project.

CHAPTER 25

# HOW TO SURVIVE
# THE CANCELLATION POINT

With all of the threads of work in iterative development, a task list or re-source allocation chart is futile. Staying on top of it would be nearly as much work as the development effort itself.

Release cycles demonstrate progress. A release is a discrete chunk of functionality delivered at a specific time within the project timeline. De-velopers determine a feature set to implement at alpha 1, alpha 2, beta 1, beta 2, etc. and provide a date for that release. They measure progress by whether implementation occurs on that date and whether they deliver all functionality. Working in this way gives managers, customers, and the project team clear targets and clear progress indicators.

In "Threads of Work," I mentioned that the phases are in wedge shapes. Let your stakeholders know that, generally speaking, the first third of a project is heavy on analysis, framework building, and process refinement—particularly if their project is a new venture without established code frameworks in place and a body of modules to rely on. If so, there might only be one code release—and an underwhelming one at that—in the first third of the project. By the time the last third of the project rolls around, most iterative projects are humming along and doing frequent code releases with lots of features.

Let's take those very same wedges from the model and look at them a different way. This graph shows a hypothetical release cycle within the overall project timeline of a new venture:

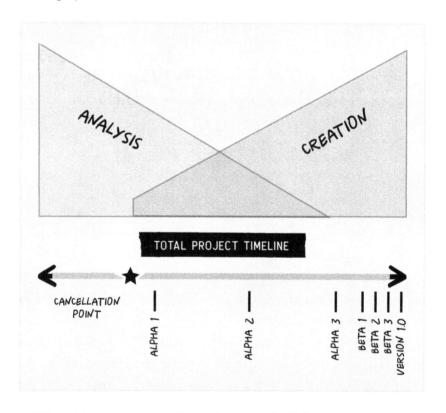

What this means practically is that a third of the way into the project—particularly greenfield ventures where no infrastructure frameworks exist yet—there may be very little actual development to show. Building frameworks and object-oriented base classes allow creation of a lot of functionality near the end of the timeline. But the early months might be scarce in terms of delivered functionality. This makes people nervous if they don't understand the nature of the team's development philosophy. Ironically, the point at which iterative development begins to yield the richest rewards is the same point that a project is in danger of cancellation due to perceived insufficient progress.

So it's a good idea to communicate to all stakeholders the likely cadence of release cycles.

A few months in, everyone gets antsy. Lots of money went into hiring developers, getting space, and querying customers. But so far, there's crickets from the dev team. They say they're working on stuff, but there's nothing to show.

Well, an iterative process isn't like a traditional process. The developers are doing a lot of heavy conceptual work: synthesizing requirements, designing frameworks, and deciding on interfaces and standards. None of that is demonstrable.

And when the alpha 1 release rolls out, it's not going to wow you. There might only be one screen that says, "Hello, world." And that is probably not going to make anyone happy.

Believe it or not, that "Hello, world" is a huge achievement. The dev team was sweating whether they'd get it to work. And now they can proudly get on with the work of delivering features and achieving a cadence of speedier releases.

I've seen projects get canceled right around alpha 1. In every case, I've felt that was a mistake based on the stakeholders not understanding how iterative development worked. Canceling early is not the same as failing fast.

My advice is to expect slow results at first. How long depends on the overall scope of the project and the maturity of your code frameworks. As a manager, project manager, or customer, prepare yourself for scarcity up front. Be explicit about being patient. Trust but verify that your dev team is getting somewhere. Tell customers and executives things like "Because this is a new direction for our company, based on an iterative approach, we must lay the groundwork. We need to work on the underwater parts of the iceberg first. Expect a lot of sprints or design sessions at first that don't have anything to do with tangible features. And the first release of the software may seem underwhelming. We fully expect that, and it does not mean the project is failing." Then show them the visualizations for phase proportions, release schedule, and the cancellation point.

As a developer, be sure your stakeholders understand that the lack of tangible features does not mean lack of progress. Give them some kind of indicator as to what parts of the iceberg below the water you're working on and what it means for the upcoming tangible features. Say something like "We wrote an asynchronous processing queue. You can't see it, but this is going to dramatically speed up the creation of features X, Y, and Z and also give us lots of opportunities for real-time customer communication interfaces." Or maybe tell them, "We spent the last two weeks designing the model structure for the sample processing system. Doing so saved us a couple months of rapid prototyping effort, and we also realized features A, B, and C will not be necessary to work on because we found a better way."

## CASE STUDY: THE CANCELLATION POINT

I was once hired to convert a legacy application into a dynamic object-oriented application that could serve a varied group of customers with different requirements. The timeline was two years. But the inexperienced team had no code repository, methodology, coding standards, testing, continuous integration, or peer review process. There was no tracking system for tickets. There *were* no tickets, no documentation, and no deployment strategy or devops.

I spent the first two months alone setting up a code repository, tracking software, continuous integration, etc. It was busywork—vital, absolutely critical busywork.

Then I hired a new development team. We took a look at the requirements and spent a couple weeks creating tickets. We bootstrapped the entire backlog from scratch, for several different customers at once—without a business analyst.

When it came time for design, we had a dizzying array of conflicting requirements and dependencies. We were designing a four-tier architecture with caching, a message broker, and other complex integrations. Also (try to suspend your disbelief) this organization had no breakout or meeting rooms. There were no conference rooms accessible to us, no quiet areas for multiple people to plug in laptops and work with each other.

So we did the only thing we could think to do—we met at a coffee shop nearby. Day after day, which dragged into week after week, then month after month, my whole team parked it in a coffee shop and did one of the gnarliest, most sophisticated designs I've ever been privy to.

It took almost three months.

By then I was five and a half months into a two-year project *without writing a single line of code*.

And periodically, upper managers from some of our customer departments would see a whole dev team drinking coffee and joking around, off company property, and not producing code.

Needless to say, there was consternation. Indignation. Pointed questions in a very suspicious tone.

I'm sugarcoating things. The backlash was so severe, and I was called onto the carpet so harshly, that my supervisor told the rest of the team that I was probably going to resign that day. He fully expected me to walk out the door and never look back.

I did not resign, because I knew what my managers didn't: *my newly formed team had pulled off a miracle*. Understaffed, overtasked, with a nearly unsortable mess of requirements, we came up with a workable design. I knew that this team had highly underappreciated skills and that I could trust them with my reputation any day.

I knew that the project was going to succeed.

And it did. The project has now enjoyed a 10-year run and been adopted far beyond the original customer base.

Had I left in that moment of stakeholder outrage, leaving a handful of recently hired developers with no senior developer to run interference, the project most likely would have become one of the failures I quoted in the introduction.

We had to power through the cancellation point, which was as unpleasant as it gets. But the ecosystem, design, and infrastructure we established in those first months led to highly productive sprints for years thereafter.

CHAPTER 26

# STOP HITTING YOURSELF
# WITH THE IRON FIST

"Let's just hope we survive the cancellation point" is not how most people want to think about launching a project. Here's a more common, and really bad, pattern.

You've launched a new initiative to do iterative development. Let's say you're in a type of company known for conservative business practices, such as health care or manufacturing. (Although finance, defense contracting, and telecommunications are other good examples.) The company has heard through the grapevine that iterative development is the way to go.

So management hires a consultant to train the team in agile development. They pick a framework such as scrum, kanban, or SAFe™. Then the company spends a fair amount of time figuring out how to manage this new entity.

The managers think to themselves:

"This new initiative is a complete unknown. Better take extra care with this one. We need a really detailed road map so we know if this thing is going off the rails. And we should nail down the contract so we don't take a bath. Let's establish a series of deadlines to ensure we're getting value. By the way, let's devote Sally quarter time to keep an eye on resource utilization. We need to optimize everyone's time."

Meanwhile the dev team are having their own thoughts:

"This new initiative is a complete unknown. Better take extra care with this one. We need to really embrace the adaptive process we've selected and be flexible with the schedule. We need to step away from contracts so we don't lock ourselves into a bad design. Let's establish new frameworks to ultimately arrive at the most value. We should lay a really sustainable groundwork so it doesn't go off the rails. And since Sally's been devoted quarter time, we'll be able to get stakeholder buy-in and not waste our time with arbitrary overhead."

There's a big launch meeting, then everyone goes to their separate corners.

The dev team hunkers down and starts designing frameworks. They sizzle their own brains to come up with flexible object models, research best practices, prototypes, and refinements. The team teach themselves languages they don't already know.

A month goes by.

"So, how's the code coming along?" Sally asks nervously.

"Code? Oh, we don't have any code yet. We've been designing frameworks."

Sally goes back to the boardroom.

"They, um, haven't written any software yet. They're designing frameworks.

"No software?! This is an outrage! We need to have a status meeting."

And so the micromanagement begins. Management recruits babysitters or spies, imposes deadlines, and calls for resource utilization. I'll spare you the ensuing angst and cultural clashes and just spoil the ending for you.

Management closes the iron fist, not allowing the dev team to iterate freely. The project fails. And everyone blames the other side for the failure.

## THE FIVE FINGERS OF THE IRON FIST

So, what is the iron fist? It's the five fingers of predictive management meant to exert control over the process:

1. Contracts
2. Deadlines
3. Gatekeeping
4. Resource utilization
5. Context switches

Recall this observation in the "Statement of Problem": "Governing iterative software development through predictive means such as schedule, contracts, timelines, and work breakdown structures is like trying to hold sand in an iron fist. The harder you tighten your grip, the faster the sand falls through."

In this analogy, predictive techniques are fingers that tighten reflexively into a fist when the development process becomes unpredictable or otherwise *suspicious*, untrustworthy, or idealistically detached from the real world of business. So the fingers tighten to exert some form of control, reigning in spending and getting back on track.

The sand in this analogy is whatever you care about the most: money, data, or scientific results, perhaps. It is the delicate, fluid, ever-shifting dance of iterative development—both the process itself and also resources of time, money, and people. This tightening of the fist causes the sand of optimal flow and resources to squeeze out between the cracks. The process slows. More time is spent overall trying to iterate as before while meeting these new demands of gatekeeping meetings and artificial deadlines. The attempts to optimize resources only bog the process down, erroneously filling white space in the process with additional tasks that derail the whole.

For an excellent illustration of that point, watch "The Resource Utilization Trap" by Henrik Kniberg of Crisp Agile Academy.[75] This video is legendary among agile coaches. We secretly wish every manager would watch it and embrace it.

And whatever you do, don't forget about the worst programmer in the world, Tim Mackinnon, mentioned in the Threads of Work section in part 1.[76]

When you squeeze the iron fist, whatever you value most disappears faster. So the fist tightens more. People burn out and leave. The project fails.

The whole time, management believes they're doing the right thing. The fingers of the iron fist are great approaches to use in a manufacturing

75    Henrik Kniberg, "The Resource Utilization Trap," Crisp Agile Academy, November 3, 2014, YouTube video, 5:33, https://www.youtube.com/watch?v=CostXs2p6r0.
76    Dan North, "The Worst Programmer I Know."

environment or very large-scale project. If you have control of the process, and know the expected inputs and outputs, those approaches help a lot.

They are detrimental to a small or midsize iterative project with less definite outputs, which embrace flexibility and change. Just look at the term "road map." It implies there is a road and that you're in a car. You know where you are going and how long it should take to get there.

If you know all of that stuff, why are you doing iterative development? Iterative might tell you to hop in a dune buggy and go over that sand dune to get to the endpoint faster. Or it might tell you to float in a hot air balloon and take an extra week to reach the final location, which, by the way, is now in Toledo instead of Miami.

Don't just take my word for it. In "Why Trust Is More Than Agility," Peter Malina characterizes the struggle for team self-management like this:

> If management requires teams to adhere to a common agile standard, they likely don't trust the teams. Instead of fixing their relationship with the teams, management slaps a process on top, creating a sense of control. This will seemingly work for a scaling company sitting on a revenue stream because money still flows. However, from then on, the company will rely on the value created in the past and a vast marketing/sales spend. A breaking point will come when they hold all the meetings they are supposed to, all the sprints have 100% committed delivery, and the company is bleeding money. Damnit agile! We are supposed to be making it right according to our KPIs, OKRs, MBOs, CSFs, ROIs, ... ![77]

## JUST HOLD ON LOOSELY

I have a metaphor for this concept that is a bit silly, but it never fails to

---

77   Peter Malina, "Why Trust Is More than Agility," *Peter Malina* (blog), accessed September 21, 2023, https://petermalina.com/posts/trust_vs_agility.

help me remember the dangers of the iron fist. It's a manual can opener. You know, those two handles with a couple gears and a round blade that you clamp over a tin can and crank, thereby slicing the top out in a circle.

I've been using those things my whole life, cursing them the whole time. Who invented this cheap junk? The blade always skips around, leaving a dotted circle of cuts and bent metal. I have to try over and over, circling the can lid until it looks like a crumpled mess. The thing keeps popping off the can lid, pinching my fingers while I scream at the kitchen walls. No matter how tightly I clench the handles, no matter how hard I bear down on the crank, it makes no difference. No matter which brand I use, or how sharp or dull the blade is, it makes no difference. The blasted things barely work.

Recently I was at mixed martial arts practice, and the punching drills got a little out of hand. I was facing off against a black belt, and I asked him if I could go full out—give 100 punches and receive 100 punches. The end result was that I gave myself a rotator cuff injury. Over a couple months, I lost a lot of hand strength.

One day I needed to open a can, and I was dreading it. My hand just didn't really have the strength to close all that well. Nevertheless, I grabbed the can opener as best I could and weakly cranked the crank. The can lid almost freed itself. The opener cut like a dream, creating a perfect, unbroken circle with hardly any effort from me.

At first I thought it was a fluke. But no. Ever since then, I have loosely held the handles and lightly turned the crank, and the can opener works flawlessly. No matter which brand I use, or how sharp or dull the blade is, it makes no difference. The things work perfectly.

Now you might think this next part is too good to be true, but sometimes situational irony really happens. Spotify was playing 38 Special. And right around the time I was using my weakened hand to open that can, the chorus of "Hold On Loosely" came on.

I kid you not. The universe was telling me how to open a tin can. My whole life I was convinced that more pressure, more control was the way, and success eluded me. It took a literal whack to the face for me to get it.

And now I am telling you something similar about managing an iterative software process. No matter how convinced you are that more pressure and more control are the keys to managing an iterative process, they aren't. The key is to use the lightest touch you can get away with. Guide the gears. Don't drive them to greater speed or pressure. Look on in wonderment as the tools you put into place (the can opener) and the dev team you hired (the hand using the tool) seamlessly deliver value (open the can.)

## EXCEPT...HYBRID AGILE IS A THING

Ahh, exceptions. Thought we were done with those, eh?

Now that I have thoroughly demonized predictive management approaches, let's take a step back. The blur box indicates that there are prelaunch and postlaunch efforts that are not the focus of the model.

Getting your organization to the starting line (the divergence point) is not at all the same thing as managing an iterative software development process. Prediction and control are detrimental in a venture where you are explicitly admitting you don't know the answer in advance. But prediction and control might be perfectly fine in the context of organizing an enterprise effort.

It's a little more complicated where postlaunch (after the convergence point) activities are concerned. There's a problem that there's no getting around: downstream people and processes—sales, marketing, distribution, advertising, documentation, trainers, etc., and the customers themselves—need to know when the software is going to be "done."

It's entirely plausible that those downstream efforts are more predictable than iterative software development is. Traditional, established approaches such as deadlines might be an excellent fit for a deployment and release process that you know well. The further away you move from an iterative process, the better a fit the iron-fist techniques become. In fact, senior executives might never directly manage an iterative process, depending on the type of business you're in.

Unfortunately, there is still a thorny issue to resolve: how to manage the handoff between an iterative process and a traditional environment. You can't arrive at a convergence point until you know the criteria and timeline for that point.

I delve into this issue in a later section called "Sliding Timeline (Fog of War)." But I wanted to acknowledge the utility of predictive approaches here because they probably factor into the overall organizational culture.

CHAPTER 27

# CATCH YOURSELF WITH THE OPEN HAND

Let's look at a more agile way of managing projects. Responsive values are more effective than predictive in an iterative process. A much better approach is the open hand. This seeks to respond and prevent, replacing the iron fist and its desire to predict and control.

The open hand aims to catch the sand and only keep as much time/ effort/resources as needed in play at any given time. It values five elements:

- Collaboration over contracts
- Stop signs over gatekeeping
- Priority shifts over deadlines
- White space over utilization
- Flow over context switching

I'll discuss these ideas more in later sections. If you take an overall sense of it, the open-hand approach aims to keep things moving in a fluid way. Boxes and barriers are reduced so there is maximum freedom to innovate and iterate. You aren't so much proclaiming how things should be but guiding efforts toward the top value with the best outcome.

If you do things right, your project will become a fuzzy blur. It's exhilarating—and troubling if you're used to control. But that same troubling blur is a really good sign that your team is in flow. You no longer need to motivate, marshal, kick-start, or utilize. That horse has already left the barn. Excellent work! You're blurring now. Shift your focus to maintaining and curating.

Seek adaptive rather than predictive methods
when managing an iterative effort

# CHAPTER 28

# ESTIMATION...OR GUESS-TIMATION?

OK, project managers, tell me if this sounds familiar:

> You: "When will the software be done?"
> Your dev team: "AAAAARRRGHHHHHHHHHHhhhh …"

For my teams, the keys to making our managers and stakeholders love us are to provide accurate estimates of what we're going to do, then stand behind those estimates. If we're not going to make our estimate, we set up cots in the break room and eat canned beans in shifts until we deliver what we promised.

So when estimation time comes around, we are very serious. It's part game, part debate, but 100% concentration. We all have decks of playing cards with possible estimates on them, known as estimation decks, which we sit around with and show our estimates at the same time like some twisted version of Texas Hold'em.

I love estimation poker. I love all of the trappings that go along with it. I'm so pumped about this process that I custom made my team's decks. We each have our own personal card backs with amusing medieval/modern puns about agile development. If you didn't think I was a hopeless geek before, this should cinch it for you: a dragon drinking coffee while chained to fatigue, knights jousting with mechanical pencils, a royal coat of arms featuring an elementary school protractor, knights giving it the old college try, and whiteboard markers providing the waters of life.

It occurs to me that I did these print on demand back in the day, so I guess technically you could have them too, if you want. I don't remember if I get zero cents from them or a handful of cents from them, so this is either a cool at-cost giveaway or a shameless ad. Also there are no coffee dragon backs in that set. But the front sides have cats and centaurs and stuff, so there's that:[78]

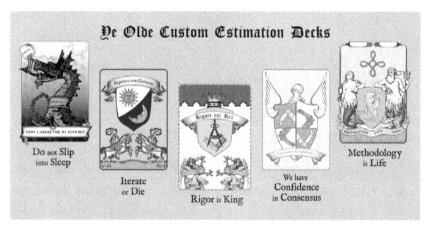

Regardless of what deck you use, there are two ways to estimate a ticket. One is time, such as "That will take 2 days." The other is relative effort, where you say, "That's 2 story points." Let's take a look at those two types.

## EFFORT ESTIMATION: WHAT EVERYONE TELLS YOU TO DO

Effort uses comparison between tickets to gauge complexity. For example, ticket 123 (table won't wrap) is only half as complex as that other ticket we

---

78  Find the cards here: https://www.makeplayingcards.com/sell/marketplace/estimation-poker-deck.html.

did last week.

In order to gauge complexity, it used to be that T-shirt sizing was the advised approach. The team would say, "That's an extra-small ticket," or "That's a large ticket." But numbers made a bit more sense to people because relative complexity is easier to grasp.

So, come sprint-planning time, we developers all sit around a table with our estimation decks and come up with a number called a "story point" selected from the following choices in a modified Fibonacci sequence:

**0  1/2  1  2  3  5  8  13  20  40  60  80  100 INFINITY**

Okay, fair enough. What does a story point mean? Generally speaking, it's a reference to some barometer of that team's past effort. One point for team A is not the same as one point for team B.

Tyler Hakes at the *7pace* blog and Sam Perera at Momenton wrote up excellent examples of the prevailing wisdom when it comes to estimation poker. They go through the pros and cons of time vs. effort estimation, why you should treat story points as relative numbers, and why you should avoid treating a Fibonacci sequence as a number of days.[79] I don't know Tyler or Sam, but their articles are both really excellent write-ups that capture the current conventional wisdom as I understand it.

The key point here is that by using an abstracted number such as story points, the whole estimation process becomes more flexible. You pick a baseline story, talk about it, and set it to "5." Then you compare the effort of the other stories in the backlog to that one or other reference stories your team builds up over the years.

This estimate of effort decoupled from time lets you do a lot of interesting math with velocity and refine your efficiency as the project matures.

---

[79]   Tyler Hakes, "Ideal Days vs. Story Points: Which Is Better and Why?," *7pace* (blog), January 25, 2021, https://www.7pace.com/blog/ideal-days-vs-story-points. Sam Perera, "Effort Estimating: Person-Days or Story-Points?," *Momenton* (blog), Medium, November 18, 2019, https://medium.com/momenton/effort-estimating-person-days-or-story-points-4c5301277423.

## TIME ESTIMATION: WHAT MY TEAMS ACTUALLY DO

In time estimation, you simply estimate how long a ticket will take in terms of hours, days, or whatever granularity your team prefers. In this case, you are not limited to a specific sequence of numbers.

Time estimation is my preferred approach because the game of relative-ticket sizing gets old fast. New people aren't going to know about that ticket you did three months ago that was three times as big as the other one from six months ago. So you need to reset the estimation with new stories, which may or may not link in scale to past estimates.

You want to know what an excellent reference point is for relative complexity? Days. You *could* say, "This will be twice as complicated as my prediction for the story we did last year for updating test procedure specification reports, which took eight hours." Or you can say, "This will take two days."

When a new developer comes on, you can explain all the past stories, how complex they were, and how the ticket ended up taking 16 hours. Or you can ask, "How many days do you think this will take?"

You can go to your project manager and say, "We've completed our estimates. This sprint is a 108. Last sprint was a 72. Our velocity is 78%, and the 72 last time took 17 actual days, so if we carry the two and divide by 11.333, this one will take 26.25 days with our current staffing." Or you can add up the points and say, "This sprint will take 26 days."

Obviously you can use a calculator or software to do the agile estimation math. You can use project management software to tell you the values. But it's a layer of abstraction that ultimately doesn't prove itself worth the mental gymnastics of thinking in abstracts rather than concretes.

I think in terms of days. You think in terms of days. Your project manager thinks in terms of days. The junior dev you just hired thinks in terms of days. Your Chinese team and Indian team and West Coast team do, too.

Now, everything is much simpler and more descriptive.

For example, when doing sprint planning, you have to decide the number of points the sprint has available. Well, points are days. So if Jake is on vacation that week? Knock five points off the sprint. Is your whole team of seven developers in an all-day training one day? Knock off seven points. Are two developers going to pair program on a story all day? It's a 2-point story. Is one person going to work two days on a ticket? It's a 2-point story.

A lot of agile consultants out there are probably cringing right now, so let me discuss my reasoning.

Ideal person days are not a new concept. An ideal person day (IPD) is the amount of work that one developer can complete when left uninterrupted with everything going well. But the current conventional wisdom is that IPDs are unrealistic and also limit the flexibility of the estimation process.

One benefit I see often quoted for story points is that they are quicker. Instead of thinking in terms of time you just say, "That is more complex than our index user story #153." You know what everyone grasps? Days. What don't they grasp? Index user story #153.

Some say that using story points allows you to build a more and more accurate library of past estimations. You know what is a 100% calibrated barometer? A day. It doesn't matter which sprint you are in now or 10 years from now, which makes reports such as the burndown chart much more useful.

## THE BURNDOWN CHART IS YOUR BEST FRIEND (SOMETIMES)

A burndown chart has the number of calendar days in the sprint on one axis, the number of estimated points on the other, and a diagonal line connecting the two. If your sprint is ahead of schedule, your trendline will be below the line. If you are behind, your trendline will be above the line.

A burndown chart is really good for tracking progress. Now let's do a simulated conversation between upper management and the project manager:

"How's the sprint going?"

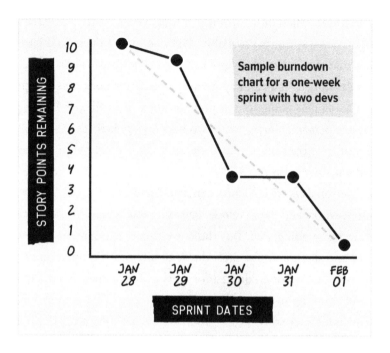

Sample burndown chart for a one-week sprint with two devs

STORY POINTS REMAINING

SPRINT DATES

"Well, we're above the line. So we're behind. We're behind by 4 story points."

"How long is that?"

"Well, given that reference user story #167 took 2 points at a velocity of 92%, carry the 11, subtract 6, OK, we're roughly 4 days behind."

Compare it to this:

"How's the sprint going?"

"Hmm, 4 points above the line ... we're 4 days behind."

I think you understand some of the reasons I prefer this approach by now but just to be explicit, consider this:

Days are explicit.

Days are simple.

Every human instinctively understands days.

Team A and team B both understand days.

A day in China, India, California, New York, Sandusky, and Durham are all the same.

A day from your sprint six years ago is the same as a day from your sprint next week.

## PLOT TWIST: IT WAS NEVER ABOUT TIME

But simplicity is not the only reason why I do this. It's for building trust.

I have tried T-shirt sizing, story points, and relative-complexity measures based on effort instead of time. And you know what happened?

My team's estimates got worse—much, much worse.

Now it's entirely possible that I did it wrong and, therefore, missed out on the benefits of agile estimation best practices.

But, I have a master's degree in iterative development methodologies, and I've been running agile teams for two decades. So, yes, I might have missed something, but if so, it wasn't something straightforward.

You know what is straightforward? Days.

I tell my team they are in trouble if we finish a sprint later than promised. I also tell them they are in trouble if they deliver earlier than we promised.

We all get the first one. Late is bad.

But delivering early also gives upper managers a reason to doubt my team's estimates. If we consistently sandbag, management will no longer trust my team's estimates. They'll give us extra work. And then we're right back in the nasty cycle of fake deadlines and buffered estimates.

If we are half a day out, and the work is done early, I send my team home. Good job everyone, we made great estimates and earned a break. And voilà! We delivered the software exactly on time as promised.

If we are running a day or more of sprint time early (which means our estimates were blown by at least 1 × number of team members), celebration time is over. We need to decide which negative outcome to choose. We can keep pulling tickets from the backlog and deliver extra features in the sprint. Then we can bend over backward to explain to management why this is actually bad and pretty please with sugar on top do not expect such extra output in the future. Otherwise, they'll risk the sanity of the dev team.

Or we can context switch to some other project, losing momentum and energy, to work on remedial tasks such as code cleanup, possibly doing a poor job that puts us behind because our brains weren't in that space.

If we are running half a day late, people need to do a gut check and dig deep—skipping lunch or working late. If we're running a day or more late (which again, means our estimates were blown by 1 × team size), then we have even more negative consequences to select from. We can pull features from the sprint to move into the backlog. Then we can bend over backward to explain to the customer why their feature didn't get done. If that isn't possible because of dependencies or release stability, we might extend the sprint, thereby announcing to the whole company that we blew our estimates. Then we can explain to management why this is bad, but pretty please with sugar on top, do not introduce extra overhead of status reports in the future. Otherwise, they'll risk the sanity of the dev team.

But I don't make people work weekends. We just have to live with the consequences of delivering late.

It doesn't take very long for everyone to become comfortable with the realities of estimation. Very quickly, by using estimated IPDs, a modified list of time choices, a burndown chart, and promised functionality within a sprint and by having to do damage control for early or late delivery, the estimation process gets very accurate.

I can relax, my managers can relax, and my team can relax. We are building trust—with numbers everyone can understand.

CHAPTER 29

# AVOID LATE-DISCOVERY SYNDROME

The main benefit of the blur box approach is avoidance of the late-discovery syndrome of the waterfall methodology. Teams revisit design, user requirements, and development so frequently that there is a very low probability of implementation failure.

Looking at it a different way, agile is one of the best ways to help you fail fast. That's a relatively recent goal of entrepreneurial efforts, where containing resource spending as tightly as possible helps determine the overall success of the venture. When a team tackles a project with lots of unknowns, the goal is to either prove the concept has legs or to fail fast so as to not waste resources.

For those exploratory ventures, agile approaches protect you by giving you early insight into success through tight customer interactions. For larger-scale projects that you're committed to seeing through, agile also protects you by preventing late discovery of problems and dramatically increasing the success of implementations.

# CHAPTER 30

# ASSEMBLING A BLUR-READY TEAM

Your goal is to build a self-managing team that can not only survive the blur box but thrive in the dizzying blur of shifting threads and phases. There's a huge overlap between this and simply hiring the best software development professionals you can find, regardless of methodology or organizational culture. So this section is not an exhaustive guide to hiring talent but rather some unique characteristics to keep in mind when hiring a blur-box-ready team.

## EXPERIENCE REQUIRED

The fuzzy blur is a welcome controlled chaos for seasoned developers who lean toward that mindset. They appreciate the flexibility and freedom, while also assuming more responsibility for their own outcomes. New developers, or developers who prefer a regimented approach, can be very uncomfortable with iterative development. New developers in particular don't have the insight to know what they don't know, avoid pitfalls, or know when to drop something that isn't working.

A large part of the success of an agile approach is having experienced developers. Without such leadership and guidance at the helm of development, the guidelines presented from this model will not work.

## CROSS-FUNCTIONALITY GIVES YOU A SAFETY NET

Another key requirement besides experience is cross functional team members. If you have a business analyst who analyzes, an architect who designs, a few developers who develop, and a tester who tests, that is siloing. The guidelines presented from this model will not work in that situation either because you have bottlenecks. You need people who can analyze *and* test, design *and* develop.

We often call this dichotomy "generalists vs. specialists." A specialized business analyst or software tester is almost certainly going to be better at their specialized tasks than a generalist developer. If you have a critical need for very refined analysis or extremely precise testing, a generalist is not the best person for that job. Hire a specialist.

The trade-off of having specialists is the constant handoff of findings. The chain of custody becomes quite burdensome. Whereas a team of generalists will seamlessly hop between analysis, design, and development.

Cross-functionality is the perfect embodiment of the adage "Jack-of-all-trades," first mentioned in 1410, as a compliment for a multiskilled worker. The term later became a snub in the late 1700s, when "master of none" was added to highlight the inferior skill sets of the generalist when compared to the specialist. And recently that snub has reversed so that the whole phrase reads "Jack-of-all-trades, master of none, is oftentimes better than master of one."[80]

Undoubtedly another stanza will be added to praise specialists in the future.

80    Gary Martin, s.v. "Jack of All Trades," The Phrase Finder, accessed January 19, 2024, https://www.phrases.org.uk/meanings/jack-of-all-trades.html.

As far as agile project leaders are concerned, the takeaway here is there must be a core of experience on the team. The team must be internally motivated. They must have personalities that embrace change rather than seek predictability.

According to Scott Ambler, you ideally want a team of *generalizing specialists,* the sweet spot between generalists and specialists. The concept of generalizing specialists originated in Scott Ambler's book *Agile Database Techniques*[81] and was further discussed in *Agile Modeling.*[82] In his *Agile Modeling* blog in a post titled "Generalizing Specialists: Improving Your Effectiveness," Scott describes the benefits of generalizing specialists on team collaboration like this:

> A generalizing specialist is someone with a good grasp of how everything fits together. As a result they will typically have a greater understanding and appreciation of what their teammates are working on. They are willing to listen to and work with their teammates because they know that they'll likely learn something new. Specialists, on the other hand, often don't have the background to appreciate what other specialists are doing, often look down on that other work, and often aren't as willing to cooperate. Specialists, by their very nature, can become a barrier to communication within your team.[83]

Scott Ambler and Mark Lines discuss this same idea in their book *Disciplined Agile Delivery:*

> There are many general strategies to improve your learning capability. Improved collaboration between people correspondingly increases the opportunities for people to learn from one another.

81    Scott W. Ambler, *Agile Database Techniques: Effective Strategies for the Agile Software Developer* (New York: John Wiley and Sons, 2003).
82    Ambler, *Agile Modeling.*
83    Scott W. Ambler, "Generalizing Specialists: Improving Your Effectiveness," Agile Modeling, accessed January 19, 2024, https://agilemodeling.com/essays/generalizingspecialists.htm.

Luckily high collaboration is a hallmark of agility. Investing in training, coaching, and mentoring are obvious learning strategies as well. What may not be so obvious is the move away from promoting specialization among your staff and instead fostering a move toward people with more robust skills.[84]

Speaking of agile coaching, if you want to follow the advice above, you owe it to yourself to read Bob Galen's book *Extraordinarily Badass Agile Coaching: The Journey from Beginner to Mastery and Beyond*.[85] I attended the Agile Coach Camp RTP and heard Bob speak on the Agile Coaching Growth Wheel. I can attest that he is the kind of agile coach you want to enlist, and he can probably hook you up with some great resources.

With the above understanding of the generalist vs. specialist trade-off in mind, here is a cautionary tale regarding the negative consequences of siloing in an agile environment. It was posted by an anonymous redditor on a thread that no longer exists. So, you know, word-on-the-street type stuff. Take it for what you will, but it strikes me as an authentic report of the issue.

An organization attempting to be agile implemented scrum, yet had silos within teams and across teams. Quality assurance specialists could only do quality assurance. Developers were only allowed to develop software. The managerial explanation for the siloing was, if the devs helped out with anything else, they wouldn't be producing value-add work. The result of the siloing was counterproductive, however. Overly large "agile" teams of 12–20 people—that were actually very good at navigating the siloed environment—did not produce a whole lot more work than a truly self-organizing, four-person team that followed agile practices.

---

84    Ambler and Lines, *Disciplined Agile Delivery*, 8.
85    Robert L. Galen, *Extraordinarily Badass Agile Coaching: Beginner to Mastery and Beyond* (RGCG, LLC, January 27, 2022).

## HIRING CONSIDERATIONS FOR AN AGILE TEAM

Team building is a little bit art, a little bit science, and a little bit luck. Even so, there are some specific considerations in building a team to confront the blur box.

First off, for the absolute lowest entry-level requirements, you must have at least two developers. That's the bare minimum necessary for doing code reviews and paired programming. I suggest at least four. That lets you split pairs off to tackle the highest-priority tickets in parallel and also have sufficient code review.

Of those four, at least one must be a seasoned developer—preferably two. Seasoned developers have seen how requirements can hide behind customer's words. They have the guts to push back against stakeholders or management. They have the experience to know why best practices are best. They've learned to avoid traps. All of those qualities are necessary for navigating the blur box. In the rush of iteration, experience is often the deciding factor between success and failure.

When interviewing junior developers, there are a few things I've learned to look for. The most important thing is to look for signs that they code because they want to. They have an inherent drive for it. It's pretty easy to spot someone who got a computer science degree just because they thought they'd get a good job from it. If you find someone who talks about programming remote controls as a kid or writing software to organize their music collection, those are very good signs. Such signs outweigh any specific languages or platforms you want them to know.

To give you an example, I was the senior developer on an enterprise dev team who needed to fill a programmer position. I was given the opportunity to hire anyone I wanted, no matter how experienced. The sky was the limit. I had one chance to pick whomever I wished. One of my options was a programmer I knew by his excellent reputation, who had 20 years of experience in our technology stack, whom management wanted to hire.

I opted for a programmer named Ben Phillips who'd been an intern at a consulting company I previously worked for. On paper, Ben had a biology background, graduated from a coding school, and had only three months of software development experience. However, in that time, he had contributed to the Django core (the primary technology we used) and had also devised a strategy to get 100% test coverage in an application. Not unit tested, which is not easy, but straightforward. I mean automated web testing, which simulates user interactions. So I said "I want Ben Phillips." My manager at the time looked at me like I was detached from the realities of business. His reply was "If this doesn't work, I'm going to throw you under the bus."

Spoiler alert: I did not get thrown under the bus. Ben is now a senior who is leading me on one of our apps. And by hiring a junior dev, I was able to finagle getting the senior guy as well with a little political shenanigans.

Another good sign is contribution to an open-source project. If your interviewee mentions an open-source project they wrote code for, that means they are already familiar with how to work within a team. Also, open-source projects have code standards.

The final quality I look for is curiosity. Have they dived into something just to see how it works? Do they have lots of hobbies? Did they solve a tricky problem through research? The blur box doesn't leave anyone much time for easing in. Programmers who have the mindset of seeking solutions through self-reliance and curiosity will excel.

## LARGER SCALE HAS ITS OWN CHALLENGES

Now let's say you don't have a tiny team as I described above. Let's say you have an entire enterprise with hundreds of developers. Does agile work in such an environment?

In my opinion, no. And yes. It depends. (Come on, you knew that answer was coming.)

One of the worst-kept secrets in software development is that it's hard to be agile in a bureaucratic environment. And the larger the organization, the more bureaucratic it tends to be. Agile is fundamentally a revolution against bureaucracy.

Larger groups are less agile. It's just a reality. The more communication pathways, the more people to coordinate, the more features to simultaneously deliver, the less agile you can be. You are constrained by the laws of time and space, the nature of human communication and collaboration, time zones, sleep schedules, and varying degrees of experience. A six-person team has 15 communication pathways. A ten-person team has 45, which is almost unmanageable. Remember, the final reveal of the blur box is that it's three-dimensional.

There are frameworks out there that claim to help enterprises scale their agility. I do not endorse any specific framework or methodology. My own experience is that the more your process resembles a published framework, the less mature your agile process is—for two reasons. First, no one in the world knows your organization the way you do. Second, the entire point of being agile is to iterate. As I've mentioned once or twice, "iteration" means starting from a certain point, figuring out what worked and what didn't, and changing your process accordingly.

Recent adoptees of an agile process rightfully cling to a framework as a guide. It makes perfect sense. If your organization knew how to be agile, you wouldn't be hiring consultants to implement a framework. You have to start somewhere, and a framework is a great place to start.

It's a horrible place to end up.

What does this have to do with enterprise agility?

Smaller teams are more agile. So a widely accepted technique in large organizations is to structure the development team into smaller teams that act independently of each other. They have their own culture and ways of working that are not imposed at an enterprise level but self-managed at the team level.

Amazon has most notably characterized this concept as two-pizza teams. Your team size should cap out at the number of people two pizzas can feed. Amazon is widely considered the most successful agile organization the world has ever known, so this concept is worth exploring.

Daniel Slater, the worldwide head of innovation at Amazon Web Services, describes the concept in an article titled "Powering Innovation and Speed with Amazon's Two-Pizza Teams":

> The concept of Amazon's two-pizza teams is straightforward: no team should be big enough that it would take more than two pizzas to feed them. Putting aside the number or the nature of toppings (we don't have time and space to solve the "does pineapple belong on pizza?" debate here), ideally, this is a team of less than 10 people: smaller teams minimize lines of communication and decrease overhead of bureaucracy and decision-making. This allows two-pizza teams to spend more time focusing on their customers, and constantly experimenting and innovating on their behalf—the biggest priority of high-performing teams at Amazon.[86]

A similar approach worked at Spotify, which is another of the world's most successful enterprise agile organizations. In "What Really Happened at Spotify," Brendan Marsh discusses how "the model is all about empowered teams, constantly trying new ways of working and organizing themselves to find the best way to move faster."[87]

OK, so what does that mean for those of you trying to implement agile on a large scale?

---

86   Daniel Slater, "Powering Innovation and Speed with Amazon's Two-Pizza Teams," AWS Executive Insights, accessed January 19, 2024, https://aws.amazon.com/executive-insights/content/amazon-two-pizza-team/.

87   Murray Robinson, Shane Gibson, and Brendan Marsh, "#0077 - Brendan Marsh - What Really Happened at Spotify," March 31, 2023, in *No Nonsense Agile*, podcast, MP3 audio, 60:00, https://nononsenseagile.podbean.com/e/0077-brendan-marsh-what-really-happened-at-spotify/.

I have a few suggestions for you, which I'm certain will ruffle some feathers, but so be it. First, I recommend that you shy away from any solution that claims to implement agile at an enterprise level. Instead, treat each of your smaller teams as … a smaller team. Then do all the stuff I talk about in this book. Grab a team-oriented framework or methodology—I recommend scrumban—and iterate from there.

Organize your teams into groups oriented toward a subset of your overall feature set or align them with specific customers. Assign a customer liaison to each team. Then assign a project manager to each group to help guide each of the teams.

Then take an organizational approach to instilling a culture of agility rather than bureaucracy. *Disciplined Agile Delivery* provides a lot of wisdom toward that end that is based in decades of implementations and metrics.

# CHAPTER 31

# BUSINESS ANALYSTS WILL PRESERVE YOUR SANITY

Speaking of customer liaisons, that's our next point of discussion. Aside from programmers, one role will dramatically improve your dev team's effectiveness: a dedicated business analyst embedded in the dev team itself—but with a twist. The business analyst's sole task is to make sure the dev team is working on the right thing based on customer requirements. That role appears in various ways in various methodologies (for example, product owner in scrum.) So for the sake of standardization I will refer to this role as "business analyst."

Customers will say things like "We need feature X as soon as possible." The dev team will say things like "We need to write framework Y as soon as possible." The business analyst needs to sit with the dev team long enough to understand their mindset, then sit with the customer long enough to understand their problems. Then the business analyst needs to synthesize these differing viewpoints so they can effectively guide the dev team.

Without a business analyst, you will lose money as multiple of your highest-paid developers spend extra weeks interacting with the customers to gather requirements and verify the usefulness of the software. They also won't be as effective.

There are also technical reasons for having this role. A business analyst is an ideal person to test the software when the sprint ends. They are the most knowledgeable about the customer's needs.

Another technical benefit comes in at sprint-planning time. One of the sacrosanct mandates of agile development is that somebody is responsible for requesting and prioritizing features, and the dev team is responsible for estimating and performing the work to deliver them. Without someone responsible for requests and prioritization, you are setting up a situation where the dev team tells itself what to work on.

That can be OK. Experienced dev teams will make good faith efforts to get inside the customers' heads and deliver value. In greenfield development or entrepreneurial efforts, there may not be a clear customer mandate. The venture is all about making a new market open up, so a self-directed dev team might be fine. But invariably, this approach will fail given enough time.

The best thing you can do to ensure your own success is to hire or repurpose an full-time equivalent (FTE) to be the product owner / business analyst / whatever term you want to use. Embed them in the same reporting structure as your developers, or perhaps in a value management office (VMO) if you have one. That person either already knows the customer's needs, or it's their full-time job to learn them. That person feeds the dev team tickets in ranked order.

These are some things that will not work:

- Not hiring/repositioning a dedicated FTE
- Asking Sally from finance services to add "dev team liaison" to her job responsibilities in between all the other stuff she's doing
- Taking on the responsibility yourself as a C-level manager
- Thinking you've got it covered by hiring a project manager
- Scheduling routine customer interactions and calling it good enough

If you do any of the above, here is what will happen in reality. Your dev team will get a sloppy batch of half-baked requirements. They'll go into extended design sessions to uncover the truth. They'll create prototypes for the customer, get the response, then scrap the whole thing and start over. They'll ask questions, get crickets in response, and do busywork or play video games until someone provides an answer.

If you want two or more of your highest-paid people to waste 25%–50% of their time, and produce worse software than they would otherwise, then by all means neglect the business analyst role.

An example from my own experience illustrates the point. I was leading a team in an established medical department at a top-tier university. I'd been hired to redesign a departmental application to scale across the entire medical school. We did so successfully and gained a lot of credibility—too much credibility.

One day, a C-level executive asked us to implement a new module that extended the functionality of our app. Let's call it the "process review module," which was meant to produce an annual report highlighting the performance of various teams within the enterprise.

"No problem," we said. "What features should it have? What should it look like?"

"Just build a process review module."

"We don't know what that is. Can you give us more detail?"

"Just ask around."

With those requirements in hand, we went forth and asked people what a process review module is and how it should behave. We talked with middle managers, people on the teams being reviewed, the HR rep, and whoever else might shed some light on this. We got back a vaguely aligned set of answers with lots of conflicting requirements. We asked the C-level exec again, but they didn't have time to reply other than that the process review module was our number one priority and to just make it happen.

So my team spent the next four months synthesizing the messy requirements into a flexible review module. We intuited how it should probably work and built the interfaces.

At 6:30 a.m. the day that year's process review cycle began, I got a call from the exec. I knew it was trouble the minute the admin assistant told me to hold. The exec asked me what the app was doing, where was feature XYZ, where was report ABC, and how did it handle the university's process review required metrics?

See, the exec had one thing in mind. They'd used a process for several years and assumed we'd be able to figure it out by talking to others. They trusted us because of our track record.

But the software we spent four months blindly developing was a hot mess. It made no one happy. And that year's process review was a disaster for multiple departments.

To our credit and the credit of the agile process, the second we got those new requirements, we were able to immediately start modifying the software. But the core design was simply flawed. No matter how much we polished the ... well, you know ... it didn't shine.

Had we a dedicated business analyst whose job was to discuss requirements with everyone—instead of a team of software developers asking ad hoc questions of whomever was handy at the time—we would have saved 10 months of development time. We had spent four months on the initial release, two months polishing the flawed design, and four months creating an entirely new process review module based on the requirements that came at us like a firehose once the initial release went out.

By the way, that process review module is now our most successful feature set in the history of the project.

CHAPTER 32

# TEAM CHEMISTRY CAN MAKE
# OR BREAK YOUR PROJECT

In this book I've given some highly biased advice to steer away from traditional management practices and to instead embrace the adaptive nature of iteration, trust your team, and clear their way. That message is intended to keep you from inadvertently getting in your team's way through well-meaning—but inefficient—ingrained practices.

However, I don't advocate for unquestioning faith or abandoning your own managerial instincts. Taking the uncomfortable steps toward working in a new way is different from surrendering complete control of the process. One of the easiest ways to lose control and dive off the cliff toward failure is building the wrong kind of team and then handing them the keys.

There are many ways a team can fail while still looking OK from the outside. The anecdotes below are meant to show how team dynamics can be a good or bad fit within an agile environment.

> I worked with a company switching to scrum with feature teams, but [they wanted] to keep a "center of excellence" with a lead for that role. A coworker and I were brought in to help genericize some of their code for the "80%" scenario and share it among the

new teams. The lead was dictatorial (in all the wrong ways), to the point he forced us to use some code he wrote a decade prior that he couldn't explain the benefit for and then started forcing the other 20% use cases in while everyone else was clocked off (which resulted in feature teams having to actually override his code to do the custom, specific thing they needed and bloated the source library with unused code.) When I called him out on a couple different occasions, including in standup at one point, the attitude was essentially "Well, he's the lead, he can do what he wants." It totally ruined the "self-organizing" aspect on the actual feature teams and made for several demotivated employees.

I joined a team where the tech lead who was the project manager/ scrum master spent 20 minutes explaining waterfall to me only for him to end with "and that's how we do agile here."

Most of our team adjusted to the culture of pair programming and code reviews. But there were two guys who refused to use the issue tracker, refused to pair with others, and got very prickly whenever they were asked to work with the rest of the team. On the outside these guys both acted and seemed the same. But they had different reasons for their refusal to work in an agile way.

The first guy acted that way because he was a terrible programmer. He knew it. He also knew that by pairing or undergoing code review, his strategy (make really obtuse code to camouflage his inadequacies) would be revealed. Shortly after forcing him to undergo code reviews, he got really defensive and quit. We found out at that time how horrible his project was, and we needed to redo it.

The second guy (whose behavior was seemingly identical to the first guy) thought he was a terrible programmer and that he was going to be revealed as a fraud. But he was a perfectly fine programmer; he just had impostor syndrome. He was terrified of the few easily teachable criteria his code wasn't meeting. Once we started pairing, he was relieved. He started following the process and writing better code. He turned out to be a good asset to our team.

The moral of this story for me is that pair programming and code reviews both forced good outcomes. One is we lost an FTE that was better for us to lose. It also helped another FTE thrive.

# CHAPTER 33

# UNDERSTAFFED TEAMS WREAK HAVOC

I have sprinkled advice about understaffed teams throughout this book. But I want to collate and restate them here because understaffing is a common—and perilous—reality in many organizations.

In any business venture, you want the right team in place. Even so, there are cases where understaffing isn't a death knell. In sales, for example, an insufficient number of sales representatives will not inherently lead to your product being a failure. Your growth might not be as fast as you want, but the downside is not total project collapse. In manufacturing, not having enough line workers will slow your output. But the product you're building isn't any different. In short, there are many situations where understaffing slows progress but does not stall it.

In agile software development, there are a few bare minimums that absolutely must be met for a project to succeed. I'm talking absolute-minimum floor. Without these in place, you are risking the entire venture.

Lone developers, for example, are red flags. In my experience, any time you have one single developer working on a project, you are taking a gigantic risk. There are exceptions. For example, Linus Torvalds wrote the initial Linux kernel in isolation.[88] One of the beta readers of this book is a lone developer who is very successful. I'm not saying it's impossible for one person to develop your software.

However, I have personally been a lone developer, and I have also dealt with lone developers many times. It's always been a train wreck. The advantages of having multiple developers compounds in an agile process. Via the magic of paired programming, code reviews, design sessions, sprint retrospectives, and more, you gain an immense buffer against failure and burnout. You gain redundancy in case a developer gets sick or goes on vacation.

Some of you out there might be laughing and thinking, "Who in their right minds would only have one developer on a project?" I salute you. But it happens more often than you might think—perhaps in your very organization right now.

88  Glyn Moody, "How Linux Was Born, As Told by Linus Torvalds Himself," arsTECHNICA, August 25, 2015, https://arstechnica.com/information-technology/2015/08/how-linux-was-born-as-told-by-linus-torvalds-himself/.

# CHAPTER 34

# A PROJECT MANAGER IS THE GLUE THAT HOLDS EVERYTHING TOGETHER

In agile frameworks, there isn't always someone named as project manager. There are various terms for a person whose job is a liaison between the development team and the rest of the stakeholders. This person knows what is being worked on and where it makes sense to go next. They step up and get others out of their comfort zones and past the fear zone. This person isn't a subject matter expert. They aren't a technical lead. They're not one of your other people (from finance, HR, sales, etc.) who occasionally peeks their head in and says, "How's it going, folks?"

No. This person is dedicated to communication, prioritization, cat herding, and redirection. They are the lifeguard who watches everyone swimming around at the beach. They're the administrative assistant to the dev team, scheduling (and rescheduling) meetings, sending project updates, intercepting angry customers, or whatever else might get in the dev. team's way.

You need that person.

CHAPTER 35

# THE PSYCHOLOGY OF THE DEVELOPER

Programmers think of themselves as the kids who did the group project while everyone else was out partying. We partially think that because we *were* the kids who did the group project while everyone else was out partying. So that's reassuring. But the key part is the sense of responsibility and accountability programmers put on themselves. Programmers want to do things the right way because it's part of our identity.

For that reason, manufactured pressure is completely unnecessary with us—no need to make up deadlines or extra check-ins to ensure we're working hard. Such tactics are already slowing us down. We work as fast as we can at all times because that is part of the life. It's a point of pride.

If you really want to make a programmer's day, compliment them on their efficiency, clean design, or elegant solution. If you want to lose a programmer's respect, let them know implicitly that you don't value their input.

CHAPTER 36

# HOW TO KILL SPARKLES

The blur box conceptual model draws a picture of how lines that seem like predictable threads of effort are actually fuzzy, teleporting blobs that together form a fuzzy blur. You can't see with accuracy where things are going because the threads are highly dynamic.

A drawing cannot show movement or the sparkling lights of the blur box, that beautiful, unpredictable iteration just humming along like little sparkles.

Can you picture it? Can you picture the sparkles?

OK, now tell the team, "Everybody stop what you're doing. We have an urgent need to work on feature Z that just came up."

Now watch the sparkle die. Watch the pulsing lights slow. See the purple light settle down into distinct red and blue dots. Watch all of the colors get murky, struggling to maintain momentum as they screech to a crawl and slowly pivot into a new cadence.

That is a context shift. And it tanks your team's productivity.

In "Context Switching Is Killing Your Productivity" by Software.com, the penalty is described like this:

"Similar to computers, the human brain needs time to adjust focus from one task to another. It must unload and reload context—costing developers energy and mental resources—when switching between tasks.

Unlike computers, humans experience context switching hangovers— the lasting effect of the mind being unable to completely forget a previous train of thought in favor of a new one. These hangovers decrease cognitive performance long after switching tasks.[89]

The hangover effects from context switching are pervasive, leading to developer fatigue and burnout. My dev team will sometimes just sit there for an hour, talking about movies after a context shift because we are so unprepared to tackle this new foolishness that's been dumped in our laps midstream.

And we are conscientious professionals. We really don't want to waste your time or money. It's just that our brains are locked up. You don't slam the race car into the wall and expect the driver to immediately hop on a bike and take a leisurely ride through the park. It doesn't work that way.

There are different kinds of context switching. One is to give an individual two priorities for the day in the same arena of work (analysis, design, specification, creation.) "I need you to develop feature X for the XYZ project but also develop feature A for the ABC project." You are asking the developer to spin up one code environment and write software, then spin up a second environment and write software.

The developer will probably be able to handle that, no problem. Yes, there will be a slight productivity hit from switching environments, but it isn't the end of the world. But if you do the same thing tomorrow and the next day—or if you add three or four different programming tasks across projects in one day—the productivity hits add up. Every repetition of a context shift leaves a residual effect that compounds every time. That is why sprints typically focus on one project. Even so, most programmers would

89    "Context Switching Is Killing Your Productivity," Software.com, accessed September 20, 2023, https://www.software.com/devops-guides/context-switching.

probably agree that coding for multiple projects in one day is not a huge burden but a minor one.

But let's say you give an individual two incongruous priorities for the day. "Sally, I need you to develop a ½-point feature X for the XYZ project. But at 11:00 I need you to meet with the customer and gather requirements for feature Y, also on the XYZ project. Write up your notes from that meeting so I can see what's involved."

You're probably thinking something along these lines: "A ½-point ticket is four hours. The meeting is one hour, and let's say an hour to summarize it in an email. That leaves a couple hours' buffer in the day! Should be fine."

It might be fine. But it might not be. Your programmer, Sally, comes in, looks at the ticket for feature X, reads the spec, then sits at her desk for a half hour planning. She makes a feature branch and starts coding.

> "Oh no, it's 10:00 already. I need to look at my notes about feature Y so I can ask the right questions in the meeting. Uh, let me stash this code real fast, push the branch …. OK, feature Y, what are you all about?"

Then there's the meeting with the customer. There were some wrinkles. Sally does her best to summarize. But her findings also mean a couple other features in the backlog need notes added. Her brain is now in analysis mode, not creation mode. The time is now to update the tickets while she can see all of the relationships in her mind with a fresh understanding of the implications.

Then it's time to code again. But Sally has her analysis brain going.

> "Oh no, it's 3:00 already. Lemme unstash this code for feature X and see where I was. What the heck is this line doing? I was going somewhere with this. What does it all mean? What was past me thinking? This will never work! Arghhhh!"

The day ends. Feature X is not done. Sally goes home dispirited. The next day it takes another 30 minutes just to untangle where she was going with feature X, and things get back to normal. Two-and-a-half hours vanished. You're now at less than 75%, for no gain whatsoever, all via the magic of shifting contexts.

The take-home message I'm trying to convey isn't to never ask your programmers to do more than one thing in a day. That's perfectly reasonable and expected. But don't expect the hours to line up the same way as an uninterrupted flow would. Incongruous context switches impose a, let's say, 1.5× time penalty.

OK, now let's say your ask is more like this:

"Sally, I need you to develop a ½-point feature X for the XYZ project. But at 11:00 I need you to meet with the customer for ABC project and gather requirements for feature A. Write up your notes from that meeting so I can see what's involved."

That's two different types of work on two different projects in one day. The penalty for switching modes and projects in one day is not 1.5×. It's more like 2.5×. Expect an entire day of nothing obvious to fill up Sally's time.

Again, I am not saying you can never ask a programmer to switch modes and projects in one day. We're professionals; we can take it. But the context switching penalty is real. It adds up. If we are constantly switching lanes, and the rest of the team is too, it's even worse. This is partially why sprints were invented, to protect the team from context switching.

Eventually, with enough context switching over time, the development team becomes ants that just lie on their backs on the sidewalk and wait for you to bring out the magnifying glass again.

## FLOW

It would be perfectly understandable if you were thinking something like this right now: "But you said that iterative software development is a fuzzy blur with people hopping all over the place, switching threads and phases in a matter of hours. You're contradicting yourself!"

There is a significant difference between a context shift that is externally imposed onto someone's brain and a programmer's internal monologue and process of discovery leading them to hop over to a different thread. The way the programmer feels when you tell them to switch context is probably the same way project managers feel when you thought your team was doing devops design but now they're doing BPR specification. You might feel a little disoriented, perhaps irate that no one clued you in, as you mentally shift gears to figure out why your team is doing something completely different from what you thought they would be.

Software developers are always seeking flow, a state of euphoric calm where code flows from our fingers and we are one with the universe. I'm not exaggerating. It's why many of us picked this job. Getting into a flow state is one of the greatest human experiences. And some programmers can drop into it fairly well. It's really good for your bottom line when we do. Time vanishes, and we work extra hours, happily. We see connections between tickets and eliminate inefficiencies.

The way to achieve a flow state is deep focus—no interruptions. We have enough of a comfort level to understand what is happening but enough uncertainty that our minds must engage. A river analogy is probably fitting here, with information flowing freely in a fairly navigable path.

Your dev team can even get into flow together, and that is truly beautiful. Everyone picks up on each other's thoughts, and the code knits together as if it were writing itself.

That is when the team might bop around wildly between analysis, design, and coding in a blur of unpredictability. But that's not context shifting so much as the team self-directing through the proper path, keeping the threads of work alive in their minds and doing what it takes to proceed.

## INTERRUPTIONS

Which leads to another kind of context shift, which is interrupting the whole team. That was all the drama earlier about the twinkles dying.

That type of context shift is a tenfold magnification of a developer switching gears. The residual hangover is more pervasive. It severs a bunch of tiny connected threads that will have to be rewoven later—much more slowly and probably not as accurately.

How do you prevent context shifts to maximize flow?

When it comes to a single developer, try not to interrupt them if they are in a zone. If they are vibing and coding and generally loving life, leave them alone if you can. In practical terms that might mean focusing on one project or task per day.

Paradoxically, giving a developer a second task might be just what they need to get a change of pace. If they are dragging on one thing, offer them another. The goal is to get them to an energetic, productive zone and then just let them roll with it—one day, two, three, however long you can make the ride last.

Obviously, sometimes you have no choice but to interrupt people. I know every company isn't like a Montessori preschool. But be aware of the side effects, and try to minimize them.

As for team context shifts, consider the following:

- Don't shift gears midsprint if you can help it.
- If the team is in design, it's a particularly horrible time to turn the ship around. Design is very cognitively challenging and not like other tasks.
- A context shift from one phase to another, combined with one project to another, is four times as bad, not twice as bad.
- Going from analysis to design to specification to development is generally easier. If your team is in the middle of specification, and you ask them to go back to analysis, they are swimming backward.
- If you have a choice of whether or not to follow a sprint up with another sprint from the same project, it's probably best to do it

instead of switching to a different project—unless your team is burned out on that project.

CHAPTER 37

# VIDEO GAMES ARE IN THE DNA
# OF YOUR SOFTWARE PROJECT

It's amazing how intrinsically linked video games have been with my career. And I'm not alone.

I am a software developer because of video games. In 1982, at nine years old, I wrote my first computer program in BASIC. It was a text-based wizarding adventure game, called *Merlin's Revenge*. I drew cover art for it in those scented magic markers that smell vaguely like grape soda (in the five minutes before they dry out and lose their scent).

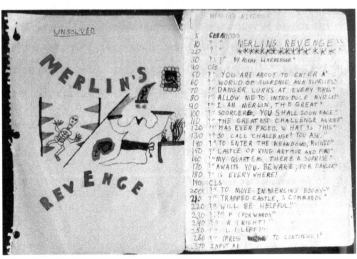

Over the next several years, I learned more-advanced BASIC techniques. I started hacking the source code of an open-source dungeon crawler called *Telengard*. I spent hours upon hours hand-typing machine language code featured in magazines like *Compute!'s Gazette* to reproduce video games like *Air Hockey* or *Pong* clones. Just to give you an idea, it was 10 pages of code, six columns each, in 10-point font that looked like this, and I was 11 years old:

```
0x 60 00 00 80 0x 60 04 00 00 0x A4 01 01 00 0x 20 00 00 03 0x 60 00 00 80 0x 60 04 00 00
0x A4 00 00 00 0x 60 05 00 01 0x 60 02 00 00 0x 20 04 04 05 0x A4 00 00 00 0x 60 05 00 01
0x 60 01 00 84 0x 08 00 00 02 0x 60 03 00 04 0x 11 20 04 01 0x 60 01 00 84 0x 08 00 00 02
0x A4 01 01 00 0x 20 00 00 03 0x 60 00 00 80 0x 60 04 00 00 0x 60 03 00 04 0x 11 20 04 01
0x 60 02 00 00 0x 20 04 04 05 0x A4 00 00 00 0x 60 05 00 01 0x 60 00 00 80 0x 60 04 00 00
0x 60 03 00 04 0x 11 20 04 01 0x 60 01 00 84 0x 08 00 00 02 0x A4 00 00 00 0x 60 05 00 01
```

In college I learned how to document software by playing thousands of hours of *The Bard's Tale*, which required you to hand annotate maps and game features. I learned networking by buying a 600-baud modem, connecting it to my phone line whenever my parents were away, and hacking into BBS systems and telephone companies in 1988.

In college, I studied the impact of video game violence with psychologist Dr. Mary Ballard. Our paper, "Video Game Violence and Confederate Gender: Effects on Reward and Punishment Given by College Males," was published in *Sex Roles*, one of the most prestigious journals in the field of social psychology.[90] The American Psychological Association asked us to present this paper in a roundtable discussion at their 105th annual proceed-

---

90    Mary Ballard and Robert Lineberger, "Video Game Violence and Confederate Gender: Effects on Reward and Punishment Given by College Males," *Sex Roles* 41, no. 8 (2004), 541–558, https://doi.org/10.1023/A:1018843304606.

ings.[91] In recognition of this work, I received the Distinguished Senior in Psychology award from Appalachian State University.

Fast-forward to my time at Purdue University when *Unreal Tournament* came out. It was seismic. Every programmer I knew was playing it in secret. So we finally decided to play it not in secret. Our lunch hours were spent right there in Freehafer Hall, the building that inspired the *Dilbert* cartoon, playing *Unreal Tournament* on the university's network infrastructure. And management was not happy at all.

And in an ironic bookend, my current team may or may not have taught ourselves a bit more about docker container deployments by installing a "simultaneous access engagement server" that may or may not be running that very same 1990s version of Unreal Tournament. And it wasn't even my idea.

So, what's the point of all this video game talk?

Video games are intrinsically linked with technology. Most programmers treat video games as a gold standard to achieve, emulate, or at least understand. Technology improvements are often driven by video games. For example, graphics processing units, which are so crucial in machine learning, data analytics, and other artificial intelligence work, owe their meteoric rise to video games. If programmers get behind in keeping up with the video game landscape, we are getting behind in our careers. Our vocabulary is stunted, and we miss out on design patterns.

The installation of *Unreal Tournament* on the Purdue University network was a mind-boggling technical feat at the time, taking four network engineers and several programmers days to implement in our off hours. You can't pay for that kind of coordinated deep dive. By the way, we found some network instability issues and fixed them. I learned 3D modeling to make maps.

---

91    D. R Rubin, "Don't Touch That Knob!" (symposium, 105th Annual Convention of the American Psychological Association, Chicago, IL, 1997).

Also, discussing and playing video games is how programmers bond. We decompress and keep our minds fresh so that we can tackle your problems with a new perspective.

So if you see your team playing video games on your nickel, take a moment to decide what that means. It could mean that you are paying a bunch of grown-ups to play games and waste your time in some sort of slacker defiance.

It could mean that their brains are completely fried from handling the mountain of context switching that has been thrown at them. They need a break so they don't make a mistake that will cost your company tens of thousands of dollars.

Or you could be witness to one of the best outcomes you could possibly hope for—a phenomenon that money can't buy and you can't force with any amount of team-building consultants. You might be watching your team bond, forming communication patterns as they learn how each other approach certain shared situations.

Congratulations! You have created a safe environment. Pat yourself on the back, and let any ire you might have had dissipate in the warm glow of team building.

CHAPTER *38*

# THEY'RE CALLED DEADLINES
# FOR A REASON

Before I tell you my approach to deadlines, I want to share with you someone else's approach. Ron Jeffries, one of the founders of the agile movement, wrote a blog post called "Making the Date." "Blog post" might not sound like the most trustworthy source in the world. But this is a blog post from the person who founded Xtreme Programming and changed the face of software development forever.

In this post, Ron makes the case that an overall deadline is important in a project, but management's job—not the developers'—is to see that it is met. Not by sweating the dev team, but by making trade-offs and decisions based on emerging reality:

> Management? What do they have to do with the date? Well … just everything. Management is the process of setting objectives and goals, applying people and resources, and measuring results, in order to meet the objectives and goals. Management is not a process of shooting an arrow into the air, to fall to earth we know not where. Management is a process of steering, of guiding business activities to provide the best results possible.

This is the fundamental purpose of management. While delegation of responsibility is a key approach in management, there are two major problems with the idea of delegating "make the date" to the development team. First of all, delegation of responsibility requires delegation of commensurate authority. Second, development teams are not managers, and it's not a good idea to delegate management responsibilities to them: we should delegate development responsibilities to development teams.[92]

As a senior software engineer on a few enterprise software development projects, I developed a rule of thumb when it comes to deadlines:

I'm not selective either. The deadline can come from my manager, their boss, or their boss's boss's boss's boss. It can come from a committee of the top 1,000 most powerful and influential people on the planet. The deadline goes *right in the trash* almost the same moment I hear about it, and I rarely give it a second thought.

Isn't that egregiously irresponsible? No. It's not. Deadlines for deadlines' sake are meaningless.

---

92    Ron Jeffries, "Making the Date," *Ron Jeffries* (blog), November 10, 2005, https://ronjeffries.com/xprog/articles/jatmakingthedate/.

I used to care. If someone gave me a deadline, I took it to heart. The team would work around the clock in a montage of late nights and cold ramen.

Then certain observations started surfacing. For example, why are we working toward this deadline? Who is it for? How important is it?

The more time went on, the more the answers worked out to this: We're working toward this deadline because management/customers/stakeholders are nervous. The deadline is for the managers. It's not important in terms of the project, core value, or some external dependency. It's important for someone else to feel reassured or to make an artificial milestone. And at worst, it's a dog chasing its own tail, where a new "emergency" deadline immediately emerged to keep everyone motivated.

You don't need to motivate us. We are motivated. You don't need to set an arbitrary date. You need to *set our priorities* and *clear our way*. The date will take care of itself.

I cannot count the times I have gone into a boardroom as the senior developer to discuss the results of meeting the deadline only to get the distinct impression that no one actually cared whether it was met. They just wanted to see progress. Or other stakeholders changed their priorities, so the deadline wasn't really important anymore, but no one bothered to tell us.

So I started to ignore deadlines and just worked on the software. I frequently communicated with everyone and delivered quality software.

Mysteriously, the deadlines dried up.

An arbitrary deadline is one of the most antithetical practices to iterative development—the pinnacle of foolish pride. It's saying, "I know in advance when something should be done by, and I'm putting my foot down to make sure it does."

You might not mean it this way, but it comes across as an insult, a lack of trust.

I can already imagine some people reading this thinking, "Don't you have any idea how business works? There are critical reasons for deadlines! It's ridiculous not to have deadlines! How will everyone plan and work together?"

If you are working on a project and about to proclaim something like "Feature X must be done by the end of next month," here's what I'd encourage you to do instead. Tell your team, "Feature X is now our number one priority, and the customer is anxious about it. Please keep me updated on its progress so I can run interference for you."

One of two things is going to happen.

The customer being nervous makes us dig deep. (That is, unless you tell us that all the time as a scare tactic or habitual bad planning, in which case we become immune to it. We no longer care about the customer's discomfort and instead lie on the sidewalk like ants waiting for the magnifying glass.) You wanting to run interference for us warms the prickly cockles of our hearts. Feature X might get done far earlier than whatever deadline you were going to impose.

That is because you *shifted priorities*. Agile processes are excellent at responding to shifting priorities. So now the team has refocused its laser sight on your biggest problem. And like the homing beacons we are, we are hammering away at that feature.

Of course, the second thing might happen instead: Feature X might not get done in the time frame of whatever deadline you were going to impose. That means it was never going to be done by your desired deadline, no matter what, and thus the deadline was spurious in the first place. Setting a date and saying a feature needs to be done by that date, generally speaking, has no influence on whether that feature gets done by that date.

What is so brilliant about all of this is *you're now embracing the agile process and steering it*. You're letting go of the predictive hubris that just gets in the way. You're honestly communicating with the team, which they respond to.

And the team now *showers the customer with attention*. The customer doesn't just get some arbitrary date in the future when they get to figure out if their stuff got done or not. No, they're now getting daily sprint updates, with burndown charts and project managers saying, "Here's where we are on feature X." If the invisible deadline didn't get met, the customer probably won't mind as much for two reasons:

1. They didn't know about the deadline in the first place.
2. They feel very well taken care of and can see exactly where things stand and why.

So what about real deadlines? The nonarbitrary kind?

Obviously, agile processes exist within a business, and sometimes there are real-world factors that affect the purity of the agile process. If there is a true deadline, obstacle, date, or contractual obligation, encode it into the DNA of the project, as early as possible, to take those factors into account.

The dev team are professionals. They will do everything possible to meet those external criteria. Just know that each restriction you place like that is hampering the efficacy of the process. You're putting a dam in the path of the river. It's a trade-off, albeit a very reasonable trade-off. I'm encouraging you to clutter the flow as little as possible.

What about all the other people downstream, or higher up in the management hierarchy, who need to see regular progress?

Anyone can see progress any time if you bake that into your process. My team provides four different ways that anyone can know anything they want at any time: daily standups, sprint burndown charts, kanban boards, and an open-door policy for the project manager.

For example, we have a daily standup that lasts 15 minutes. Anyone in the enterprise can hop into that remote meeting. And they do—customers, my boss, my boss's boss's administrative assistant, whoever is curious. They get to hear the following from everyone on my team:

- What did you do yesterday?
- What will you do today?
- Do you have any roadblocks?

It's amazing how quickly anxiety and busywork dissipate when people tune in and hear what's actually happening. We developers are accountable to ourselves, our customers, and our stakeholders, and a daily standup is one of the promises we make. I've been doing a standup every day for almost 15 years. I have rarely heard anyone say, "Wow, it seems like you all aren't working hard enough." I have heard people say we should shift our priorities, so we do, and things get better.

If you've read this far, are you curious if I really, truly just ignore deadlines? The answer is, I try to make them irrelevant. But if—despite my best efforts—one is there, I make a business trade-off: what is the risk of me tossing this deadline in the trash and going on about my day?

If the risk is something vague, like "You'll get in trouble," then I toss it. If the risk is "We might lose our licensing," or "XYZ customer only has 3 months left under contract, so we'll owe a million dollars if it isn't done by then"—yes, of course I treat it with respect.

# CHAPTER 39

# STOP SIGNS ARE THE NEW DEADLINES

OK, project manager. You have done your job well. You have constructed firm barriers to protect your team's white space. Your handpicked team is self-managing. The team is in flow. The fuzzy blur is blurring.

Time for you to start reaching for the stop sign.

But … what about flow and context switching and stuff?

That all still stands. But you have a critical role to play now. Think of your team like a bunch of Forrest Gumps. What does Forrest Gump love to do more than anything? Run. Give Forrest the ball, and he will run all the way down the field, through the end zone, under the goalpost, out the locker room, and all the way to California.

Someone in the crowd needs to hold up a sign telling Forrest when to stop running. And that person is you.

When they're in flow, programmers will crank out code like nobody's business. They will speak to you in rapt tones about the code's beauty, the inevitability of the next module and the next. All of time and space are related in harmony, and they can see the plan.

You have to walk the line between believing them and not believing them. Trust but verify:

"What will be the impact of what you're working on next? (What business value does it deliver?)"

"Is this helping out with our number one priority, which is feature X? (Are you getting down in the weeds and losing sight of the top priority?)"

The double-edged sword of creating the fuzzy blur is that you need to shape it and guide it. You need to focus on the biggest business value and ask questions of your team to ensure they're focused on that.

Asking a team if they are correctly focusing their effort is different (and superior) to giving them a deadline. Think of it this way: what are the intent and implication of a deadline? To me, a deadline means something along these lines:

- We need to marshal our resources so we have enough time to produce X amount of work in Y number of days.

- Without a deadline to motivate people, the bus might not start on time. The passengers might not all get on. We'll waste time, and we won't get to the destination in time.

- Maybe we should publish the deadline as Wednesday, but really we all secretly know it's the following Monday. Let's give ourselves a buffer.

- If we don't feed the team a steady supply of deadlines, the team might not maximize their efforts. They might just laze around at the bus stop or ride the wrong buses willy-nilly, and we'll have to do a massive coordination effort later. Best to just keep everyone focused on the next milestone.

In other words, a deadline mostly focuses on generating momentum. As the gamesmanship increases, the resources are more finely manipulated to keep everyone moving toward a previously stated goal. The deadline gives everyone plenty of warning that important thing XYZ is approaching, and everyone needs to gear up to be ready for it.

But the blur box shows us that the bus is already moving and everyone's on it. There is no need to generate momentum. The fuzzy blur is in motion already. The bus driver is cranking some tunes, and the passengers are humming along.

Only it isn't a bus. It's a hovercraft that floats a foot above the ground and can effortlessly pivot in any direction to head for a new destination. The game is no longer "How can we make up a bunch of milestones to keep things moving?" The new game is "How do we make this hovercraft ride last and show us the scenery we most want to see along our journey?"

In this analogy, where the scenery is your customer's top-requested features, the passengers are your dev team, and you are the hovercraft pilot, you should be thinking along these lines: "We've been heading deeper and deeper into feature ABC scenery for a couple weeks now. Is it a better use of our time to look at some feature XYZ scenery now? Are we getting too focused on the details of cactus flower cultivars and not focusing enough on the map as a whole?"

Scott Ambler and Mark Lines put this risk into practical terms in their book *Disciplined Agile Delivery*. It boils down to processes and practices and how an unfettered team might dive too deeply into their own rabbit hole: "Although people are the primary determinant of success for IT solution delivery projects, in most situations it isn't effective to simply put together a good team of people and let them loose on the problem at hand. If you do this, then the teams run several risks, including investing significant time in developing their own processes and practices, ramping up on processes and practices that more experienced agile teams have discovered are generally less effective or efficient, and not adapting their own processes and practices effectively."[93]

As a project manager, you need to reach for the stop sign when your radar warning is sufficiently strong enough to indicate that the team is now laser focused on the wrong thing. Or, if you are really good, be like a

---

93    Ambler and Lines, *Disciplined Agile Delivery*, 7.

sweeper in the ice sport known as curling. Brushing the ice with a broom, seamlessly redirecting the team without breaking flow.

# CHAPTER 40

# FAILURE BY FAILURE TO COMMUNICATE

Given the controlled chaos of the blur box, the most critical success factor is communication between developers, testers, business analysts, managers, customers, and other stakeholders. Communication is one of the difficulties of most business processes, but in the case of iteration, it's both more critical and more complicated.

Alan Davis wrote in "The Software Company Machine," "Software development companies do not function themselves as systems. Instead, they function as a set of totally asynchronous and rarely communicating divisions, which succeed only by accident, not by design."[94]

So for the blur box to succeed, the role of management should shift from managing development to managing communication and facilitation. At some point, the development team has to be trusted to deliver the functionality it promises.

Managers who focus on communication are more likely to succeed in the middle of the blur box. Why are deadlines and road maps made in the first place? For comfort, security, or informed decision-making.

---

94    Alan M. Davis, "The Software Company Machine," *IEEE Software* 17, no. 2 (March 2000), https://doi.org/10.1109/MS.2000.10005.

With predictive scheduling ripped away, there is now a vacuum. Upper managers and customers will feel disconnected and at the whim of a development team they don't necessarily trust. Effective agile managers fill that vacuum with a different kind of information: updated priorities, progress, velocity, or early discoveries and successes.

The agile project manager becomes a hub, routing the proper types of communication up and down the chain. They diffuse the fuzzy blur, hiding the wild whirling lights and giving a more palatable description of what is happening to those not on the bleeding edge of the dev process. The astute agile manager will also bring information to the dev team, helping refine their focus and curtailing unfruitful avenues of development. They keep the dev team honest.

The development team has new responsibilities as well. They must take responsibility to inform all stakeholders of what is going on. Specifying formal communication responsibilities is a possible way to enforce communication. For example, the development team has to communicate with the technical managers and business analysts, who are responsible for notifying other managers and customers. Even if such formal processes are not in place, the dev team must actively and transparently advertise where they are at any given time.

The dev team *cannot hide*. They must proactively inform other people of how things are going.

*Customers* cannot hide either. Customers must become inquisitive about implementation status rather than delivered functionality. They can no longer lob their requirements over the wall and wait for results to roll their way. Customers are now part of the project team—or at least tightly coupled to it.

# CHAPTER 41

# DON'T TRADE ANALYSIS PARALYSIS FOR UNENDING DEVELOPING

There was a line in "Threads of Work" that introduced the concept of a convergence point: "don't trade analysis paralysis for unending developing." What's that all about?

Analysis paralysis is when a team gets locked in a round robin of conflicting design questions or requirements. They go around and around trying to figure it out, getting deadlocked. Great news: agile software development is fantastic at overcoming analysis paralysis. We *know* we don't know. We don't pretend to know. Not knowing doesn't bother us.

We pick a thread up and run with it, discovering stuff. Slowly but surely, the whole emerges.

Here's more great news for you: Previous development leads to even better development later. Features start humming along. Requirements that our analysis paralysis were obscuring come to light, and we design and implement those.

That process iterates and continues.

But now *your money is all gone.*

You have twice as much software as you were expecting, and the dev team is happily humming along on iteration 137.

Agile is excellent at telling itself what to do next. It's not good at telling itself when to stop. Like Forrest Gump, we will just keep running out the back of the end zone and down Main Street to the Pacific Ocean.

If you wish to prevent this, these are good things to do as a manager:

- Keep a close eye on acceptance criteria. Be vicious with the stop sign.
- Don't get drawn into the self-serving drama of the dev team. Be rigorous about whether their next focus is the right focus.
- Be a hard-ass about limiting scope.
- Redirect the dev team to the new number one priority.
- Be very specific in requirements about the definition of "done."

# CHAPTER 42

# YOU CANNOT ESTIMATE DESIGN

Design is the spark of creation in terms of software development. It's the eureka moment. Developers stare into the void and glean meaning from it. Software is a mere manifestation of the true achievement software developers seek to attain: a good design.

Sooner or later (let's be honest, it's sooner) the dev team will need to develop a feature that they don't yet know how to develop. They've gathered requirements. They understand what the customer wants. There's just one problem: the dev team has no idea how to do it.

So they move into a design mindset. In design mode, developers become sleuths, mind readers, scientists, archaeologists … whatever is needed to get to the bottom of how to implement the feature so that they can write specs and begin coding.

Managers inevitably ask me, "How long will it take you to design that feature?"

My answer is always the same: "I have no idea."

"Really, though," they might say, "we need to know how long so we can tell marketing when to expect the feature."

"Really, though, *I have no idea.*"

Nothing you can say will give me that idea. Nothing you can threaten me with will make me magically understand how to implement that feature. No pressure is great enough to inject that wisdom into the gray folds of my brain.

I don't know how long it will take me to design what I don't know how to implement.

*I don't know.*

Stop asking.

Let's dig deeper. Someone hands you a bucket. Then they hand you a pint glass full of water.

"How long will it take you to pour that pint of water into that bucket?" they ask.

You have held glasses of water before. You've probably dumped one out before.

"About 2 seconds?" you say.

"OK, prove it."

You pour the water. It takes one and a half seconds. They hand you a quart of water.

"How long will it take you to pour this quart of water into the bucket?" they ask.

"Three seconds!" you say, with more confidence, and indeed, it takes three seconds.

Then they hand you a bralph and seventeen scallamajiggers of trazzlemorph.

"How long will it take you to pour these seventeen scallamajiggers of trazzlemorph into the bralph?" they ask.

What do you say?

Do you say, "Oh, about three seconds?"

Or do you say, "I have never seen a bralph before. I don't know how it works. I don't know what trazzlemorph is or how it behaves. Someone else might know, but I don't. So I need to investigate and learn about bralphs and scallamajiggers and trazzlemorphs before I can answer that for you."

"But marketing really needs to know. I'm afraid I have to insist. How long will it take?"

This is how developers feel when you ask us to estimate how long design will take. Just because the feature is ultimately going to be coded in a computer doesn't mean we know how to do it, and guessing how long it will take to figure it out would be unprofessional of us.

As a manager you might think, "OK, fair enough. Let's do a design sprint. Two weeks of uninterrupted design time."

I really appreciate you for that. It does absolutely nothing to alter the situation. I don't know if it will take two hours or three months. My team has spent one week before designing how to change a background from green to blue. Management assumed it would take an hour. We have also spent four hours planning how to completely redesign a complex system, which management thought would take a month.

If we knew how long it was going to take, we wouldn't be in the design phase.

I can estimate with decent accuracy how long gathering requirements will take. I can estimate with pretty good accuracy how long writing specs from a design will take. I can tell you with high accuracy how long developing specified features will take. I can tell you with very high accuracy how long testing and implementation will take.

I can tell you with *zero accuracy* how long designing something will take—less than zero accuracy, plus or minus one year.

Managers, these are your takeaways:

- Never include design in a sprint—unless you are OK with the sprint going over by 16 weeks or being done 13.5 days early.

- Never timebox design—unless you are OK with having no design at the end and having misspent that timebox effort.
- Never write a ticket that says "Design feature X."
- Never write a road map that says you'll spend one month in requirements gathering, one month in design, and six months in development.
- Never pressure your team to give an estimate of how long it will take to design a feature. At best you will get a completely useless guess, and you will later look like a fool to your upper managers for posing it as anything real. It's not real.

When your development team says they are moving into design, it means something important. It means that they, as a collective team, have reached a point where bopping around between phases like electrons is no longer cutting it. They have come to a crawl. They can no longer guess, circumvent, or charm the problem away. They are at an impasse where the only solution is to put on the brakes, get everyone in a room, and figure out how to solve this.

This is your moment of gravest uncertainty. You have to take a leap of faith and simply let the team design. Ask how it's going, and break down roadblocks. Buy them two pizzas. Give them a pressure-free, interruption-free bubble.

If they want to go for a walk, play video games, or go home and meet back up a few hours later, cool. Their brains are fried.

If you walk in, and they are talking heatedly, or everyone is silent, turn right around and walk back out.

If you have a good dev team, they aren't wasting your time or money. They're not being lazy. They aren't being ornery.

Cradle that uncertainty in your hands like the precious bubble it is.

# CHAPTER 43

# GETTING TO THE DOTTED LINE

Fixed-price contracts are a horrible fit for iterative development processes. They require a detailed description of the subject matter of the contract in advance—details such as time, money, resources, and delivered functionality. But the blur box shows us three things:

- You can't predict the overall timeline.
- You don't know how many resources will be on any given thread at any given time.
- The top-priority features change with each sprint as the team makes new discoveries.

Fixed-price contracts aim to minimize the potential risk caused by unpredictable, later changes. The blur box mitigates risk by embracing unpredictability (a.k.a. early discovery) and changing almost everything about the outcome in real time.

Fixed-price contracts are just *a horrible fit for iterative development*. They're antithetical.

So the business world has come up with other forms of contracts besides fixed price, called "agile contracts." Peter Stevens describes several alternative contract structures that work well with agile to a certain degree. I agree with the conclusion he made of opting for phased-development contracts:

> I have worked quite happily for years with a phased-development contract. The original contract was a fixed-scope contract with a cost ceiling, but as we worked together and built up the level of trust, the surrounding text just withered away. Trust, a bit of boilerplate, the sprint contract, and a quarterly sign-off from top management worked quite nicely.

> "Money for nothing, changes for free" contract turns the advantages of the scrum and agile development processes into a competitive advantage.

- By prioritizing and delivering business value incrementally, the chances of an outright failure are dramatically reduced. This advantage is passed on to the customer.
- Furthermore, it's a cooperative model, so it offers incentives to both parties to keep the costs down.
- The early cancellation clause rewards the higher productivity achieved with scrum teams. On the downside, this clause feels a bit like a "golden parachute," which may not be politically acceptable in the current economic climate.[95]

I encourage you to read the article in its entirety.

---

95    Peter Stevens, "10 Agile Contracts," Agile Software Development, December 9, 2019, https://www.agilesoftwaredevelopment.com/posts/10-agile-contracts/.

CHAPTER 44

# STRESS-FREE DEMOS. NO REALLY.

Demos can be nerve racking. Nervous, expectant customers wait to see how all of the time, money, and effort have come together to meet their requirements. Upper management rap their fingers on the desk. Lots of pressure is all tied up in this high-visibility moment of truth.

Pretty stressful, right? Not for an agile team. Demos are an afterthought.

One of the key mantras my teams follow is to deliver functioning software at the end of every sprint. You could drop by for a demo on Tuesday afternoon, and I could pull up the latest stable build and show you how the software is going. Then I could point to the kanban board and show you where it's going next.

Not only are demos unstressful, but they should also be anticlimactic because they are so routine.

CHAPTER 45

# WHEN THE GOING GETS TROUGH

A project is like an empty trough that needs to be filled with water. There are many ways to get the trough filled.

The waterfall methodology attempts to fill the trough with five or six huge buckets: The analysis bucket, the design bucket, the development bucket, etc. Having poured all of those buckets in, you may find that you filled the trough to overflowing, and much of the water has spilled on the ground. Or you might find that the trough is only half-full, and you need more buckets than you planned for.

The blur box says filling the trough is more like a steady drizzle of raindrops. Each particular raindrop could be an analysis, design, or development raindrop, but it will keep raining only until the trough is full enough.

Now think of the water as resources (e.g., time, money). The raindrops represent incremental development. We stop when the trough is full. You spend less money because no water sloshes to the ground from predictive buckets—especially if you keep a close eye on acceptance criteria and avoid the agile trap of unending developing.

CHAPTER 46

# SLIDING TIMELINE (FOG OF WAR)

The effort you put into making a schedule is wasted almost the minute the ink is dry. But people need to have an idea where things are going so they can make adjustments and decisions, especially when it comes to the overall project timeline.

## TRADITIONAL VS. AGILE

When it comes to timelines in traditional projects vs. iterative projects, there's good news and bad news.

Traditional projects:

- Are better fits for having timelines. Everyone expects it and participates.
- Are unpredictable with regards to the time required. Guessing the end when projects are at the beginning is particularly difficult.
- Have certain trade-offs baked into the project structure that make timelines more reasonable. There is slack built in.
- Account for how the project overhead will be devoted to things like making schedules and having status meetings.

- Are less efficient overall, but everyone is a little happier because they can see where they're expected to be by a certain time.
- Emphasize predictability, thus willing to sacrifice efficiency (also suspend disbelief that predictions will match reality.)

Agile projects:

- Are abjectly horrible at making overall timelines.
- Are abjectly horrible at predicting how long things will take at the beginning of the project.
- Are good at predicting how long things are going to take in the middle portion of the project.
- Are fantastic at predicting how long things are going to take near the end of the project.
- Emphasize the value of adaptability. They are willing to sacrifice the security of having a schedule.

## SLIDING TIMELINE

There is a glimmer of hope in the way iterative development helps increase predictability as the project moves forward. Here's an image that helps illustrate the phenomenon:

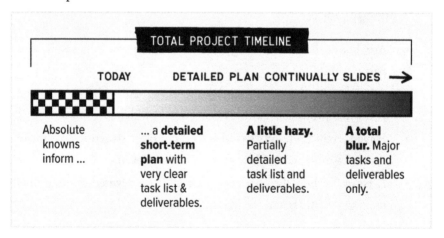

As you can see from the figure above, there is a "fog of war" effect in the future. But agile is all about learning from previous iterations. It's also focused on the upcoming features. This means an agile team absolutely knows where it has been and uses that to get a really good idea of how the short term is going to play out. So by the end of the overall timeline, that fog of war disappears entirely.

Obviously, traditional projects also benefit from this same discovery as time marches forward and things become clearer. The difference is in mentality.

Traditional projects with a timeline made up in advance invite people to work toward that timeline. It can be helpful in some cases, but agile teams generally consider it to be prescriptive and harmful. As a traditional project team moves forward, the team keeps trying to meet milestones. An agile team just works on whatever the top feature is. The schedule emerges as time moves forward.

The reality of iterative development demands a culture change within the project development team. The primary concession is that IT needs to not only endure change but also embrace it. What does this mean practically?

## SIZE YOUR TIME WINDOW

Use a sliding timeline, periodically revisit and update the sliding short-term plan. How long is short term? It depends on your comfort level with risk and the strength of your downstream relationships. Agile proponents make the short-term window as short as possible. Traditional business culture would say to make it as long as possible. Four years is good.

Put another way, an agile mindset would say that two weeks is risk averse because there is a high chance of satisfying the incremental deadline. Six months is practically meaningless. Unless you're OK with saying, "Oh well, if we're wrong, we're wrong, carry on." The traditional engineering mindset would say that two weeks is so short as to be meaningless. There's no way to align downstream resources in that amount of time. Six months to them is risk averse. It gives everyone time to plan and is the more wise, conservative choice.

So, what window of time do you select as a reasonable time frame for providing schedule estimates?

Assuming you do sprints, start with the sprint length. For the purposes of this discussion, I'll say two weeks. That is the minimum amount of time you should commit to, and in a way, you already have committed to that by agreeing to a sprint contract.

Many agile teams, mine included, estimate so they can pull more tickets in if things go ahead of schedule. (This is actually bad if you are trying to build trust through accurate estimates.) If you're comfortable estimating individual tickets, which I am, and you are comfortable agreeing that the next sprint will do XYZ, then congrats! You have bought your sliding timeline two more weeks of wiggle room.

If you want to live a little dangerously, tack on another sprint's worth to bring the sliding timeline up to six weeks.

## ADJUST FOR CULTURAL FACTORS

If your team follows the agile mandate that customers and developers should work with each other *every single day*, then you are better positioned to lengthen the sliding timeline window. Since everyone is on the same page, fully aware of where things are going, they should have a similar understanding of the risks and probabilities involved in the schedule estimates. You're indicating, "Hey, we trust each other and have a shared focus, so we'll share some risk and predict further out."

If you do not work alongside your customers every day, then you need to subtract the interval of customer interaction from the sliding window. For example, if you only talk with the customers at the end of a sprint (which is what my team does), then you subtract two weeks from the time window.

It only makes sense. How can you expect your team to commit to a certain timeline when they don't even have the opportunity to find out if they were right or wrong except every two weeks? Two weeks becomes the absolute earliest point at which adjustments can be made.

Take penalties into account as well. What is the *penalty for being wrong?*

If you are asking for a timeline because you like to know where things are going, or that's how you make decisions, those are personal reasons with little financial impact. Go ahead and lengthen that window. As long as no one is being punished for being wrong, you can ask for more of a vision statement with a longer window.

If you want a timeline because you are making downstream deals and spending money based on the timeline, shorten it to capitalize on early discovery. If you push that sliding window out too far, you risk overpromising and underdelivering.

My advice is the short-term window should be as long as two sprints. For us that is four weeks. My unscientific impression is that if my team had promised certain milestones three to six months in the future, we'd be wrong approximately 99.999% of the time—which speaks well for my team's flexibility.

*Do not plan tasks or deliverables at all beyond the sliding plan,* because there's no way to know what those will be.

CHAPTER 47

# ITERATE OR PERISH

I started part 2 by saying everyone needs to step out of their comfort zone. That is the overarching theme of these observations. But I haven't yet explicitly endorsed the biggest benefit to this whole process: you should iterate your business processes the same way the dev team is iterating their code.

Lots of people talk about improving their processes. There is a lot of hand-waving to it. But when was the last time you actually changed a fundamental part of how you do business?

If it was recently, my compliments to you, and apologies for pigeonholing your organization. If you are like the rest of us, it probably doesn't happen very often. People do not typically like change. Inertia is comfortable. But great things happen when a well-reasoned change is implemented. Seek out change. Embrace it. Implement it.

For example, in the early days of agile, one of my colleagues was able to convince management to abandon a multimillion-dollar investment to the betterment of the entire organization:

> I have been completely convinced that defect-tracking systems are the bane of software development for some time now. They're deemed so necessary by companies that they'll invest millions of

dollars in licenses and training, often more than they'll invest in any other tool.

Way back in '99 I joined a new team for a greenfield project. I don't remember why, but we collectively decided we'd give this new Extreme Programming thing a try. We collectively agreed we were going to work by the book, do it all, and see how things went. So, that meant unit testing, TDD, pair programming, the whole jug of Kool-Aid.

One of the other agreements we made was regarding defects. All of our stories were simply written on 3"×5" index cards, but defects had to also be entered into the inevitable defect-tracking system. Anyway, we agreed that the product owner (or, in this case, the XP customer proxy) would immediately review any new defect and decide if it needed fixing. If it did, we would fix it immediately. If not, we'd delete it.

We soon noticed we were running with three or fewer defects (usually just one or zero) at any given time. Using the defect-tracking system was such a pain, we went to the powers that be and asked for permission to stop. And we got it.

You do not know joy in software development until you no longer are saddled with a defect-tracking system. Or maybe that's just me.

Lessons

- Quality is speed. If you want to go fast, focus on quality. If you focus on speed, all you get is poor quality.
- Defect triage, management, prioritization, etc. is a massive source of waste (in the lean sense) for most software development teams.
- Don't "manage" defects. Just fix them.

# PART 3:
# THRIVING IN THE BLUR BOX

NOW THAT WE'VE UNCOVERED THE PROBLEM AND RIFFED ON A BUNCH of talking points, how does this actually look day in and day out? How does a software development team successfully work in an iterative way?

# CHAPTER 48

# A BIT OF WARNING FIRST

This is the part where I show you what's in my cupboards and you wrinkle up your nose and say "You actually eat that stuff?" In this part of the book I will detail the specific techniques that my teams have used for years to produce enterprise software on time and within budget with chronically understaffed teams working within a nonagile business culture. Let's call them the "agile circus escape practices," hereafter abbreviated as ACEPs. Note that I am not calling them "best practices." That's because I don't think they are best practices. They are compromises and workarounds that confront the blur box inside the traditional business mindset we're working within.

I think you'll soon see that my process has a long, long way to go. Because I typically find myself working in non-agile organizations.

The point of this section is *not* the ACEPs themselves.

It's the *thought process that led to the ACEPs.*

Agile is all about refinement. I have refined my approach many times and discarded documentation that seemed useful but wasn't. I've brought back steps that seemed redundant but in retrospect were critical. The 12 practices outlined in this section are my bare-minimum practices necessary to deliver functional software in a sane way. If any of them are left out, my approach will fail.

Speaking of the Agile Manifesto, it's not a methodology. There are no required artifacts, documents, processes, or tools. What I'm about to lay out in part 3 is more methodology-like, but this is still not a methodology. Scrum, kanban, and SAFe™ are methodologies or frameworks—but if you listen to me, and you use them, they will become unrecognizable as you alter them to suit your organization. In other words, I'm not trying to tell you what to do. I'm showing you how you might think about this overall puzzle and arrive at a workable solution. The only place I know where to start such a conversation is by showing you what I do and how it adds value.

You already know that one size does not fit all. Not every team/project/company is the same. I have used this approach in teams of 2 to 10 (the maximum viable team size in my opinion) in start-ups, health care, manufacturing, and higher education across a very wide array of projects. You should know up front that much of what I do flies in the face of current agile thinking. Some of what I'm about to say will countermand the best practices recommended in agile trainings.

I'm also not recommending you adopt my approach. The value of this section isn't the ACEPs themselves. It's the thought process behind why these procedures work and how they confront the fuzzy blur.

## 100% GUARANTEE

I've expressed precious few guarantees or absolutes in this book. But now I'm going to put my money where my mouth is and offer you a 100% guarantee, without equivocation:

*If you follow the steps I'm about to outline in part 3 of this book, I guarantee you that your agile initiative will fail.*

Utterly and completely fail. Because my teams, my customers, and my problems are not yours. Also, because I did most of my agile thought processing years ago, got the gist of it, then went off to use the ideas in my own practice without closely following the refinements that emerged. I use a folksy mixture of decades-old techniques, cutting-edge post-agile trends, hard numbers, superstition, and personal preference based on my team personalities. Now I'm about to open my kitchen cabinets and show you the mismatched array of stuff in there.

Why? It is definitely not to persuade you to follow my lead. Rather, it is to show you the train of thought I went through to arrive at the final-ish product.

Every tool, technique, artifact, and ceremony you employ had to come from somewhere. Someone suggested it, mandated it, or invented it. In any case, you have to evaluate it and determine: does this add value to my organization? Does this make us more agile and responsive?

As you read this section, pay attention to your own reactions. Perhaps you think to yourself something along these lines:

"That's not news at all. Everyone knows it is essential to use a code repository. That's hardly a groundbreaking revelation!"

If so, congrats! You have decided upon and internalized something that you and I both agree is a critical practice for modern software development. The anticlimactic nature of that revelation is a really good sign that you're doing things right, in my opinion.

Now pause and think, "well, why did he write that into this book in the first place? Surely there aren't people out there who don't use a code repository? That is ridiculous!"

Then quietly go verify within your own organization that everyone is, in fact, using a code repository. Because you might discover that the best practices you have internalized are being ignored. Right in your own backyard. Don't ask how I know.

Perhaps in reading part 3 you think to yourself something along these lines:

*Estimate using days instead of Story Points? What utter madness is this? Is he a fool?*

If so, congrats! You have decided upon and internalized something that you and I *completely disagree* is a critical practice for modern software development. Your indignation is a really good sign that you've given this lots of thought and made a decision that works for your organization.

Now pause and think, "well, why did he write that into this book in the first place?" Then consider whether your reaction is a protective instinct. Maybe something I wrote is provoking you. Maybe it's something to reconsider about your process.

Ultimately I don't care whether or not you estimate using days, or story points, or even forego estimates altogether.

I do care about you examining each of these twelve ACEPs and deciding/ verifying how they fit into your overall picture. I've arrived at this suite of techniques and it works very well for my teams as a system of inter-related tools. Maybe some of the actual techniques will be helpful to you, and that would be a nice bonus. Yet the focus of this chapter is the thought process of evaluating approaches to see how they fit into an iterative mindset.

About that thought process—my key guiding principle is simplicity. I make trade-offs that always favor simplicity. The big hammer. The ACEPs try as much as they can to go with the flow of how people think. This is best explained by one of the 12 principles in the "Manifesto for Agile Software Development:": "Agile processes promote sustainable development. The sponsors, developers, and users should be able to maintain a constant pace indefinitely."[96]

A sustainable pace is best achieved with something similar to the *principle of least surprise*. Or in this case, we'd use the most natural, least effort, way-people-think, densest hammer we can find that does the job. Each ACEP is the ratio of least effort to largest payoff I can manage.

---

96   "Manifesto for Agile Software Development."

Just so you know, the first time I stepped up to the plate to lead an agile software development team was a spectacular failure. I'd been studying the principles for years, and I did a lot of things right. At first, it was glorious. We made excellent estimates and delivered quality software right out of the starting gate. But I did not take sustainability into account. I inadvertently put myself on a treadmill that was not paced to everyone's liking. So now I look for the simplest, easiest, lowest-friction, inherently understandable, steadiest-pace techniques I can find.

Let's look at an example ACEP, "Organize your Sprints using the bluntest approach possible," to see what type of trade-offs this approach takes. You'll read more about sprint planning below. But as a teaser, we base sprint planning on an independently prioritized backlog (features ranked by the customers) and estimated features (estimates provided by the development team). We figure out how many days are available in the sprint, count up the estimates to match, draw a line in the backlog demarcating the highest-priority features within that time frame, and commit to those features. It's a quick and dirty way to hit higher-value tickets and also a quick and dirty way to plan.

There are arguably better ways to accomplish some of those same goals. For example, David Griffiths explains bang for the buck score as a third aspect of agile sprint planning in his excellent YouTube video, "Learn Agile Estimation in 10 Minutes." This metric is calculated with this formula:

*Value rank* of a ticket's priority
(expressed as one choice from a Fibonacci sequence)

*Divided by*

*Story point estimate* (expressed as one choice from a Fibonacci sequence)[97]

---

97    David Griffiths, "Learn Agile Estimation in 10 Minutes," May 9, 2014, YouTube video, 11:55, https://www.youtube.com/watch?v=Hwu438QSb_g.

The purpose of this metric is to deliver maximum value early with the least amount of effort. By hitting the tickets with the highest bang for the buck score first, the team delivers the most value it can.

David's approach is more sophisticated than mine. It definitely arrives at an optimized sprint schedule. I am fully aware that this metric exists. I've known about it for a decade. But I don't use it. Why not?

Because *my customers aren't entirely dependable*—from my point of view.

I love you, customers. Without you I'd have no job. But let's be honest: you probably don't consider one of your top daily priorities to be shuffling my backlog around and assigning Fibonacci priority numbers to the tickets.

Customers don't think about what they want with the technical rigor that software development requires. Rightfully so. They aren't developers. So part of the developer's job is to talk to the customers and figure out what it is that they *really* want, which may be different from what they *say* they want. And part of the reason we should design software to be easily changeable is that the customers' requirements will shift as they start to interact with early versions that the dev team delivers.

If I were depending on customers to add weight values to the tickets in my backlog, my process would slow to a crawl. I'd be calling them daily and saying, "Hey, could you log in and look at our project tracker, and maybe rank order stuff? Thanks!" Then I'd wait two, three, or even 15 days for them to comply.

It's important to have independent prioritization—critical even. But my organization simply does not make that a priority. My team's solution has been to meet with the customers after every sprint, get them to sort the backlog tickets, then we draw the line as previously mentioned.

This isn't optimal. But it's a reality my team exists within. More agile teams than not probably also exist in some form of this uncomfortable agile-meets-reality culture.

If you have the luxury of a dedicated product owner, business analyst, or daily integration with the customer (another Agile Manifesto principle), then by all means, please use the bang for the buck score. And by the way, I am envious of you.

If you are scraping together whatever agile foothold you can, keep in mind that *sustainability is your salvation*. It all goes back to sustainability. The ACEPs are a combination of radical removal of processes and artifacts, with some inefficiencies tossed back in to acknowledge estimation and promising deliverables. Those aren't in vogue if you listen to many agile consultants. They may not be fashionable in the current agile software development climate, but nevertheless, I still have them in the ACEPs.

The development team's job is to listen, be curious, design, specify, make short-term promises on the top features, and deliver on those promises in a predictable, sustainable way. In this sense, "predictable" means able to make estimates—better yet, able to make excellent estimates.

"Sustainable" means the dev team does not burn out but looks forward to coming into work every day. The customers don't get burned by having their needs ignored or promises-unfulfilled. Management doesn't lose trust in the dev team and start the counterproductive cycle of arbitrary deadlines and status meetings to maintain order.

And all of that takes place in an environment that only partially supports the agile process.

So in the case of this ACEP example, "Organize your Sprints using the bluntest approach possible," the thought process behind my decision went something like this:

- We really need sprint planning. It's a critical business communication tool that shows the stakeholders what's coming up. They already have a much fuzzier road map than they are comfortable with, so we have to give back some detail about what's happening. So this is a must-have process for us in order to establish and maintain trust.

- Hmm, let me research sprint planning. Oh look here! David Griffiths recommends the bang for the buck score as the best way to plan sprint value. This makes a lot of sense. This is "the best way" for sure.

- Uh-oh, it says here that the customer has to continually maintain feature priority scores on an ongoing basis. Our customers return maybe 10% of our phone calls and cancel three-fourths of our meetings together. Our company culture just isn't ready for that kind of tight collaboration.

- Therefore we will sadly put the bang for the buck score on the shelf and willingly follow a process we all agree is inferior. Instead we will get as much information as we can from the customer, then pretend as if we aren't the developers. We'll get our project manager to rank the tickets the way we think the customer would.

Is this ideal? Absolutely not. But if it's the sticking point that is holding up the rest of an agile process, we'll accept that inefficiency so that we don't have to worry about constantly seeking input from a customer who has no cultural pressure to listen to us. That's more sustainable. Then we can work on improving the organizational culture to get even better value delivery.

CHAPTER 49

# OVERVIEW OF THE AGILE CIRCUS ESCAPE PRACTICES

My approach for developing software in an agile way within a nonagile-friendly environment looks like the diagram below. It pulls key techniques from scrum, kanban, extreme programming, and other sources.

The 12 practices are as follows:

1. Code repository
2. Issues
3. Branching
4. Feature development
5. Code reviews
6. Project tracking
7. Backlog combing
8. Estimation poker
9. Organize sprint
10. Deliver functional software
11. User feedback
12. Deployment strategy

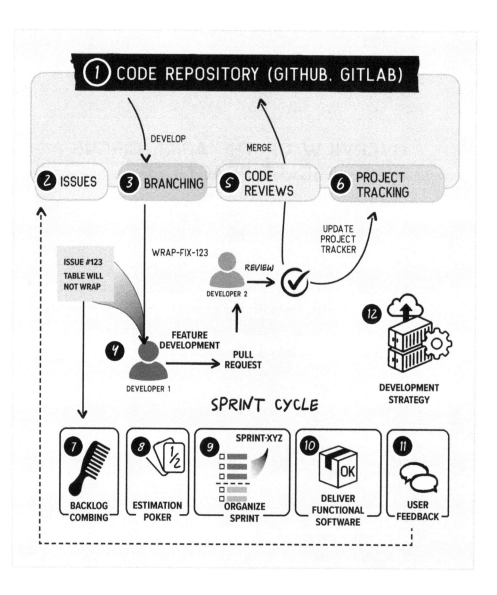

① CODE REPOSITORY (GITHUB, GITLAB)

DEVELOP

MERGE

② ISSUES ③ BRANCHING ⑤ CODE REVIEWS ⑥ PROJECT TRACKING

UPDATE PROJECT TRACKER

ISSUE #123 TABLE WILL NOT WRAP

WRAP-FIX-123

REVIEW

DEVELOPER 2

FEATURE DEVELOPMENT

④ PULL REQUEST

DEVELOPER 1

⑫

DEVELOPMENT STRATEGY

SPRINT CYCLE

⑦ BACKLOG COMBING

⑧ ESTIMATION POKER

⑨ SPRINT-XYZ ORGANIZE SPRINT

⑩ OK DELIVER FUNCTIONAL SOFTWARE

⑪ USER FEEDBACK

I'll talk in greater depth about each step, but the overall flow is like this.

1. The project begins with the establishment of a code repository. That is the bedrock of the entire project. I and 15 quintillion other developers rely on GitHub.

2. Once the code repository is in place, the team needs to add issues into it to form a backlog. Derive the issues from user stories or developer notes.

3. A developer pulls an issue (say issue #123) from the backlog and makes a feature branch tagged with number 123 in the code repository.

4. The developer works on the code, then says, "I'm finished!"

5. Other developers look at that branch in a code review and say, "OK, looks good." The feature branch merges into the develop branch and is now part of the code base.

6. That completion triggers an update to the project tracking.

7. When it becomes necessary, the team curates the backlog of issues to refine what is important. They remove outdated tickets and reprioritize all tickets.

8. When there are a decent number of tickets ready to be estimated, the dev team plays estimation poker and reveals how long each feature will take to develop.

9. When the time comes to plan a sprint, the project manager determines how many developer days are available in the sprint. They draw a line at the number of estimated points down in the prioritized backlog and say, "This is what we are committing to in the next sprint."

10. The team works on the software. They deliver functional software at the end of the sprint.

11. The team asks users/customers to review these latest improvements. Their comments drive the creation of new issues into the backlog.

12. When the customer accepts the new changes, the deployment process kicks in to deliver the newest software to the customers.

These practices then begin again, in whatever order the status of the project dictates.

It all seems simple, right? In a way, that simplicity is why these practices succeed. Each practice only does the minimum of what's needed for its thing to be done right. Each practice depends on all the others. Not a single one of these practices can stand alone. We can't do 11 of them and expect to succeed.

But, of course, it isn't really simple. There's a lot of work, like technical effort and business process redesign, to set this all up.

CHAPTER 50

# ACEP 1
# CODE REPOSITORY: FREE INSURANCE

The code repository—an external site that backs up and manages your code—is the beating heart of your software development process. Its importance cannot be overstated. Even so, even today, I encounter software projects that don't have version control tracking. I've seen side projects run by lone developers who don't see the point, and legacy software created back when repositories were not the norm. Without a code repository, you will fail.

## A CAUTIONARY TALE

I'd just taken a new job to redesign the software development process for a company with little experience in software development best practices. One of my customers came forward with some urgent updates needed to fix an inventory-tracking program. This software retained 10 years of institutional knowledge critical to the enterprise. None of the original developers still worked there.

I went in to make the requested changes only to find that the software had no repository. Changes were made directly on the file system, and the web server pulled from that directory.

Concerning. Very concerning.

So I moved the code to a fresh repository, then went in to make updates. But I couldn't do it. The entire codebase referenced a custom-built Python module—let's call it "inventory_updater.py"—which I could not find for the life of me.

I searched the codebase for any reference to inventory_updater.py. I looked on the web server's file structure for it. I looked for imports that might be referencing external software. No matter what I tried, inventory_updater.py eluded me.

It simply did not exist.

The only, and I mean only, evidence that it ever existed was a file called "inventory_updater.pyc" in one of the temp directories on the web server. A .pyc is a compiled file that helps the software run a little more efficiently.

No. *Oh no.*

I told everyone on my team to freeze. Do not blink. Do not breathe on the web server. I called central IT in a panic to see if any impending updates were scheduled that would take the server down.

Then, as if I were playing the board game Operation and waiting for the buzzer, I carefully extracted the compiled .pyc file from the temp directory. That file was the only living record of a mission-critical module referenced by an entire inventory system. If I somehow messed up this file transfer, accidentally erased the file or something, a thousands-line business rules module would be gone with no way to reverse engineer it.

I used a Python decompiler to extract the human-readable code back out of the temp file and added it to the repository with relief.

You must use a code repository—even if you are one person working on a server you have complete control over.

## WHAT IS A REPO?

With that importance in mind, let's take a look at a brief history of version control and why it's important. A repo (combined code repository and version control system) is a file storage service for code. A version control system manages historical states and versions of a codebase. The term "repo" has come to encompass both since they are so intertwined.

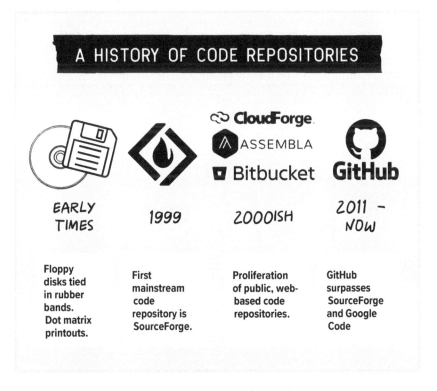

Version control systems (VCS) developed alongside code repositories.

And that leads us to 2023, a glorious time where Git consolidated its hold on the VCS arena, and GitHub has provided a peerless interface to it. So for once, we IT people don't have to rack our brains to figure out the best choice of which software to use.

So why should we use a repo?

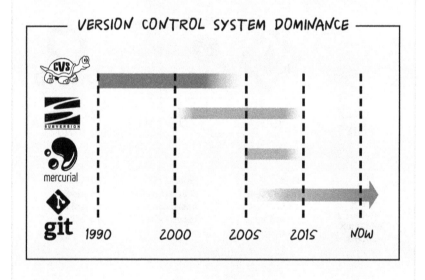

VERSION CONTROL SYSTEMS

CVS, the initial second generation (centralized) VCS kicks of the modern era.

Based on the principles of CVS, Subversion is launched in 2000 and quickly dominates the industry.

Launched simultaneously in 2005, Mercurial and git prove the benefits of distributed version control systems.

In 2015, Stack Overflow removes the annual survey question "Which VCS do you use?" because git had overtaken all others.

VERSION CONTROL SYSTEM DOMINANCE

## QUALITY OF LIFE

It used to be that software teams did what they could to ensure good practices. Before the advent of distributed VCS in 2005, developers literally yelled down the hall to each other. "Don't touch sys.txt; I'm working on it!" We'd put sticky notes on a computer: "DO NOT TOUCH: compiling!" We had floppy disks and printouts. I literally have re-created thousands of lines of code by retyping the program from a printout I am grateful to have printed.

Now we're free to work on any file at any time. We can tell who made a change. We can compare versions. We can focus.

## DISASTER RECOVERY

Before repos existed, code was mostly stored on shared file systems. If you overwrote your code, or the server died, so did your code. Reverting to a previous version? Forget about it.

True story: in one of my jobs at a manufacturing plant, one of the shift managers was responsible for storing backup line data. He had a box full of meticulously organized floppy disks in a filing cabinet. One for each day, clearly labeled in sequence. He was also responsible for sometimes retrieving very large and expensive metal tools that fell into awkward nooks on the manufacturing floor. He used a magnet the size of a human head, which he stored on the side of the filing cabinet. Over time, the data backups got corrupted because they were being stored next to a huge magnet. No matter how careful and well-meaning your people are, data can get lost.

## CODE QUALITY

Repos are a natural fit for continuous integration services, pull-request reviews, integrated project tracking, code linters, and more. A repo saves you in so many ways. If you have ever asked yourself any of the following questions, a good repo has your answers:

- When did this feature get added?
- Who wrote this line of code?
- Oh, no! We messed up. Can we go back to the previous version?
- Oh, no! We messed up a little over here, but we want to keep the stuff over there. Can we make a new version that does that?

- Did the thing I just wrote break our entire codebase?
- We want to add a new team in India to contribute to the code. Is that OK?

Those are all great questions. Your repo also answers a hundred questions like that, that you didn't think to ask. It's just humming along, saving all of our butts on an hourly basis in ways we don't even comprehend.

## HOW A CODE REPOSITORY HELPS YOU ESCAPE THE AGILE CIRCUS

So what does this all mean to you? A code repository is a must-have for me. But the ACEPs aren't about what *I* should do. They're about what *you* should do and what decisions you need to be mindful of.

The blur box shows us that context switches are a reality. There will be times that your team pivots itself away from a certain feature set or is forced to by outside pressures. When that occurs, how will you pick the pieces back up later?

A code repository is like a fancy way for a bunch of people to hit the save button on a shared document and come back to it later. Only each person gets a chance to include their thoughts when they hit save. Via the magic of commit messages, each developer can say something like this: "I was refactoring the inventory_parts tree to make it more efficient and was about to write a test for edge cases."

Now when the next sprint comes along, and the developer checks that code back out, they'll see the message to their present self from their past self and be like "Oh, yeah, I remember that." The repo even has diff tools that highlight the code changes, making it even clearer what was happening.

The blur box also shows us that resources may hop onto a thread or away from it in a thick/thin way. If you have a code repository in place, a newly joining developer can read over the commit history and get a good sense of where the project was headed as of the last active development period. The sheer amount of metadata that a repository provides you helps the handoffs to be as warm as possible.

The blur box also shows us that a lone developer working in isolation is a recipe for failure. A code repository makes it easy for multiple people to work on the same codebase. It also makes it easy for anyone to peek in and see what is being done by whom and how. That greatly mitigates the risk presented by a lone wolf developer. Finally, repos make it easy to do code reviews, which, as you'll see in a bit, is one of the ACEPs.

## ITERATING THE CODE REPOSITORY ACEP

One of the key principles of agile is to iterate. To adapt to change, try new things, and always improve your process in light of new information. So for each of the ACEPs I will provide you with real-world examples of how my team has refined and iterated that ACEP over the years.

At first glance it wouldn't seem like a code repository is particularly flexible. Not the sort of thing you want to go into and start poking around. But our repo has been more like a living process over the years and changes quite frequently.

First of all, we have tried different repos from time to time just to verify whether something else is better. We use GitHub, but we put some of our projects into GitLab just to see how it would go. We ended up not choosing GitLab. But using it for a while, seeing the slight philosophical differences between the two, led us to organize our GitHub repos differently.

We've also periodically tried some of the features we don't typically use, such as epics or bulk actions. Doing that led to small but meaningful efficiencies in our process over time.

I just added a new tag to our code repo this week to help us distinguish external dependencies, and it really clarified our sprint planning.

Finally, AI is starting to be integrated with GitHub. It will suggest tags, and it even does some automated pull request reviews.

There are always things you can evaluate and tweak, even in your code software packages, that might improve your process. Iterate or perish!

# CHAPTER 51

# ACEP 2
# ISSUES: BUSINESS VALUE IN A NUTSHELL

Issues are the results of your requirements gathering or the developers discovering new things to develop. An issue is a discrete chunk of effort that will lead to an improvement in a software system. In software development, that effort usually refers to development.

But an issue could also be devops, scaffolding, documentation, etc. Issues can be feature enhancements, new features, or activities to reduce technical debt. (Incidentally, if you are not actively managing technical debt, you owe it to yourself to check out Jon Kern's thoughts on his blog, appropriately named *Technical Debt*.[98])

Issues must have three components:

- A number
- A title
- A description

---

98   Jon Kern, "Got Technical Debt?," Technical Debt, February 13, 2013, https://technicaldebt.com/got-technical-debt/.

Issues should have four additional pieces:

- Enough detail to let the dev team know what the bug or expected feature behavior is
- An indication of what criteria should be met to consider the issue complete
- Who has been assigned the issue once it's in development
- An estimate of how much effort it will take to complete the issue

Estimate size dictates when to demote an issue to a task (a trivial amount of work) or promote it to an epic (an issue that encompasses several smaller issues):

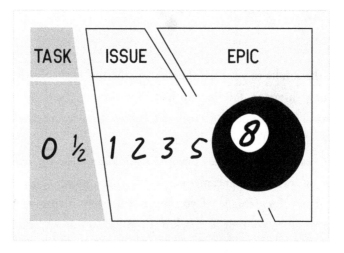

Below is an example of an issue that we will track throughout this section of the book. Notice that it has a number and title (although a better title would be something like "Account status table on the main financial dashboard will not wrap"). It has enough detail for the dev team to understand what is happening, with a screenshot showing the problem.

There is a solution that the dev team discovered while analyzing the issue: getTableData is not accounting for breakpoints. The issue has been assigned to someone and has an estimate. All things considered, this is a healthy little demo ticket for us to talk about.

It's also important to understand what an issue is not. Here are some warning flags to keep in mind when writing tickets:

ISSUE #123: TABLE WILL NOT WRAP

When users look at the account status table on screens smaller that 1024 x 768, the status column text does not wrap. It goes off the side of the screen like this:

| account | status |
|---------|--------|
| acme ltd | Account has been f |
| bank 5 | active. |

This is because the getTableData method needs to account for breakpoints. Fix the method so that when text is longer than one line at small resolutions, the text wraps inside of the status column. **Assigned to: Jane Estimate: 1/2**

- A bug report is not an issue. The bug report is an indication that something is wrong. It's not a design for fixing the bug. When you understand the cause of the bug, then you can make an issue.

- Underdescribing an issue because you think it will be handled quickly can bite you a year later.

- Issues that depend on the effort of another entity are not issues. If you need to interact with another team or company that is not under your direct control, do not write those interactions as tickets. They cannot be estimated or controlled.

- Analysis, design, or training are not issues. They cannot be estimated. They are done when they're done.

Getting issues right is one of the most critical aspects of software development. If your issues are vague, too broad, or impossible to estimate, you are setting your team up for failure. If your issues are well thought out and easy to estimate, your software development process will flow downhill.

INVEST is a popular acronym to help you decide whether a ticket meets the best criteria:[99]

| | |
|---|---|
| **I** | Independent |
| **N** | Negotiable |
| **V** | Valuable |
| **E** | Estimable |
| **S** | Small |
| **T** | Testable |

INVEST falls under the umbrella of a concept called "definition of ready," a.k.a. DoR, which is a fence erected to keep immature tickets out of the sprint so we don't waste time tracking down unknowns in the middle of the sprint.

You could argue that tracking down unknowns is the purpose of a sprint. And being too restrictive on what is allowed into a sprint is not agile. Mike Cohn writes about this in "Definition of Ready: What It Is and Why It's Dangerous." Mike is in the same category as Scott Ambler and myself: people who did not help author the Agile Manifesto but were involved in the discussions leading up to it and have been writing about it ever since. So he's a good person to listen to.

Mike shares my opinion about external dependencies:

> For example, suppose your team is occasionally dependent on some other team to provide part of the work. Your user stories can only be finished if that other team also finishes their work—and does so early enough in the iteration for your team to integrate the two pieces.

99    Wikipedia, s.v. "INVEST (Mnemonic)," last modified July 18, 2023, https://en.wikipedia.org/wiki/INVEST_(mnemonic).

If that team has consistently burned you by not finishing what they said they'd do by the time they said they'd do it, your team might quite reasonably decide to not bring in any story that has a still-open dependency on that particular team.

A definition of ready that requires external dependencies to be resolved before a story could be brought into an iteration might be wise for such a team.[100]

But Mike cautions against being too restrictive with DoR. It can lead to a water-folly way of establishing phase gates:

Here's an example of a definition of ready rule I'd recommend that a team rewrite: "Each story must be accompanied by a detailed mock-up of all new screens before we start work."

A rule like this is a gate. It prevents work from overlapping. A team with this rule cannot practice concurrent engineering. No work can occur beyond the gate until a detailed design is completed for each story.

A better variation of this would be something more like: "If the story involves significant new screens, rough mock-ups of the new screens have been started and are just far enough along that the team can resolve remaining open issues during the iteration."[101]

There's a lot more wisdom in the article, so I encourage you to read it.

## HOW PROPER ISSUE TRACKING HELPS YOU ESCAPE THE AGILE CIRCUS

---

100 Mike Cohn, "The Definition of Ready: What It Is and Why It's Dangerous," *Mountain Goat Software* (blog), May 23, 2023, https://www.mountaingoatsoftware.com/blog/the-dangers-of-a-definition-of-ready.
101 Cohn, "The Definition of Ready."

The reason I'm bringing this DoR topic up now is that your organization needs to carefully consider what is a good issue and what is not. Then you must do the minimum required to keep yourself from getting trapped later in the process, while keeping your options as wide open as possible. It's a dance that no one but you can perform.

Issues are the reason why you're doing software. They are mini versions of your customer being taken care of by your team. You need to spend a sufficient amount of time thinking about how you will grow, manage, and harvest them amid a fast-paced, iterative process.

The blur box shows us that our arena is three-dimensional—multiple projects, locations, time zones, etc. How is your issue approach dealing with that? How do you ensure that the fuzzy blur of iteration does not eat through all of your tickets, leaving your funnel dry?

The blur box suggests that experienced teams are more likely to succeed in the blur. Is your team experienced enough to handle vague tickets? To resolve competing feature requests? Are they emotionally intelligent enough to read between the lines and deliver what the customer actually wants? If your team is experienced, you can be quite permissive where tickets are concerned. If they are less experienced, you'll probably need some scaffolding in place to support issue curation.

## ITERATING THE ISSUES ACEP

It's amusing to look back over our issue history. When we first started out, we were all gung-ho about structuring the issue names with roles and value adds:

*Issue 101: As an author writing about agile software development, I want to write a book that clearly articulates the benefits and challenges of iteration so my readers will not fail in their own agile efforts.*

Over time, that structure became unwieldy. We decided as a team that the format was kind of annoying and wasn't adding much value. Now our tickets are more like this:

*Issue 101: Write a book that clearly articulates the benefits and challenges of iteration.*

Then, in the body of the ticket, we explain some of the value if it helps the developer.

# CHAPTER 52

# ACEP 3
# BRANCHING PROTECTS YOUR CODEBASE

Given the global complexity of systems and approaches, it's rare in software development to have one person define best practices in one fell swoop. Linus Torvalds did it with Git, and Vincent Driessen did it with branching strategies. You can read the genesis of the idea in Driessen's article "A Successful Git Branching Model."[102]

The developers I know all use Driessen's approach, or something based on it, even though Driessen himself offered an updated strategy after this one went viral.

So what are branches?

- A *long-running branch* is a permanent record of sequential changes to a code base over time (main, develop).
- A *feature branch* is a short-term series of commits around a feature(s) that we merge back into develop, then delete.

---

102  Vincent Driessen, "A Successful Git Branching Model," *Nvie* (blog), last updated March 5, 2020, https://nvie.com/posts/a-successful-git-branching-model/.

- A *hotfix* is a simple, clear solution to an emergency production problem.

Those three work together something like this:

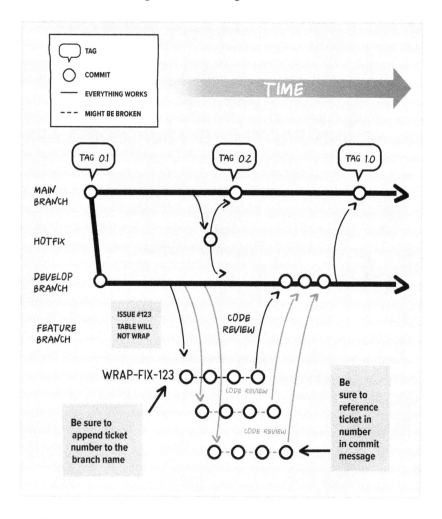

This strategy offers many benefits for an agile dev team. Having two long-running branches provides flexibility in deployment. The Main branch is a good target for devops to do deployments against. It's stable.

Development is also stable, but it's better for setting up demo sites or staging new features.

The unstable feature branches branch from and back into develop, leaving Main alone. That way there's always a production-ready branch. Hotfixes don't stall the development effort. Feature branches show where a change came from.

## HOW BRANCHING HELPS YOU ESCAPE THE AGILE CIRCUS

I used some variation of the word "iterate" well over a hundred times in this book. An iteration is a refinement of your approach in light of new information.

Each feature branch is a chance for your team to experiment with a new direction or to provide a new solution. They can create a temporary reality that the customer can see and play with and say yes or no to it. Branching is the exact opposite of commitment. It's as though you're reading a Choose Your Own Adventure book but keeping your fingers between all of the page numbers of each choice so you can go back and try a new path if this one fails. Branching gives you the chance to try things without altering the core code base. It's the very definition of iteration.

Whereas making commits directly to your production branch is the ultimate form of pride. "This is definitely the correct approach," you are proclaiming, while erasing your own footsteps so you can't go back.

Pride is not your friend here. Humility is. Think about your branching strategy in terms of your team dynamics, your customer, and how many downstream resources you have for testing, A/B marketing, etc. Then you can iterate like a pro.

## ITERATING THE CODE REPOSITORY ACEP

So far I've been all like "here's how my team is awesome about following best practices." But we have not iterated much on our branching strategy.

That's partially because it works really well for us.

But it's also because we are really, really anxious about yanking our hands in and touching the third rail that might electrocute us. And that fear, or prudent caution, is a blind spot.

For example, Vincent Driessen himself posted an arguably superior approach in the post referenced above:

> This model was conceived in 2010, now more than 10 years ago, and not very long after Git itself came into being. In those 10 years, git-flow (the branching model laid out in this article) has become hugely popular in many a software team to the point where people have started treating it like a standard of sorts—but unfortunately also as a dogma or panacea.
>
> During those 10 years, Git itself has taken the world by a storm, and the most popular type of software that is being developed with Git is shifting more towards web apps—at least in my filter bubble. Web apps are typically continuously delivered, not rolled back, and you don't have to support multiple versions of the software running in the wild.
>
> This is not the class of software that I had in mind when I wrote the blog post 10 years ago. If your team is doing continuous delivery of software, I would suggest to adopt a much simpler workflow (like GitHub flow) instead of trying to shoehorn git-flow into your team.[103]

We are a web development team with few rollbacks, so we should probably consider whether there is a business value to be gained by simplifying our branching strategy.

---

103  Driessen, "A Successful Git Branching Model."

# CHAPTER 53

# ACEP 4
# FEATURE DEVELOPMENT DONE RIGHT

I could spend a lot of time here telling you various approaches to do software development effectively. Fortunately I don't have to, because it has already been done far better by others. Let me tell you of a few influential books that I recommend. Reading them is a great way to gain vast insights into good ways and bad ways to develop software. Each has a different tone and focus, so if it doesn't jibe with your style, reach for another book and see if it fits your brain better. You can find each of these listed in the Further Reading section of the appendix.

*eXtreme Programming Explained, 2nd Edition* by Kent Beck and Cynthia Andres is an agile-forward approach to developing software, as befits one of the Agile Manifesto coauthors.[104] The first edition of this book was foundational to my understanding of coding best practices. For example, at the time I read it, the notion of paired programming was heretical. Management would ask things like "Why in the world would you have two programmers sit there working on one feature? They can't both type on the

---

104  Beck and Andres, *eXtreme Programming Explained*, 2nd ed.

same keyboard, *NCIS*-style, and achieve double speed." But we now know that codeveloping a feature can be faster and superior than one developer working alone. This is thanks to Kent Beck.

Speaking of manifesto coauthors, Robert Martin has written an entire series of books on the subject of software development. For the purpose of discussion I'll recommend *Clean Code: A Handbook of Agile Software Craftsmanship*.[105] All I'm going to say on the matter is that Uncle Bob is the one who first introduced me to the concept of "code smell," a highly scientific term for doubting a code's quality. If that intrigues you, you have much more to look forward to in this book.

Another legendary tome from two other Manifesto coauthors is *The Pragmatic Programmer: Your Journey to Mastery, 20th Anniversary Edition* by David Thomas and Andrew Hunt.[106] It got a 20th anniversary update in 2019, and for good reason: this book is widely influential in the software development industry. For example, it introduced the concept of DRY (Do not Repeat Yourself), which is a mantra our team repeats often.

Just to throw in a non-Manifesto-coauthor book, check out *Real-World Maintainable Software* by Abraham Marín-Pérez.[107] It delves into essential skills such as separation of concerns and loosely coupled architecture, two notions that you'll be glad you paid attention to when you inevitably need to refactor code.

There are hundreds of factors involved in software development that are outside the scope of *Inheriting Agile*. For purposes of discussing the ACEPs, here is a simplified overview of our approach to software development that is a natural fit for the rest of the practices I've described.

105  Robert C. Martin, *Clean Code: A Handbook of Agile Software Craftsmanship*, 1ⁿ ed. (Pearson, 2008).

106  David Thomas and Andrew Hunt, *The Pragmatic Programmer: Your Journey to Mastery, 20th Anniversary Edition*, 2nd ed. (Addison-Wesley Professional, 2019).

107  Márin-Pérez, *Real-World Maintainable Software*.

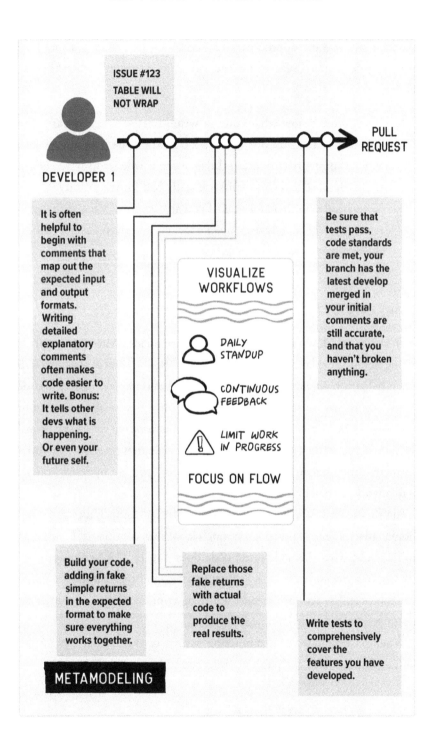

ISSUE #123
TABLE WILL
NOT WRAP

PULL REQUEST

DEVELOPER 1

It is often helpful to begin with comments that map out the expected input and output formats. Writing detailed explanatory comments often makes code easier to write. Bonus: It tells other devs what is happening. Or even your future self.

Be sure that tests pass, code standards are met, your branch has the latest develop merged in your initial comments are still accurate, and that you haven't broken anything.

VISUALIZE
WORKFLOWS

DAILY STANDUP

CONTINUOUS FEEDBACK

LIMIT WORK IN PROGRESS

FOCUS ON FLOW

Build your code, adding in fake simple returns in the expected format to make sure everything works together.

Replace those fake returns with actual code to produce the real results.

Write tests to comprehensively cover the features you have developed.

METAMODELING

As for my specific approach, I like stubbing and testing a lot. I tell every new developer I've ever trained two rules of thumb when they are starting out:

1. If you don't know what code to write, start with comments. That will help you figure out what to do in the code. But always keep those comments current, and delete them when you have code in place. Because bad comments are really bad for your sanity.
2. Tests are always there for you. If you are unsure of what to do, write tests, either of already developed code or test-driven development of the feature you're about to write.

## STUBBING

If you are staring down an empty page and have no idea what to do, start by writing detailed explanatory comments that describe what is about to happen. It helps you plan and tells other people what is happening in the code.

But comments must be updated and are only a good short-term solution. That is because *outdated comments are infuriating and hurt literally everyone.* If you write a comment, then write code that does not match the comments, then fail to update your comments, you are opening yourself up to a world of pain.

For this reason, *The Pragmatic Programmer* by Andy Hunt and Dave Thomas advises against putting too much labor into comments. Comments can lie about what the code does; code does not lie.[108] A better approach is trying to write code that is self-documenting; in other words, the names of variables and functions are sufficiently descriptive that you can infer the meaning from the code.

When starting to work on a function, write a comment that says, "Apply the transformation to each point." Then the code might become this:

---

108 Thomas and Hunt, *The Pragmatic Programmer.*

```
foreach (point in points) { point = transform(point); }
```

You can then delete the comment, because the code now clearly has the information that was in the comment.

While I agree with the above approach, there are times when you need a nudge to get the code ball rolling. So at the beginning, I recommend good comments, with brief life spans. As you fill in the comments with self-documenting code, go back and remove the comments until there aren't any left.

## DAILY STANDUP

Every day, participate in a daily standup. This 15-minute meeting is most commonly associated with scrum but can be used by anyone. In the traditional standup, each developer explains the following:

1. What they did yesterday
2. What they're going to do today
3. If they have any roadblocks

Those three talking points do a lot of heavy lifting. They force the developer to replay the last day and pick up the thread. They help to visualize the workflow for the current day. They give management warning flags of which roadblocks to clear. Sometimes, other developers will ask questions that improve everyone's understanding of where the dev process is. Daily standups are really good at providing early discovery.

The real benefit is that daily standup is armor for the dev team. Anyone in the enterprise may attend standup. But it's good etiquette for no one but the dev team to speak. This isn't the place for company announcements or management check-ins.

If you have curious customers, antsy managers, or other people who think the development process is a black box, invite them to standup.

Whether or not they show up, you can point to the process and say, "You can hear our progress any given day."

## HOW FEATURE DEVELOPMENT CAN HELP YOU CONFRONT THE BLUR BOX

There are so many ways to develop software that it's almost ridiculous for me to provide you with recommendations. So let's instead focus on how your development approach might confront the blur box.

Threads and phases are constantly shifting around each other in a fuzzy blur. It's not always good to get too scattered down multiple trains of thought because they might pivot away. One good strategy for confronting that reality is to limit work in progress. A team can get overwhelmed if they pull too many tickets and have too many balls in the air. So do your best to only break off one or two tickets and get them merged back in as soon as you can.

WIP limits comes from the lean tradition of just-in-time manufacturing. I learned of the concept when working at Subaru-Isuzu. It's a counterintuitive observation that working on fewer things at once is faster than working on several things at once. WIP is best articulated by two books: Donald G. Reinertsen's *Principle of Product Development Flow*, which is a dense and comprehensive tome describing everything you ever wanted to know about lean product delivery, and Eliyahu M. Goldratt's *The Goal*, which is a fiction novel about the theory of constraints.[109] That one-two punch will give you a rounded understanding of flow theory, which is one of your best defenses against the complex challenges of the blur box.

Because of the realities of iteration, the programming team has an onus to write flexible code. *The Pragmatic Programmer* uses this as a primary criterion for evaluating the quality of code: good code is easy to change.

---

109    Donald G. Reinertsen, *The Principles of Product Development Flow: Second Generation Lean Product Development* (Celeritas Publishing, 2014). Eliyahu M. Goldratt and Jeff Cox, *The Goal* (Gower Publishing, 1984).

Since you already know the blur you're about to confront, do everything you can to ensure changeable code.[110]

The blur box does one thing really well: it throws change into our faces. (Not actual change, like quarters and stuff—that would sting.) Knowing that, you can alleviate some of the side effects through continual feedback. Here's a foolproof recipe for failure: make one developer work in isolation on something. A better approach is to encourage continuous feedback. This can be as simple as "Hey team, I'm stuck on this test. Anyone got a minute to talk me through it?" It can be as complex as a mid-sprint pull-request review by the rest of the team.

## ITERATING THE FEATURE DEVELOPMENT ACEP

### Artificial Intelligence

I mentioned that stubbing (aka pseudocode) is one of my core practices as a programmer: writing a code comment that tells the developer what is going to happen in the code. Another reason to begin with comments is when using AI tools such as GitHub Copilot. At the time of this book's writing (which will likely seem quaint by the time it sees print), AI-paired programming is starting to trickle into the market. The landscape is changing fast. In the case of GitHub Copilot, the programmer writes a detailed comment, which tells the AI what type of code to stub in.

My IT director asked me to evaluate the benefits and drawbacks of using generative AI in our software development teams. I went to a great talk on GitHub Copilot by Brent Laster, who wrote *Learning GitHub Actions*.[111] Then my team spent a day trying Github Copilot out. My hot take on Copilot thus far is that it might be useful to:

1. generate boilerplate code

---

110  Thomas and Hunt. *The Pragmatic Programmer*.
111  Brent Laster, *Learning GitHub Actions: Automation and Integration of CI/CD with GitHub*, 1st ed., (O'Reilly Media, 2023).

2. show us directions we hadn't thought of

3. translate code from one language to another

From a practical perspective, what might incorporating AI-assisted tools into our coding practice look like? Some ideas based on my initial explorations are:

1. Add a new issue field named "Prompt."

   A user story or issue could have a new section called "Prompt," where during design sessions, the team crafts the code comment that will be used by AI to generate the initial code. That way, when a developer pulls a ticket (either during a sprint or during a flow-based approach), they'll have the benefit of the group's consensus on how to generate the initial code. That will reduce the effects of context switching, which often occurs when pulling a new ticket. The developer stares at it blankly, wondering what the heck is supposed to happen next. With AI prompts in place, you're giving yourself the gift of flow by tapping into the groove that was present during design sessions, no matter how much later the ticket is pulled. That could theoretically lead to increased development speed, improved code quality, and developer confidence—as though the entire team is participating in the launch of the feature.

2. Include your chats in the pull request.

   As part of the pull request, developers should attach any AI chats they used to generate the code. That way reviewers have some context for how the code was generated, which will help them spot potential issues. It also might reduce the context switching penalty introduced by moving from feature development to code review mindsets.

That means reviewers can critique the included chat as well. For example, if a senior developer has noticed over time that a junior dev does not fully understand the concept of separation of concerns, they can keep an eye out for teaching opportunities that might be hinted at in the chat. That way, developers learn from each other how to solicit better generative code from the AI.

3.  Be highly suspicious of AI-generated tests.

    Our team explored using AI to write tests, which seemed like a no brainer when we started. GitHub Copilot uses the context of any windows open in the Integrated Development Environment (IDE) to inform its code generation. That is to say, it draws on both its training set (the millions of lines of publicly available code used to create the language learning models, or LLMs) and also whatever you have open on your computer at the time you ask it to generate tests (local context.) Theoretically—especially if you already have the code written that you wish to test—you should be able to point to a feature, provide the AI with a test case prompt, and have it produce a result that is customized to your local context.

My team has concluded that it's a terrible idea to use AI to generate tests. In fact, human-written tests become even more critical when AI is in the mix.

One of the main benefits of testing is to proclaim independently what a successful feature looks like and what results it should produce under different conditions, then ensure the code produces those results. This is particularly true if doing test-driven development.

Our admittedly brief foray into using AI to generate tests was concerning. The AI wrote really nice-looking tests that were technically accurate, but completely missed the point of what we were asking them to test. Or, even worse, wrote tests that were not technically accurate at all.

This could be due to several different factors. One, I could just be really bad at asking Copilot how to write tests. I'm new at this, and I might be missing a very large boat that would make it all work better.

Two, I might forget to close certain windows that would confuse the local context for the AI. True, that would also be user error and not the AI's fault. But when I develop, my IDE has enough open windows that the tabs no longer show all of the file names across the top. I need to use a dropdown to access all open files. Since I don't have a readily apparent visual cue of all the files that are open, I might forget that a counterproductive file is open. That will mess up the test generation.

This scenario is especially likely if I were to develop in one session (which is a conceptually complicated endeavor, juggling lots of balls at the same time) and come back later to write tests. My mind focuses on what test to write, and maybe forgets all of the windows I had open while developing the feature. Poisoning my local context is an entirely plausible scenario. Not to mention, it would be a drag to have to close all of those open windows to write the tests, then have to open them all back up when I switch back to development mode, which invariably happens when you write tests—frequently many times per hour.

There is also a third reason why the tests might fail, which is not user error at all: the AI just borks up the test. It is only as good as its LLM, and it can only draw on what the developer has available locally. It can't read minds.

But we developers know what we had in mind when we provided the prompt, so there is confirmation bias when we see what the AI spits out as a test. And that is perhaps the biggest danger of all. The developers use the prompt in the ticket to lead to the initial boilerplate, use the understanding of that prompt to interact with the AI chat to refine the code, assume that the AI understands the test prompt the way we do, and then look for confirmation that it produced the right results.

But it might not. Testing is hard.

Much of that potential misunderstanding would be mitigated through test-driven development—but that means there is no local code handy to provide local context to generate the test, which was one of the potential time savings in the first place. It would also be mitigated by not involving AI at all in writing tests.

I'm still evaluating whether AI will be beneficial to us, and I do not yet have the experience to know if the above takeaways are big problems or easily overcome. Either way, a big part of that decision is thinking through how our process will iterate in light of this new tool.

**Daily Standup**

Daily standup is another great example of how we've iterated our feature development process. It's really useful for showing everyone what is happening. But daily standup has come under fire recently. Some organizations have stopped using daily standups altogether. Some find the traditional three questions limiting, more like a book report that everyone else snoozes through. It depends on your intended audience and what you want to get out of standup.

So we've made some changes to our standup routine over the years to keep things fresh. For example, I randomly switch up the order of who goes first. That may not seem like much, but it keeps everyone honest about preparing what they have to say.

We also got rid of the roadblocks question because it was rarely needed. Doing so saved us about two minutes per standup. That was four and a half years ago, which means we've saved about one week of developer time:

(260 work days per year × 2 minutes) ÷ 60 minutes × 4.5 years = 39 hours

That's not a bad return on an investment that took us a few minutes to decide on.

# CHAPTER 54

# ACEP 5
# CODE REVIEWS: EVERYBODY BUT YOU HATES THEM

Here's the worst-kept secret in software development: Nobody likes code reviews. Done poorly, it's where holier-than-thou meets impostor syndrome. They're a perfect breeding ground for social anxiety and snark, like a gladiatorial arena where your self-worth gets battered around by your coworkers.

So your dev team might kind of slink away and not do so many of them anymore.

Danger! Danger! Wrangle them all back. Make code reviews mandatory for any branch merge. They're software development's analogue to double-blind clinical trials or double-entry accounting. Independent reviews ensure new code passes muster.

As a developer and a reviewer, you have these responsibilities:

Before I get into the nitty-gritty of code-review advice, let me first explain why you should care—what the business value of code reviews actually is.

There have been moments in my professional life when I trusted someone else's code without double-checking it. Some of the most exciting memories of my career came from such moments.

## DEVELOPER RESPONSIBILITIES

**DEVELOPER 1**

Deliver a pull request that meets the acceptance criteria. Assume that any comments given are meant constructively. Do not be defensive. Respond to comments with a "done," plan, ticket, or query.

**DEVELOPER 2**

Read all the code changes. Run the new branch and ensure that it works properly. Make constructive comments. Ask questions. If you aren't approving the pull request, state why.

One morning I woke up a couple hours earlier than usual. Was it some dark intuition causing me restlessness?

I decided to go into work early. At 7:30 a.m., as I was walking to my office from the parking deck, my cell phone rang. Odd ... who would be calling me at this hour?

Turns out, it was the director of networking for the major research university I was working at. The entire medical side of the university network had gone down. Every researcher, business person, student, and hospital patient no longer had access to the internet. Every server, smart appliance, medical device, and key card entry system had gone down.

Aside from the obvious safety concerns over patients' lives and people being locked out of their buildings, dollars were at stake. Someone once calculated how much money each minute of lost network time costs the university. I'm not going to tell you how high that figure is nor share how many minutes the internet outage was. I will simply tell you what the very irate director of networking technology told me: "The entire school of medicine network went down, and it is because of the server your team just brought online. What the fiddlesticks is going on down there?"

I'm paraphrasing. But the upshot is that an errant bit of code we'd put into production cost the university more than my entire team's salaries combined.

So my team and I dug in to find out what had happened. Our senior devops guy had taken the lead on it and was pretty sure it couldn't be our server that caused the problem. But we went line by line through the server configuration and discovered the culprit.

There is a concept called "address resolution protocol," or ARP. It means that a server on a network announces to the rest of the network, "Hey, everybody, I know how to resolve addresses. You can trust me to route your server requests to wherever in the world they may be going."

Well, our server didn't know how to route server requests to wherever in the world they may have been going. But we had put this line into the server configuration:

```
ARP = 1
```

That's it. Doesn't look like much, does it? But if you put that line into a configuration on a server that doesn't actually handle address resolution, it poisons the ARP cache. That's a fancy way of saying that our server was swallowing up every request routed through the network and sending them into a black hole of nothingness. So all of the servers kept redoubling their efforts at computer speed, until the network was swamped with requests going nowhere, and they had to shut it all down. The hospital has a code for it: code black. It's one of the most severe colors out of all the colors. It brings with it a slew of meetings, probably with lots of yelling.

By walking through the server configuration line-by-line and explaining to us what each line did, our senior devops guy was able to definitively explain what had happened, so we could fix it and mend fences with the networking team.

Walking through the server configuration line-by-line and explaining what each line does isn't too far away from a code review. I know absolutely nothing about server configurations, which is why I trusted his code in the first place. But had we all taken just a few extra minutes to discuss the new code, perhaps that error would have come to light. Perhaps we could have saved hundreds of thousands of dollars—and not endangered patients.

If we had enforced a policy of code reviews, not allowing code to go into production until we approved it, we might have avoided the entire snafu.

Don't take my word for it. Here are a couple similar stories from my contemporaries regarding the importance of code reviews, from an online discussion I had with anonymous software devs that has since been taken down. You know, word-on-the-street type stuff.

> I was on call, and our entire legacy application went down at 2 a.m. Some network call was failing because a service had gone down in a region, but there was some failover logic in place.

When I read the code closer, there was a simple if statement checking if the response existed, instead of an error property on the response object. The if statement always evaluated to true, so the failover logic never kicked in.

When I looked at git blame, the author YOLO merged a two-line code change without review or adding any tests.

> At a start-up there was a bug with our API endpoint that would send email notifications via a third-party email API. After adding a try/catch clause (which we should've already had), I saw if you added the same email in the To and CC lines (same for To and BCC), it would cause an exception on the provider's end. A user could add multiple recipients—so if they happened to add duplicate emails, there was a risk of it crashing. So we refactored so all email lists were converted to a set so the emails were unique. Initially having the error check would've saved more time.

When approving a pull request, look for these acceptance criteria:

1. New code doesn't break the existing codebase. This is mostly ensured by continuous integration bots. Another pair of eyes never hurts.

2. New code is able to be merged. Again, a good repo will tell you that in advance. If not, a code reviewer needs to merge the feature branch into their local copy of the develop branch and make sure there are no conflicts.

3. New code is standards compliant. My Python team uses PEP8 as a code standard. Find something similar that makes sure all of your developers are using the same conventions. It makes reading and maintaining code much easier.

4. New code doesn't have a "code smell." "Code smell" is Bob Martin's highly scientific term for "something ain't right." Maybe the variable names seem weirdly specific or convoluted. Maybe the indentation levels seem a little extra. Something is setting your radar off.

5. New code has adequate test coverage. We maintain a floor of 90% test coverage, which means that if new code causes our total code coverage to drop below 90%, that new code must increase test coverage to stay above that water line.

6. New code has the proper comments. Recall above when I said outdated comments are infuriating and hurt literally everyone? Here's the place to catch those misleading comments.

7. New code works. Funny that it took us this long to get here, but yes, you need to make sure the new code actually functions. Typically, you'll run it in your local dev environment and poke around.

8. New code meets the acceptance criteria (explicit or implied) in the issue. It's always best practice to go back and think about the original issue or user story to ensure you've met the user request.

## HOW CODE REVIEWS HELP YOU CONFRONT THE BLUR BOX

Software development is about solving human problems. Human problems are often nebulous problems. So the dev team does their best to codify them—literally.

How do you know that you got it right? One way is to write the code, add it to the main branch, do a bunch of testing, then at the end of the project a year from now, put it in front of the customer to find out if you got it right.

Well, we know about the realities of iteration. We can do better. The blur box lets you get something in place far earlier and present that to customers in an incremental way.

How do you know that you got it right? One way is to write the code, add it to the development branch, do a bunch of testing, then at the end of the sprint two weeks from now, put it in front of the customer to find out if you got it right.

Well, we know about the realities of iteration. We can do better.

We can write the feature, submit it as a pull request, then get it in front of another developer's eyes that same day. That developer knows the customer's problem, too, and which way they think the feature should have been done. They are a test audience that prevents obvious problems from getting to the customer's eyes.

## ITERATING THE CODE REVIEW ACEP

Our first iteration of reviewing code, in hindsight, seems obvious: we weren't doing them in all cases. We had a couple developers who were each lone developers in a specific language not used by the rest of the team. We kinda shrugged and said, "OK, we trust you, I guess?"

That was not wise.

When I began sitting with these lone developers and asked them to walk me through their code, I saw horrors that will keep you awake at night. (If you're on the hook for the final product, at least.)

For those of you who like discussing code, I'm talking hardcoded variables. Nested loops within nested loops within nested loops just to avoid the simple step of writing functions. Hardcoded pixel counts. Unused subroutines. Obfuscations galore.

At first I thought perhaps I was a fool who just didn't get it. But over time I came to realize they were likely doing the "nobody can understand what I do because it is so hard" schtick. It was not long before that mess was shut down, saving us money and eliminating risk. We redeployed the apps in our own language and boom! Bob's your uncle.

Speaking of Uncle Bob, for lots of ideas on how to improve code review effectiveness and code in general, you owe it to yourself to peruse chapter 21 of *Clean Code* by Robert C. Martin.[112] And while you're at it, read the rest of the book as well.

(I'm certain that Uncle Bob had never heard that pun before.)

---

112  Martin, *Clean Code.*

# CHAPTER 55

# ACEP 6
# PROJECT TRACKING:
# YOUR SUIT OF ARMOR

Somehow, some way, you need to know where you are trying to go and how far you are along that path. Otherwise, your venture will be aimless, and you'll just be tossing money down a pit. Just as in the feature development section earlier, I'm going to hand-wave a little bit here because there are hundreds of approaches you can take, and I'm not the person to tell you which one to choose.

Especially if you follow my advice and eliminate deadlines as much as possible. If so, I will put in a plug for kanban boards. A kanban board is a wonderful project management tool. It's just so ... nice. Streamlined. Clean. Anyone can see at a glance how things are going. I started using them at Subaru. Then throughout the rest of my career, inspired by the floor-to-ceiling rolls of paper I'd seen at Subaru, I made my own kanban board out of wood trim, fabric, and foam board. Year after year, the little tickets would march past.

Well, now they make software with kanban boards built in. I use Zen-Hub, which integrates with GitHub and provides us with a digital kanban board for our ticket management.

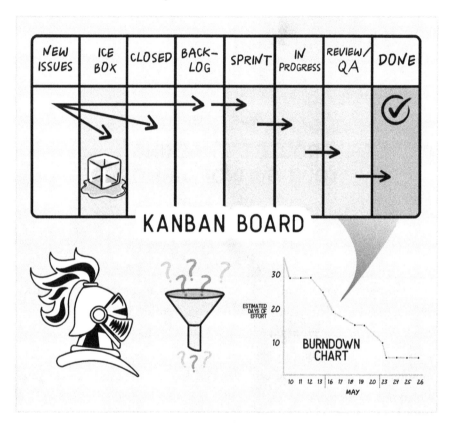

## HOW PROJECT TRACKING HELPS YOU ESCAPE THE AGILE CIRCUS

OK, enough hand-waving. I'm not the one to dictate which project-tracking approach you should use. I *am* the one to talk about how the blur box affects project tracking. There are three primary benefits agile developers derive from project tracking.

## *Protection*

I tell my team that certain practices we follow are like putting on a suit of armor. When the rest of the company comes charging in with pitchforks, we can point to our project tracking. It's very easy to prove that we have been working on the right stuff at the right pace. Without project tracking, it's our word against the company's darkest fears.

"Charging in with pitchforks" is a metaphor for added overhead—update reports, status meetings, fine-grained deadlines, or pressure. In other words, inefficiency. These tasks take up time better spent in software development and add no value. The blur box has no time for such speedbumps. Project tracking is our shield meant to deflect busywork.

## *Question Funnel*

"Hey, did you guys ever get that table-wrap issue fixed?"

"How's the sprint going?"

"Are you ever going to fix the white space issue I brought up in 2009?"

Questioners, meet our friendly kanban board. The blur box moves fast and lean. Any questions that you can handle with self-service speed us up.

## *Clear Progress*

There's no better feeling in the world than being accused of something (which the dev team seems like an easy target for, I guess?) and then pulling out the last five years' worth of burndown charts to shut that mess down.

For example, a recent worldwide pandemic caused our team to suddenly become 100% remote. There was apprehension about that from upper management, who were understandably nervous about not being able to keep an eye on things.

Via the magic of burndown charts, I was able to demonstrate that our team is now 9.5% more effective on average than in previous on-location sprints.

It makes sense if you think about it. My commute is about 20 feet. The bathroom is closer. Getting lunch takes five minutes instead of a half hour. I don't have a water cooler to hang around and talk to my coworkers. Otherwise I work the same basic hours I always have, but my time is much more focused.

It might make sense. But having the proof of progress in hand is next-level clarity.

Incidentally, our team had absolutely no transition penalty when switching to fully remote work. We had already accounted for uncertainty and distributed work by facing the blur box. We just happened to be sitting next to each other. Going 100% remote had almost no impact on us, except improving our efficiency. So I advocate an agile approach for any remote team.

## ITERATING THE PROJECT TRACKING ACEP

We did a lot of iteration on project tracking in the beginning. We tried demo periods for several commercial kanban-style trackers. We held meetings at the end of each trial and asked the team what they liked and didn't like about each.

That's how we eventually landed on the one that sucks the least for us, ZenHub. It integrates with our repo. It does a lot of the stuff my team finds valuable. So when the value-to-annoyance trade-off was acceptable, we went with it.

Since then, I have quietly iterated our project tracking in a different way: we no longer produce burndown charts. Once we'd made our reputation, people stopped asking to see them. Over time, it became a ritual. Then an artifact. Then a ghost. If you listen carefully on a dark night, you can still hear our old burndown charts rustling in the storage room.

I'm fully aware that somewhere up there I said burndown charts are your best friend and did a whole section about them. When I needed armor, burndown charts were there for me. They helped us establish credibility and trustworthiness. But at that point, they weren't culturally necessary anymore. So we iterated.

Nothing is sacred in an agile shop. Not even the stuff I said a few chapters ago.

# CHAPTER 56

# ACEP 7
# BACKLOG COMBING:
# GET BACK A FEW BUCKS

Issues/tickets/stories are the fuel of the development process. It's vital to have quality fuel feeding in at a steady pace. Your backlog gets out of sync without maintenance. So when your backlog is no longer feeding your development process effectively, take a break and refine the backlog. What should you do?

## *Reduce Size*

Do a first pass through the backlog for any quick wins. We have a couple dead-end columns in our kanban board, such as "icebox" (nice-to-have features we might get to someday but are extremely low priority) and "closed." If we can easily sort a ticket into the icebox or closed columns, our burden just got lighter.

The blur box encourages iteration of process. Revisiting tickets and eliminating outdated ones is a rudimentary form of iteration.

## Return to Sender

Do a second pass looking for any tickets that no longer make sense. Has iterative discovery changed the original landscape? The team may need an explanation from the product owner—or even need their permission to close the issue. Any ticket you can punt back up the chain lightens the burden further.

## Prepare for Launch

Do a third detailed pass where the product owner or stakeholders—not the development team—prioritize each remaining ticket. The dev team does the estimates. Someone else prioritizes.

Otherwise, people naturally fall into the trap of thinking, "Well, this is only going to take a day. Let's bump up the priority." That means that the true priorities keep getting pushed down.

## HOW BACKLOG COMBING HELPS YOU ESCAPE THE AGILE CIRCUS

Something wonderful happens when the entire team sits around the virtual table and combs through the backlog: They remind themselves of the value they're providing to the customer. They uncover or rediscover trends that show either where they're getting off track or directions they're taking that are helpful. Unlike estimation sessions where we scrutinize one ticket in isolation, backlog combing gives a 10,000-foot view of the entire suite of tickets. Patterns emerge. False starts reveal themselves. Cruft floats up to the top for us to discard. Empty holes in the overall picture surface.

Agile is primarily concerned with two things: delivering maximum value and eliminating wasteful processes. Every ticket that we close or put in the icebox during the backlog-combing process leads to the best kind of code there is: code that was never written in the first place. No design, estimation, creation, pull-request reviews, or maintenance are needed. And any trends that we uncover help the team focus on the best value.

## ITERATING THE BACKLOG COMBING ACEP

Stop me if you've heard this one: we realized we weren't doing backlog combing sessions often enough. It's like going to the dentist for regular checkups—except its other people's teeth. And you kinda forget about them rotting back there in the drawer.

Have I have grossed you out? Good. Mission accomplished. At least one of you is going to think about that and decide to refine your backlog.

Now that we're doing the dentist analogies: if you were taking a bite out of ten or twenty candy bars at a time, just cramming them in your piehole at once, your dentist would probably tell you to cut that out.

If you replace "candy bars" with the word "tickets" and "piehole" with the word "developers," then you have a work-in-progress metaphor. You want everyone to finish the candy bar they started first and then get another one. That's called a work-in-progress limit, or WIP.

WIP is a feature development practice, but it also helps with your backlog combing. If your devs are used to just grabbing whatever they want whenever, and then leaving half-finished candy bars laying around, there isn't much incentive for them to worry about the supply. But when they have to pick and choose, suddenly the backlog column gets more important. WIP is a natural fit for keeping the backlog of tickets palatable to everyone.

So we have iterated by unofficially introducing WIP limits. Not a hard threshold like better team leads would recommend you do. For example, Jim Benson and Tonianne DeMaria Barry have a lot of work on the subject. For the sake of providing a reference, try their most popular book, *Personal Kanban: Mapping Work | Navigating Life*.[113]

---

113   Jim Benson and Tonianne DeMaria Barry, *Personal Kanban: Mapping Work | Navigating Life*, (self-pub, 2011).

According to the Kanban Maturity Model, my refusal to make current policies explicit puts me on the cusp of the step 2 > 3 transition. But there are, like, five steps. So my team has some iterating left ahead of us.

In the post "Why Limiting Your Work-in-Progress Matters" by *Planview Blog*, that very thing is explicitly called out:

> When it comes to setting WIP limits, we made a half-hearted attempt to limit ourselves to three cards each, but agreed we'd come back to that later as it's really for more advanced Kanban teams. Right?
>
> The importance—and urgency—of setting WIP limits all changed for me after a recent conversation with Jim and Tonianne. Jim pointed out, "If you're not limiting your WIP, then there is no flow. Your Kanban board is no more than a to-do list." That was the "aha" moment I've been needing. If we don't limit our work, how can we see where the bottlenecks are? And if we don't identify the bottlenecks in our process, how can we fix them?
>
> If we're really committed to improving our workflow, then it's time to step up. Setting WIP limits shouldn't be an after-thought that sounds good in theory; on the contrary, it's a necessity to avoid the penalties of wasted time, effort and resources.[114]

---

114  "Why Limiting Your Work-in-Progress Matters," *Planview Blog*, March 3, 2014, https://blog.planview.com/why-limiting-your-work-in-progress-matters/.

CHAPTER 57

# ACEP 8
## ESTIMATION:
## WHERE BUSINESS VALUE AND
## PROGRAMMERS COLLIDE

I often hear this question asked: "Should my agile team estimate in terms of time (ideal developer days) or effort (story points)?"

An even better question is this: "Should you even do estimates at all?"

This is possibly the most important consideration in all agile development. The decision to estimate or not—and if so, what types of estimates to do—defines the rest of the process.

Estimates are undeniably inefficient. They take time away from development. They often aren't worth the air they are spoken into. Yet as a dev team, if you can estimate accurately, you buy yourselves a ridiculous amount of freedom to pursue your agenda. So let's take a deep dive into this most critical of decisions.

## FORGET ABOUT ESTIMATING ALTOGETHER

In pure, enlightened, next-level agile development, there are no estimates.

The time the team would spend to produce estimates (of dubious accuracy) is just wasted effort all around.

An excellent summary of this concept can be found at Ron Jeffries's blog—yes, the very same Ron Jeffries who introduced to the world the concept of story points. Management wanted his team to do estimates, and the team kept adding a velocity multiplier to the estimates. Management was getting confused why one day was taking three days. Or said another way, why a three-day estimate indicated one day of actual work. So Ron's team stopped using days and just called them points.

And the estimation world changed dramatically. Teams across the world started decoupling estimates from time measures. They now estimated in terms of effort. Scaffolding was erected and entire schools of thought formed around this decoupling.

Then Ron apologized to the world for creating story points—but not for the reason you might think. Not because story points are too abstract and confusing. Ron, and many other highly respected agile thought leaders, decided that estimation itself is not agile.[115] Stop estimating altogether and watch your productivity soar.

That is exactly the same kind of madness I preach elsewhere in this very book. Don't use schedules. Don't have gatekeeping meetings for each phase. But get rid of estimation? That's silly talk.

Is it?

It's a gut check for sure. It would be very hypocritical of me to say, "Don't make a road map," but then throw shade at the suggestion to abandon estimates. So in a pure sense, in a fully autonomous agile process, I endorse the idea that you should consider not doing estimates altogether.

---

115  Ron Jeffries, "Story Points Revisited," *Ron Jeffries* (blog), May 23, 2019, https://ronjeffries.com/articles/019-01ff/story-points/Index.html.

## OR DECIDE TO USE ESTIMATES ANYWAY

That said, my team definitely uses estimates. Not only do we use them, but we also use the wholly outdated concept of linking an estimate to actual hours instead of relative complexity. Not only do we use that outdated concept, but we also proudly spend an inefficient amount of time doing estimates.

Why? Agile teams rarely have the opportunity to develop in a methodologically pure agile environment—that rarefied state of detachment from established practices with complete freedom to be curious, try, fail, and iterate with as few distractions as possible. If you are in such an environment, you probably don't need this book, and I am envious of you.

The majority of agile teams need to make some concessions to established management culture. It's just too big an ask for everyone to let go of their training and instincts. People need reassurance, insight, and evidence to make business decisions. That evidence has traditionally taken the form of "Are we on schedule? Are we over budget?"

Something has to give somewhere. The agile team must decide which hill they want to die on and which hill they want to relinquish.

I choose to die on the hill of estimation. Out of the gamut of management techniques out there, from Gantt charts to resource utilization, the technique that gives my team the most benefit is estimating effort. It's a chance to play ball and give managers and customers some form of clarity. By providing hard numbers, we assuage the mounting feeling of helplessness that agile often inflicts on the rest of the enterprise.

Knowing that they need to meet some expectations around providing time/effort information to others, my team makes detailed estimates of how long each ticket will take. It's both an olive branch and armor. And we get something out of it too—but not what you might think. More on that later.

If I've convinced you to use the old-timey estimation approach, here are the ACEPs.

## MY CONTROVERSIAL RECOMMENDED ESTIMATION PROCESS

At the end of backlog refinement, you will have a cruft-free, prioritized list of top features. Ideally, you should make estimates of effort independently of estimates of value so as not to influence the dev team's estimates. But in a shared project management tool, that's not really realistic. So we pretend not to know the priority when we do our estimates. OK, time to estimate!

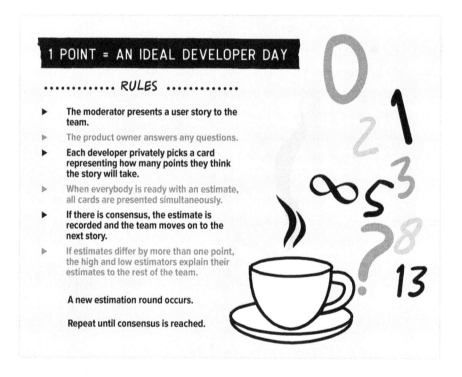

**1 POINT = AN IDEAL DEVELOPER DAY**

············ RULES ············

▶ The moderator presents a user story to the team.

▶ The product owner answers any questions.

▶ Each developer privately picks a card representing how many points they think the story will take.

▶ When everybody is ready with an estimate, all cards are presented simultaneously.

▶ If there is consensus, the estimate is recorded and the team moves on to the next story.

▶ If estimates differ by more than one point, the high and low estimators explain their estimates to the rest of the team.

A new estimation round occurs.

Repeat until consensus is reached.

### Points

We say that one point is equal to one ideal developer day. That is, if the team is left uninterrupted, what could one developer accomplish in one day?

It's possible that the team will be interrupted. Because of that interruption, our one-day estimate might take two days. That's not our problem.

That's your problem, stakeholders. We will gladly decrement one day from our sprint time for the interruption and keep on working afterward.

We don't pad our estimates to account for interruptions. But we do list them in the sprint retrospective. This way stakeholders see the consequences of their interference with the sprint, and the team and individual developers don't take a hit to their productivity record.

Regarding estimates, the only choices of numbers to pick are listed below. Most agilists would consider this constrained list of time estimates as completely ridiculous, but it works for us and we achieve very accurate estimates.

**0**: This is already done, doesn't need to be done, or will take a trivial amount of effort to do.

½: This will take about four hours.

**1:** This will take one day.

**2**: This will take two days.

**3**: This will take about three days, which is getting up there in terms of complexity and attention span. Will I magically get it done on day four and then pull a 1-point ticket?

**5**: Or will human nature kick in, and it actually takes a whole week? Or will it take me three days, if I pair program some (bumping it up to a five)?

**8**: This ticket is far too complex for one person to handle in a week. So maybe we put a couple people on it or break it down.

**13**: I think I've only used the 13 card once in my whole life.

**20**: I don't think I've ever used the 20 card. If I did, it would certainly be followed by "obviously this ticket is too large, and we need to break it down."

∞: The infinity card is the drama llama of estimation poker cards. This will take *forever*. Or it's an ongoing process. Anyway, the developer is rejecting the ticket's validity.

**?**: "I have heard everyone talk about this ticket for an hour, and really, team, I have no idea. Just, no idea. Pass me this round. I defer to you." (We request that the question mark card be a last resort and used infrequently.)

**Coffee cup**: Brain full. Tummy empty. Bladder full. Me no think.

## Rules

We have arrived at this set of rules:

- The moderator presents an issue to the team.
- The product owner answers any questions.
- Each developer privately picks a card representing how many points they think the issue will take.
- When everybody is ready with an estimate, they simultaneously present their cards.
- If there is consensus, they record the estimate, and the team moves on to the next issue.
- If estimates differ by more than one point, the high and low estimators explain their estimates to the rest of the team.
- A new estimation round occurs.
- Repeat until the team reaches consensus.

Those rules are there to protect the process and give the ultimate estimate the best chance of being right.

## Guidelines

There's also a bunch of informal guidelines that are not written down anywhere—until now, in this book.

There's a guideline we use to avoid social influence. This guideline is so strict that it might as well be a rule: *Do not* bias the discussion with an estimate. Saying stuff like "This is way more complex than that 3-point ticket we did last sprint," or "This should take no time at all," will get you kicked off our newly formed island. Just don't do it. Don't bias a whole room of estimates with your own hubris.

Another guideline is that *we strongly prefer lower estimates*. If my brain is getting into 5-, 8-, or 13-point territory, I'm more likely to say, "Uh, peeps, maybe we should break this ticket down." Or "This might be an epic." Usually, you can break down the ticket, although not always, and that's OK too.

## Overhead

Each estimate includes the following overhead:

- Updating the change log
- Writing tests
- Linting the code
- Merge conflict resolution
- Pull request review time

Sometimes a ticket will be fairly simple to implement, but it means updating a bunch of tests. That ticket gets a higher estimate. In rare cases, we know there will be a gnarly merge conflict when updating certain code. So we might tack on a day.

## Multiperson Tickets

We try to account for how we'll work on the ticket. If we know that two people will work on it for two days, we have a choice to make, because 4 is not one of the options:

1. Estimate it at 3, and don't take a full two days.
2. Estimate it at a 5, and take our time.
3. Break it into two 2-point tickets.

The point is, we account for implementation strategy in the estimation process, thereby, hopefully, arriving at better estimates.

## Responsibility

An estimate is a mini contract. You are promising the rest of the team, "If I estimate a 5, I can do this ticket in 5 ideal person days. Or I know how to get it done in 5 ideal person days."

We as a team are promising something similar to everyone else when we come up with a collective estimate. Our names are on the line with each poker card we drop onto the table.

Is that pressure? Yes. Is it unreasonable pressure? No. It's accountability.

I will never be mad at a team member if a ticket takes longer than the five promised days. I will be mad at a team member if they pad their estimates or treat estimation as a joke.

Our final estimate is a promise: It will take us X days to produce features A, B, and C. At the end of X days, you can expect them.

It's not X plus or minus a week. Each day we are above or below our estimate erodes other people's confidence in us.

There have been times when I knew in my heart of hearts that I'd been goofing off at some point in the sprint when I should have been working. And I was one story point behind. So I worked on Saturday to get that point done, not because management told me I had to work that weekend but because I committed to a certain amount of work. And it's up to me to see that it gets done.

There have been times when I was one story point behind, and I knew that management had pulled me away from the sprint for some crisis or another. No problem. I marked down one day of impedance on the sprint and enjoyed my lovely Saturday.

By the same token, there have been times when my team of five developers kicked butt, and then we were collectively five points ahead. In these cases, there are two choices: each developer can pull a 1-point ticket, and we can be five points ahead of what we promised. Or we can all go to the conference room to play video games for a day.

My only questions are "Which conference room?" and "What video game are we going to play?"

Is that irresponsible? Not at all. If we pull the five tickets and are ahead, somebody somewhere will think, "Ooh, we can squeeze more work out of these folks." So they pressure us to take on more tickets, pointing to the "5-points-ahead sprint" like some sort of evidence. Then follows months of overwork and burnout.

No way in hell am I going to punish my team long term for being efficient.

Now if the one-day-early finish becomes a habit, I'm going to advocate very heavy-handedly for people to tighten up their estimates so we get back to accuracy.

## HOW ESTIMATION HELPS YOU ESCAPE THE AGILE CIRCUS

At the beginning of this section, I mentioned that my teams get something out of estimation but that it's not what you think. It's time to delve into that. The secret benefit of estimates is that they're really stealth design sessions.

Doing estimates of each ticket improves the code my team writes. When we're all sitting around a poker table, cards in hand, trying to come up with a number that won't make us look like a fool to the rest of the team, something happens that doesn't happen at any other stage of the entire software development process: for a brief moment in time, *each developer has 100% of the responsibility for that ticket.*

There is nowhere to hide. There is no team member to share the blame or glory. Stem to stern, each person must take the entirety of that ticket into their own brain, be their own project manager/customer/dev team, produce a result, and tell everyone else how long it hypothetically took.

Doing estimates mitigates diffusion of responsibility. That's a social psychology term for attributing the onus of responsibility to someone else the more people are added to a situation. It leads to the bystander effect, where no one calls an ambulance because they assume someone else already did. In estimation poker, there are no bystanders. There's you, the ticket, and your estimate.

If we leave aside the obvious trade-off that estimating tickets takes up precious time, estimation has been nothing but helpful from a code-quality perspective. Here are the types of things that often happen.

## Consensus

The team can bop right along, doing the estimate, then everyone puts down a three. Perfect. Everyone agrees. We could get into various thought experiments about how a roomful of developers coming up with the same number doesn't necessarily mean it's right. However, in my experience, consensus is a validation of the design. It's clear. The team understands it the same way. And I find that consensus estimates, practically speaking, are quite accurate.

## Dissention

The team can bop right along, doing the estimate, then half the room says, "That's a ½-point." And the other half of the room says, "That's a 3-point." Oh, no! After some discussion, we discover the discrepancy. Often, we'll break down the legitimate 3-point stories into a couple smaller tickets. Or maybe the people who pulled ½-point estimates reveal why the effort is unnecessary. In either case, by taking a few minutes to estimate a story, we effect a relatively large swing in days.

## *Redirection*

People start talking about the ticket and trying to make an estimate, and at some point it all devolves. Confusion sets in. People tell their views, and others chime in with opposite theories. Soon enough it becomes clear: the ticket is unclear. What we thought was genius-level specification turns out to have been a flimflam job, a poser ticket among the real tickets.

With that shocking discovery, we either need to punt that ticket back to the drawing board, nix it altogether, or refine it on the spot. Sometimes, the act of estimating an inestimable ticket sets off a cascade of design questions that causes the team to pull the emergency brake and go right back into requirements gathering or design.

All of those benefits arise because someone asked me to put my name to an estimate. If we'd skipped the estimation step, the sprint would have launched, and a bunch of developers who thought they each had a solid idea of the specification would have gone off and written incompatible software, only discovering the misunderstanding after expending lots of effort.

Those three outcomes of consensus, dissention, and redirection are all excellent outcomes. They *avoid late discovery*, which is an agile goal that aligns with the blur box. The three outcomes also share a secret in common: each is a trojan horse that sneaks in another round of design.

Design is critical to the software development process. But a lot of developers don't like it. Design is mentally taxing. You don't go home after a day of design and say, "By golly, I feel invigorated this evening! What say we go for a stroll?" You're more likely to stumble to the couch, cover yourself in warm laundry, and numbly stare at the crack in the ceiling.

Estimation is really a mini design session. Each brain at the table is doing a full analysis of the ticket parameters, thinking through the process and solution. We consider why and how, taking full responsibility for understanding the ticket and making a call.

That flurry of crowdsourced design at the last minute before estimating the upcoming sprint does an amazing job of revealing logical flaws. Or it suggests the irrelevance of certain tickets, which only improves the upcoming sprint. This is an excellent way to avoid late discovery—which leads to another benefit of estimation: sacrificing short-term inefficiency for overall process efficiency.

In this book, I have urged you to cut your process down to the bone. Eliminate cruft. Especially, eliminate processes that seem like they are helping but are actually hampering the project. Most of the stuff I've asked you to avoid boils down to unnecessary communication tools—particularly those that are predictive in nature.

There's a certain point at which enough is enough. The human brain can only take so much uncertainty. Somewhere, somehow, there must be an island to stand on that is based on solid evidence.

In the Agile Circus Escape Practices, estimates are the olive branch we extend to anyone who is frustrated by our culture of trimming out traditional forms of business communication—the island. We heap the sand of our knowns into a little pile and say, "OK, here is some solid ground for us all to rally on."

It's reassuring for everybody. The dev team feels more unified heading into the sprint. The project managers are relieved to have numbers to present to upper management. Estimates allow us to make commitments: "We're pretty confident we can have X, Y, and Z features done in two weeks."

If we do, we gain credibility. If we do over and over again, we gain trust. When people trust a team, trust a process, they ease off on the gatekeeping questions and practices that are detrimental.

So for me, tight estimation of the upcoming two weeks is my safest position to relent to standard business practices. It's a minor downshift in productivity with fringe benefits for my team, which also appeases upstream and downstream customers. That buys my team overall greater efficiency. We're spending a little time to provide the bare minimum in contractual obligations, which buys enough trust to prevent the detailed progress tracking that will suffocate us.

It's also why I double down on inefficiency and embrace time estimation rather than effort estimation. If I have to do estimates, let's at least talk in terms that everyone understands, and reap some side benefits from that too (easier scheduling and burndown charts with real-world applicability).

## ITERATING THE ESTIMATION ACEP

I'll go out on a limb and say that the process I described in the previous section is where I'm going to lose credibility with a lot of people. I already hinted above at many possible ways we could iterate on our estimation process. But here's the weird thing: it works. We get very, very accurate estimates. I'm talking full team, two week sprints, planned in advance finishing plus or minus four hours on target.

So much of that success comes from micro-superstitions we've baked in over the years. For example, there's no ceiling to how long something can take. But there is a floor, and that's zero. In practice, no 0-point ticket takes zero seconds. Updating a line of code, adding the change to the change log, running tests, and pushing the new branch takes some measure of finite time. But usually, a ½-point ticket does not use up a full four hours. It's more like two to three hours.

So we'll often rotate between a 0-point and ½-point estimate when dealing with a bunch of similar issues in a sprint-planning session. If we have 10 tickets that are variations on "Update the XYZ chart to use the new color key and help widget," the estimates might look like this: 0, 0, ½, 0, 0, ½, 0, 0, ½, ½. Thus averaging out to roughly two hours per ticket.

It's a subversion of the rules, but it gets us to more accurate estimates.

# CHAPTER 58

# ACEP 9

## ORGANIZE YOUR SPRINTS USING THE BLUNTEST APPROACH POSSIBLE

This part should be anticlimactic. If the other practices have gone well, organizing the sprint is a simple matter.

Now that you have a curated backlog that has been sorted by the business owner, and all backlog tickets have been independently estimated by the development team, merge them into a curated backlog. Plan sprint start and end dates. Plan availability, make your cutoff, and create an empty burndown chart. There. Now your sprint is planned.

We've already taken a look at estimates and backlog combing. With an estimated, sorted backlog in place, the next step is to plan sprint dates.

There are three strategies you can employ when it comes to sprinting:

1. Follow the structured scrum approach and always be in sprint time. Every two weeks (most common but you could also do monthly) a new sprint begins. All effort counts as sprint work, no matter what it is.

2. Follow the unstructured kanban approach and never be in sprint time. Tickets constantly flow through the board.
3. Keep an overall kanban board with some extra sprint columns in the mix, which are themselves a mini scrum board. You sprint when sprinting would be most effective, then draw the top-priority tickets when not in sprint time.

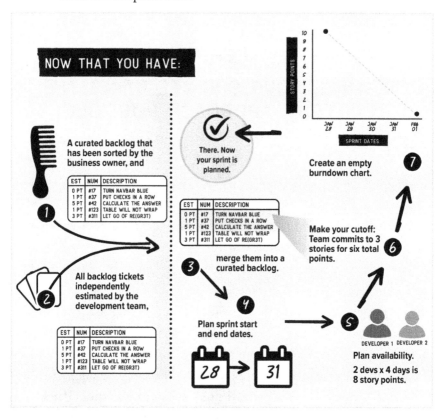

The benefit of strategy #1 is that your team will fall into a natural rhythm of prioritization, prediction, effort, and results. There is a cadence. You can plan around sprint releases with some accuracy.

The problem with strategy #1 is that you cannot estimate design. You cannot write a ticket that says "Design feature X." That's a recipe for blown estimates. Sprinting is not equally effective for every kind of developer effort. And some agile adopters also see pure sprints as restrictive.

The benefit of strategy #2 is absolute efficiency. The top-priority ticket is always there, ready to be plucked. There's no estimation or scheduling to interrupt the flow. There are the tickets, their progression, and the code. That's all. Do you have bandwidth? Pull a ticket. Don't have bandwidth? Don't pull a ticket.

The problem with strategy #2 is the relative lack of business communication that the rest of the enterprise relies on. With no estimates, no schedule, and no predictions of any kind, the process becomes the most obscure of blurred boxes.

The benefit of strategy #3 is that there's always a 10,000-foot view and a 100-foot view available. You can always see where the team is going and where it's been. You can get highly accurate estimates of velocity and past performance. When the team plans a sprint, you have the closest thing an iterative process can provide to hard numbers to pass on to others. In that sense, you are generating the data that *How to Measure Anything* recommends for making business decisions.[116]

Strategy #3 lacks the rigorous schedule of scrum and the effortless fluidity of kanban. However, in my opinion it does the best job of addressing the unknowns presented by the blur box. That is what my team uses.

## HOW SPRINT ORGANIZATION HELPS YOU ESCAPE THE AGILE CIRCUS

This might be a good point to pause and talk about sprints in a greater context. Should you even have sprints at all?

The agile circus escape practices loosely fall under the banner of scrumban, which is a made-up methodology that incorporates aspects of scrum

---

116  Douglas W. Hubbard, *How to Measure Anything: Finding the Value of Intangibles in Business*, 3rd ed. (Hoboken, New Jersey: John Wiley & Sons, Inc, 2014).

and kanban. The two approaches differ dramatically. Scrum is a highly structured approach with sharply defined roles and responsibilities (product owner, a scrum master, etc.) Sprints are tightly scheduled bursts of focused development effort on an agreed-upon list of features. In contrast, kanban is fluid. The primary structure is a simple arrangement of columns arranged on a board ("not started," "started," and "done," for example). Roles are flexible, and tickets continuously pass through the phases.

ACEPs are not officially linked to scrumban. It was an independent evolution. As my career has plinked and plunked its way down the Plinko board of life, I've run into obstacles that prevented the use of either approach.

I began with the best of intentions to use scrum. Its rigor helped tame my team's predilections to analyze things too much and not get started on the big stuff. But my team sizes have never been large enough to pull off scrum. Oddly enough, the product owner has consistently been the toughest role to fill or simulate. Without dedicated roles in place, my teams needed some way to visualize and communicate what was going on.

So for the first team I ever led, I thought back to the Subaru factory. I was early in my career, a third-shift data entry grunt for the maintenance department. After using a Windows 3.0 PC that was at least seven years out of date to produce some numbers, I'd ride a tricycle across the factory floor at 3 a.m., daily productivity totals in hand, with robotic spark showers raining down in slow motion all over the place. I'd hand the numbers to a Japanese manager. He would pencil them in on a large poster hanging on the wall and use a ruler to draw a series of tiny lines. Sometimes we'd use pencils and napkins to argue heatedly in "math," the only language we both understood, stabbing at little formulas we'd scribbled on the napkins until one of us backed down. At the end of the month, we'd roll the hand-drawn line chart up and store it in a large metal cage with other rolls of paper stacked to the ceiling.

The Japanese and Americans would all huddle around large poster boards with handwritten notes moving across it. I thought it was so strange at the time. It made no sense to track data with note cards when computers could store it all. I tried to change the Japanese managers' minds. But they were adamant that the notecards on the poster board were the way to go.

And when it came down to it, I realized the simple effectiveness of the approach. So my software team installed a physical board just like it and moved sticky notes across the columns to see how things were progressing in our sprints.

It worked really well. Sprints and estimation poker gave our process the structure my team needed to focus our efforts. Kanban gave us a flexible way to visualize and communicate.

## ITERATING THE PROJECT PLANNING ACEP

In fact, the kanban board worked too well.

The intensity of sprinting was too much for me. I'm drained after the go-go-go energy of a sprint. I appreciate downtime, when design and analysis can blossom or when we can pull tickets that are not necessarily on theme. With the security of the kanban board to guide us, I made a really bad call and declared a break from sprinting for a few weeks.

Tickets started piling up. We got overwhelmed. Without the structure of sprinting and the looming backlog of tickets, we got discouraged. The team eventually imploded.

One take-home message from that fiasco could have been to use either scrum or kanban. Do not walk in the middle of the road—or get squished, just like a grape.

But when it came time to lead my next team, I could not let go of the kanban board. It really did a great job of addressing some of the challenges presented by the blur box—especially since we did not have enough people to fill the ideal distribution of roles. The kanban board helped with prioritization, which is a critical aspect of iteration. And it truly shined at communication. The board was our silent, automated team member who told anyone interested exactly where we were in the process.

But the kanban board alone was not sufficient for my team to thrive. We needed intermediate goalposts, some tangible measure of progress. Sprints provide that. A good sprint is a mini victory. We said we'd do these 10 tickets, and by gum, we did these 10 tickets. Sprints provide a natural rhythm of retrospectives, which come the day after the sprint ends, when we discuss and make improvements.

So we made the dubious choice to walk in the middle of the road, combining the structure of scrum and the fluidity of kanban.

It shouldn't work. But it does—because it really isn't walking in the middle of the road at all. Both scrum and kanban take the blur box into account. They both have a laser focus on prioritization, communication, early discovery, and refining processes. They use opposite approaches to the problem, but their hearts are both in the right place: Embrace the unknown. Embrace change. Cease unproductive avenues as soon as possible.

Scrum is arguably a predictive methodology in that it makes estimates. And believe me, kanban advocates will throw shade at scrum for just that reason. To us, the time window of two weeks is a reasonably brief window for making predictions. And estimating that a ticket will take two days is a far cry from saying, "Feature X will be done on April 1," if it happens to be January. I'm comfortable making a promise that a bit of functionality will take a certain amount of calendar days if we are uninterrupted. I am not comfortable predicting the distant future.

## Evidence-Based Scheduling

It's only fair to give airtime to other options that are not the densest hammer in the toolbox. A related, but much more sophisticated, approach to scheduling is Joel Spolsky's evidence-based scheduling. You can read about evidence-based scheduling on the blog *Joel on Software*, written by the guy who cofounded Stack Overflow, the most important knowledge bank in software development history. He's also the guy who launched Visual Basic for Applications. So if you use Excel, thank Joel.

In evidence-based scheduling, tasks are broken down into discrete chunks less than 16 hours. Those are tracked to see how much time has elapsed. You then use that to simulate the future and arrive at a confidence-distribution curve, showing the probability that you will ship on any given date.[117]

Joel's reasoning for this approach is that the dev team is overconfident in how well they have specified the design, which leads to inefficiencies (or even outright mayhem) when it comes time to develop the software. He describes step one of his processes like so:

> When I see a schedule measured in days, or even weeks, I know it's not going to work. You have to break your schedule into very small tasks that can be measured in hours. Nothing longer than 16 hours.
>
> This forces you to actually figure out what you are going to do. Write subroutine foo. Create this dialog box. Parse the Fizzbott file. Individual development tasks are easy to estimate, because you've written subroutines, created dialogs, and parsed files before.
>
> If you are sloppy, and pick big three-week tasks (e.g., "Implement Ajax photo editor"), then you haven't thought about what you are going to do. In detail. Step-by-step. And when you haven't thought about what you're going to do, you can't know how long it will take.
>
> Setting a 16-hour maximum forces you to design the damn feature. If you have a hand-wavy three-week feature called "Ajax photo editor" without a detailed design, I'm sorry to be the one to break it to you, but you are officially doomed. You never thought about the steps it's going to take, and you're sure to be forgetting a lot of them.[118]

117  Joel Spolsky, "Evidence Based Scheduling," *Joel on Software* (Blog), October 26, 2007, https://www.joelonsoftware.com/2007/10/26/evidence-based-scheduling/.
118  Spolsky, "Evidence Based Scheduling."

I 100% agree with Joel on this point. It's why my teams estimate tickets in terms of half-day to three-day chunks (the upper limit my team strives for). This ACEP approach is less granular and more error-prone than evidence-based scheduling. But it's dramatically easier. Evidence-based scheduling requires precise tracking of how long things *took* so you can predict how long they *will take*. To me, the overhead of doing detailed recordkeeping during the sprint process is not worth the gains of measuring tickets in maximum 16-hour chunks vs. maximum three-day chunks. But if you disagree and want to gnaw yourself out of the bear trap a different way, you owe it to yourself to look into evidence-based scheduling.

## How to Measure Anything

Another approach to improving predictions comes from *How to Measure Anything* by Douglas Hubbard. Here's an oversimplified summary of the approach:

1. Break the project into several pieces.
2. Have your domain expert suggest a 90% confidence interval for the range of possible completion times for each piece.
3. Assume a normal or log-normal distribution for each piece.
4. Then put the pieces back together into a composite model.[119]

The resulting distribution of possible completion times is plausible. If you need to make strategic decisions based on your dev team's time estimates, give this a try.

Generally speaking, you can take steps to get better at making estimates. If the estimates you propose at the sprint-planning meeting are consistently wrong, you can improve.

---

119  Hubbard, *How to Measure Anything*, 121–122.

# CHAPTER 59

# ACEP 10
## ENSURE YOU WILL
## DELIVER FUNCTIONAL SOFTWARE

There are three crucial checks to perform before embarking on the development process:

## CHECK DEPENDENCIES

If a sprint ticket depends on something not in the sprint, delay it.

Imagine this. Your team is planning a sprint. The time has finally come to integrate one of your processes with an external customer. Let's call them the "Software Quality Unified Assessment Team," or SQUAT for short. Your team has been talking with Jack at SQUAT for a month or two discussing an API integration, and you're ready to code it. You set up a whole sprint's worth of tickets. The top-priority tickets are something like these:

> #2001: Get an API key from Jack SQUAT and put it into the config file.

#2002: Work with SQUAT tech support to test the key integration and API access.

Then the sprint kicks off Monday morning. You call Jack, but no one answers the phone. You email SQUAT and ping their chatbot, which sends you into a loop of "I'd like to help you with that. Have you read our article, 'The Basics of Computer Communication'?"

Tuesday, Wednesday, Thursday, and Friday roll around, and your team ain't got SQUAT.

The entire sprint depends on these two tickets. You have wasted an entire team's efforts and energy waiting for someone outside of your control to respond. Never plan a sprint around any sort of external dependency, no matter how trivial it may seem.

*Clean Architecture* by Robert C. Martin suggests a workaround where you write an interface or facade class around external dependencies. All of your internal code works with the facade, not the external dependency.[120]

The take-home message here is to solidify or create a mock-up of any external inputs in advance of the sprint.

## CHECK COMPLETENESS

If the selected tickets as a whole are going to lead to unstable software, extend the sprint scope to account for the shortfall. For example, let's say your normal sprint window is two weeks, and the top priority is to create an API to interact with SQUAT. But given the estimates, after two weeks you'll have a partial API that will not actually connect and return any useful data.

It's probably best at this point to extend the sprint to three or four weeks, whatever is necessary to achieve a stable result at the end of the sprint. Also, you could strip the planned sprint down to an absolute minimum

---

120   Robert C. Martin, *Clean Architecture: A Craftsman's Guide to Software Structure and Design*, 1st ed. (Pearson, 2017).

or spike in order to return something, anything, that proves a viable API integration.

## CHECK VISIBILITY

If the user can't see the results, they'll think you sat on your hands for two weeks. This erodes the credibility a sprint is designed to build. Remember, according to kanban, a sprint is cruft. So you need the payoff of continued trust at the end of a sprint.

When the software development team holds a sprint, they're making two promises.

1. To Deliver a Tangible Improvement

   The sprint must deliver something the user can respond to—working software, understandable mock-ups, or something the user can critique. That's the foundation of the iterative development process that the blur box represents. There must be something to demo, share, or discuss that the customer can give actionable feedback on.

   The only exception to this is in periods where the dev team needs to make frameworks to support future development, such as at the beginning of a project. This time of zero visibility should be as brief as possible. The longer time goes on without visibility, the more nervous others get. The threat of cancellation grows. In those "dark sprints," it becomes crucial to overcommunicate what is happening behind the scenes.

2. To Not Make Anything Worse

   The sprint will conclude with working software (assuming there is software existing in the first place.) If there is some sort of production issue, or the team is addressing a redesign that better matches the user's needs, the sprint delivery will not set the user back.

## HOW DELIVERING FUNCTIONAL SOFTWARE HELPS YOU ESCAPE THE AGILE CIRCUS

Unlike the rest of the ACEPs, the section above basically *is* escaping the bear trap described in the blur box. Everything I listed in this ACEP so far is inherently the thought process for confronting the blur box.

## ITERATING THE DELIVERING FUNCTIONAL SOFTWARE ACEP

In a way, my team's answer to this is way too broad to be of any use to you. We make changes all the time, and they are idiosyncratic to our needs. However, there are a couple generalizations I can make.

### *Cheating on Assigning Tickets to Developers in Advance*

One is that we've started looking out for the "battleship trap." There is a difference between having five 1-point tickets in a sprint vs. one 5-point ticket. It's like playing Battleship, and you're psychic, so you know where each enemy ship is already. However, it takes you a day to fire each shot no matter what.

In the 1-point tickets scenario, no problem. Cram those destroyers wherever you like in the schedule, take one shot per developer per day, boom! Sprint is done.

In the 5-point ticket scenario, that might pose a problem for how the completion of the other tickets go. You can have both sprints estimated at the correct number of points for the available time, but the large tickets don't line up with people's availability. Now you have empty squares where only one person is firing, and you cannot sink the battleship in time to meet the sprint end date.* You've got it lined up in your sights, you're firing away, but you simply run out of days—even though on paper you had enough time according to the number of tickets compared with total availability.

(*For those of you who are thinking "No, the carrier has five pegs, not the battleship," I congratulate you on your attention to detail.)

Anyway, certain that someone else has articulated this problem clearly elsewhere, I've looked into spillover, and the concept of swarming, which is related to limiting work-in-progress. Spillover is a scrum term, and WIP limits comes from the lean philosophy of pull-based production systems, like Subaru's just-in-time delivery. Scrum will tell you that you should not assign a ticket to a specific person during sprint planning. Lean will tell you that when a big boi is blocking your WIP flow, everyone swarms it and knocks out that carrier as a team.

So our iteration on delivering functional software is to break one of the sprint planning rules if our sprint contains any tickets over two days. In that case, we do some quick Tetris block visualizations to see if the pattern of tickets and availability is going to fit, and if not, who we need to assign each ticket to. Or decide to swarm it if that is possible. Or break up a ticket if possible.

## *Switch Modes as Needed*

The other change we made to iterate the "deliver functional software" mandate at the completion of a sprint—and this is a very big one—is that we've explicitly decided whether or not to be in kanban mode or sprint mode based on prevailing winds.

There are probably some project managers cringing right now.

If we're in a situation where one of the following apply, we will decide to not be in sprint mode and instead be in flow mode:

- the team feels like there will be ongoing or major interruptions.
- the team suspects upcoming context-switching shenanigans, like we're Charlie Brown, and Lucy is going to whisk that football away at the last second.

- there are lots of unrelated high-value tickets on the top of the back-log, and a sprint would just not make cohesive sense.
- there's a lot of bugfixes, design sessions, or other non-ticket work going on that is the top priority.
- we are in a "wait and see" mode on anything, such as external dependencies, and it could be "go!" time any second now.

There are probably some lean or kanban people out there thinking "So, you mean any given work day, then? Just do kanban all the time." *Au contraire,* friend. Here are the factors where we decide to go into sprint mode, batten down the hatches, and tell everyone to buzz off while we focus on a sprint:

- we have an honest-to-goodness deadline and we need to do our best sprint estimation contracts to give people some semblance of scheduling.
- there are a lot of conceptually related tickets at the top of the back-log and we want to get into a groove on them.
- we are tired of playing football with Lucy and we just want to focus on kicking the ball through the goalposts. The sprint is like a "do not disturb" sign for us.
- we have that rare confidence that our priorities might not change in the near future, we have more related tickets than will fit into one sprint, and we want to do a twofer of back-to-back sprints.

In those situations, sprint mode gives us more of what we're looking for from the work vs. sanity dynamic.

CHAPTER *60*

# ACEP 11

# CUSTOMER FEEDBACK: THE ALPHA AND OMEGA OF YOUR PROCESS

Leaving aside deployment strategy for the time being, customer feedback is the alpha and the omega of the development process. Software begins and ends with customer feedback. If you don't have it, you don't know what to develop. If you don't seek it, you don't know if you made good software.

It might be good to clarify the types of feedback involved in the software development process. *The Lean Product Playbook* by Dan Olsen breaks down customer feedback on two dimensions, qualitative-quantitative and attitudinal-behavioral. Before a new product gets made, you only have attitudinal data (what customers say they want):

- Interviews (qualitative)
- Surveys (quantitative)[121]

121  Dan Olsen, *The Lean Product Playbook: How to Innovate with Minimum Viable Products and Rapid Customer Feedback*, 1st ed. (Hoboken, NJ: John Wiley & Sons, Inc, 2015).

Then you make prototypes, which allow you to do usability testing (qualitative) and see what customers actually do (behavioral). Once you start to bring in large numbers of potential or actual users, you can do analytics and A/B testing (quantitative, behavioral).

At that stage, you have reached the point where developers can directly measure the impact of their changes on the performance of the business. This stage is most conducive to rapid iterative software development. However, I suspect Olsen's advice applies mainly to web start-ups oriented toward general consumers. For some companies, such as those who make physical devices, quantitative behavioral data takes a lot of work to assemble.

Let's take a closer look at customer feedback.

## FEEDBACK METHODS

Let's rank five methods of gathering feedback, from best to worst:

1.  Dedicated Business Analyst, Product Manager, or
    Company Founder

    A dedicated point of contact—embedded into the development team, and reporting either to the Value Management Office or the development team manager—is the gold standard of customer feedback. Their job is literally to interview customers and synthesize feedback, then efficiently disseminate it to the dev team.

    I'm not getting into the financials of what developer hours are worth. But if you have a bunch of developers spending time interviewing customers, hiring a business analyst or two probably makes financial sense, not just for cost savings but for quality of feedback. A business analyst or product manager can ferret out conflicting comments and trace business processes to arrive at a sane set of requirements. Whereas a dev team might have to go through a few iterations to get there.

2.  The Phone Game

    This is where customers and developers talk directly as needed. In a way, it's great. The developers get an immediate sense of what the customer values—in other words, early discovery. A good relationship between the customer and dev team is a real asset in terms of communication effectiveness and code quality.

    However, developers aren't trained business analysts. We're pretty good. We're cross functional. If we're seasoned developers, we have the experience to ferret out shaky stories, rattle cages, and get to the bottom of all this. But there are times that we ask a question, get an answer, take it at face value, and run with it—to the peril of the project.

And then we scrap the whole sprint because we didn't talk to secret customer B, who has a different story. Or we didn't realize the customer assumes, naturally, that we know about processes A, B, and C.

"Everyone knows about processes A, B, and C."

Well, my team doesn't.

For this reason, *The Pragmatic Programmer* by Andrew Hunt says don't gather requirements—dig for requirements. What customers say they want is not the same as what they really want.[122]

3. Hodgepodge

   This is the most common scenario: a hodgepodge of ad hoc feedback funnels. There is no direct, reliable communication between the dev team and customers. So the dev team grabs whomever they can to double-check requirements: project managers, grad students, a janitor who overheard Sally talking about the software after work one day—any lead we can get. It's a sad, suboptimal reality.

   The blur box will wreak havoc on the hodgepodge method.

4. Simulated Feedback

   This is the last-ditch attempt to get actionable evidence. No one returns our calls. The janitor doesn't know what Sally thinks. The dev team is on its own. So we analyze usage logs, do surveys, or grab random people to sit down in front of us to try the software.

   It's like customer feedback archaeology. The CEO spent two seconds on the SQUAT detail page. Does that mean she found the

122  Thomas and Hunt, *The Pragmatic Programmer*.

answer right away? Or rage clicked off the page? We have to scrape logs and hypothesize. It's like living on gruel.

If your dev team is at the point where they are commandeering randos off the street or digging through a server log to assess who did what and why, you have a problem.

5.  No Customer Feedback

There really isn't much point in developing software for customers if you don't have actual or simulated customer feedback.

## GOTCHAS

Now you have some actionable customer feedback, and you're ready to populate the backlog with issues. Look out for these warning flags.

*A bug report is not an issue.* A bug report indicates that something is wrong. It might directly lead to an issue if the bug is straightforward. But often, bugs require some analysis and design to figure out what is happening. And you can't estimate design. So if you throw a bug straight into the sprint, it's like throwing in a temporal vortex that might expand and squeeze out the rest of the sprint tickets. Perhaps have another column on the kanban board, or a separate document, for bugs, but do not put them into the backlog until they are converted to actionable tickets.

*Underdescribing an issue* because you think the team will handle it soon, and it's self-evident, will probably bite you eventually. Let's look at both assumptions. The dev team may not handle the issue soon. Remember, the dev team does not (well, should not, anyway) control priority. If the product owner comes around at the last minute and rearranges the backlog, suddenly your hot-off-the-press tickets grow cold.

That leads to the self-evident thing. In the current context, a ticket described like this might make sense: "Fix the SQUAT chart." But six months from now, your team might have questions. "Which SQUAT chart? What's wrong with it? How will we know it's fixed?" In short, laziness and short-cuts are not a good idea—even if you think you're saving precious hours in the short term.

*Dependencies are not issues.* If the ticket you are writing depends on the effort of someone outside the team, strike it from your backlog. Put it on a to-do list somewhere else. Email the project manager or business analyst.

Whatever you do, do not make a ticket like "Contact the SQUAT team and get an API key," then estimate that as a ½-point ticket. Your elapsed time might be much, much, much longer than four hours as you wait. You might have your whole dev team calling every hour for a week with no results. It could happen.

Similarly, *analysis, design, and training are not issues.* You cannot estimate how long it will take to design something. So a ticket like "Design the SQUAT API" is just asking for trouble. My team handles such issues outside of structured sprints.

## HOW CUSTOMER FEEDBACK HELPS YOU ESCAPE THE AGILE CIRCUS

Congrats! You have gathered feedback and filtered out the red flags. What's next? Your goal now is to delegate, communicate, and otherwise parse the feedback.

### *Direct Any Business Processes You Can to Other Business Staff*

The blur box compels you to hire a cross-functional team. But if you have a dev team that is competently cross functional, there's a strong temptation to use them for a lot of tasks better suited to others. For example, I've done the following as an IT person on the clock:

- Trained customers
- Designed marketing pamphlets to distribute at conferences

- Trained interns
- Redesigned business processes
- Analyzed financial data
- Contributed to biomedical and genetics scientific papers
- Designed logos
- Developed customer chatbot decision trees
- Cleaned out tissue-sample freezers
- Created an inventory system for maintenance part labels that were stored in a coffee can
- Edited someone's fiction novel

Those were all really interesting experiences. Variety is one of the perks of being in a creative job like software development. And you know, life is quirky and fun. But as a general rule, keep in mind who is the best person for a job. For example, say you get feedback that is suggesting a business-process improvement. The dev team is enthusiastic about seeing it through. But are they the right people for that, even if they're interested? Make a call. Should they take the initiative, or should it be handed off?

## Overcommunicate

Getting feedback is essential to creating fully realized software. The more you can test your assumptions and poke around for exceptions, the more effective the development cycle will be.

## Network with Others

In my case, I'm talking about other departments or universities. Perhaps for you, it's floating ideas by a mentor, a friendly rival, a different business team, or the internet to get an outside perspective. Maybe others have better handled the idea. Maybe an open-source solution exists. Pop your bubble and check facts.

## *Train*

Sometimes, you will save money in the long term by pausing and training your dev team now. If the feedback indicates a weakness in the team's current tool kit (say, they aren't familiar with a certain API development tool set), then get them some training. The experience will inform the development process.

## *Analyze*

With feedback in hand, analyze it for patterns, holes, antipatterns, opportunities, and what have yous. Learn the unknown unknowns. Answer the questions you have and the questions you didn't know you should ask. Be curious.

Finally, with the feedback gathering, warning-flag filtering, and post-feedback refinement done, it's time to make an issue list. You're now ready to begin software development.

Keep in mind that customer feedback is the alpha and omega of software development. The entire process outlined above needs to happen before development begins and after completion.

## ITERATING THE CUSTOMER FEEDBACK ACEP

This is less of an iteration and more of a robot voice blaring from the loudspeaker: "Warning, we are at defcon 3, hodgepodge. I repeat, we are at defcon 3, hodgepodge." We look at the level of customer interaction we're getting and always strive to get it as close to level one as possible. If we feel the relationship is getting rocky, or the business analyst we thought was on our team is suddenly being redirected, or we find ourselves scraping access logs and reading the tea leaves, then we raise the red flag.

My team typically plays in that zone between the telephone game and hodgepodge. So we have to do cultural interventions sometimes and explain to everyone why they need to answer our questions—or else get no software for the holidays.

CHAPTER 61

# ACEP 12
# DEPLOYMENT STRATEGY:
# IGNORE THIS AT YOUR PERIL

Deployment exists outside of all the other processes in part 3. It's the process by which the software reaches the customer, including physical locations, application type, containerization, playbooks, and platforms such as Amazon Web Services. Deployment strategy is crucial—and often overlooked.

Just as I hand-waved in the sections on feature development and project tracking, I'm also going to hand-wave here. This simply is not the book to help you decide on a deployment strategy. There are dozens of viable deployment strategies, across a wide variety of architectures and platforms. Me telling you how to implement is a really bad idea.

## HOW DEPLOYMENT STRATEGY HELPS YOU ESCAPE THE AGILE CIRCUS

Nevertheless, during your software development, keep in mind the considerations that will help you deal with the blur box. Your software development life cycle is built around your deployment strategy. When writing tickets, account for the method of deployment in case it affects the chosen specification. For example, ask questions like these (substituting the technologies listed here with whatever the current technologies of the day might be for you:)

- How many databases are involved? How are they distributed?
- Does your software employ caching, such as Redis cache? Are there issue optimizations to cater to Redis?
- Do you have a message broker, such as RabbitMQ? Do your tickets take messaging into account?
- Do you use Ansible playbooks for deployment? If so, are there certain code decisions that will make deployments simpler?

Such questions will help you avoid late discovery of problems. They'll also help prevent wasted effort via rework.

## ITERATING THE DEPLOYMENT STRATEGY ACEP

Devops is the sleeper issue faced by most organizations. With the proliferation of software-as-a-service platforms, scalable architectures, alternative database strategies, big-data considerations, etc., the deployment of your software has stealthily become a big problem. You need a repeatable, stable way to deploy to demo servers, staging servers, and production servers. You need a way to monitor system health and respond to issues. You need automation—lots and lots of automation.

You might be relying on your dev team to solve those problems. It makes sense. The dev team is intimately familiar with the code. They know computers pretty well. But devops is a different skill set from software development, just as marketing differs from payroll. Asking software developers to design and automate deployments is something of a risk.

We might be able to pull it off. You might pay a lot more for that convenience than you think. Or you may burn out the sensitive brains that are tuned to problem-solving rather than the pragmatic symphony that is devops.

Consider this as a plea for you to hire devops engineers and fold them into your development process.

# A FINAL WORD

Iterative development is an unpredictable whorl of color and movement. That unpredictability is precious and adds value to the organization because it means that new ideas and discovery are taking place. Highest-value tickets are always in progress. The team avoids dead-end streets. You can often reallocate planned expenditures.

This very whorl of unpredictability challenges business processes that have been established for over fifty years. The blur box flies against management practices that are so common and ingrained that they're considered basic business etiquette. The blur box is rude, alien, and preposterous. It trivializes decades of accepted knowledge.

Yet much of the conventional wisdom we rely on for managing software development was founded on a grotesque misunderstanding. When the U.S. Department of Defense codified Winston Royce's cautionary tale into a mandated methodology, the world changed irrevocably. Support structures and management solutions trickled down, from the military to the private sector to colleges.

Some of these practices are wise and timeless. They work in spite of the waterfall. Some of them are makeshift bandages on a problem that exists as a ghost behind the scenes that no one can quite put their finger on. And some of these accepted management practices are based on lies and are completely arbitrary.

These collected software development and management practices, both good and bad, have accumulated through two generations of the workforce. We're about to hit the fourth generation of post-waterfall software development teams. That generation has no easy way to know the legacy they're about to inherit.

This friction of accepted practice vs. the inherent unreliability of the foundation has caused a rift in the industry. Agile devotees have been very vocal, provoking defensiveness and derision from traditional managers. They've also transformed many businesses and delivered stunning results. Traditional managers have held on to processes they trust, which have proven time and again to keep massive projects on track and successfully implemented.

We're at the threshold of a monumental shift in the software development industry. All of the signs are there. The tension and stubbornness that often happens before a paradigm shift is happening now. People are digging their heels in to protect their own turf. But the brashness of the agile debut has mellowed into humility as we agilists realize that we haven't accomplished our vision. And traditional enterprises are quietly adopting the good parts of agile to streamline their approaches.

Both of those concessions are encouraging. Each side knows that compromise needs to occur. This is a perfect time for a reboot.

This book contributes to this shift. By exposing the myth of the flawed approaches that influenced us all, and by providing a conceptual model that helps explain iterative development, I encourage people to rethink their processes. I encourage you to ask the right questions:

- How does my organization's process handle the realities of the blur box?
- Which components of traditional engineering management work well, and which aspects of agile work well?

- Given the antipattern predictive management turned out to be for iterative processes, what assumptions should my organization take a hard look at?
- How can I best prepare myself and my stakeholders?

**It is time for us to exit the alternate timeline.**

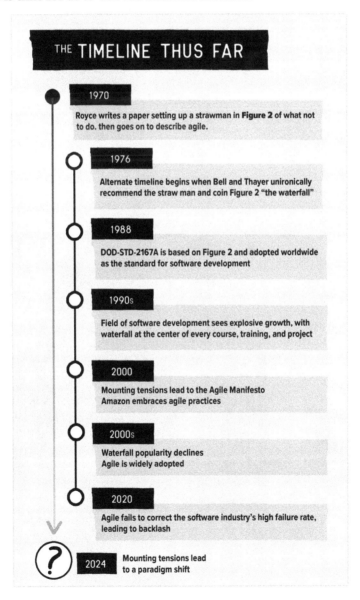

# APPENDIXES

## WHERE TO GO NEXT

When you reach this point in the book, you may be wondering, "Where should I go from here? What should I do next?"

These are the three best things you can do next:

1. Help me.
2. Help yourself.
3. Help your organization.

There's a lot of overlap in those three steps. You can help me out a lot by leaving a review on Amazon or Goodreads. I want your genuine reactions and helpful tips for others who might benefit from reading the book. I read each of these reviews personally, and they'll help me write more-useful books in the future.

You can also help me by recommending me as a speaker to your organization. I love getting in front of audiences and talking about iterative software development. You can find out more at my website, www.roblineberger.com.

While you are at the website, help us both by signing up for my email list. I use the email list to let people know about my upcoming presentations, news about the book, lessons learned from others, tips I learned by sharing the material, and things like that.

You can also help yourself by checking out some of the further reading laid out in the appendixes. I learned a lot from these sources, and I think you will too, particularly because I am not you. You know your own situation and strengths better than anyone. Go forth and read up—but now armed with the concepts you've learned from the blur box. From now on, when you read or hear anything about agile, project management, or software development, ask yourself questions like these:

- How does this handle threads of work?
- How does it handle phase teleportation?
- Does it help us get past the cancellation point?
- Is iteration in light of new discovery an inherent part of the process?
- Is this predictive or adaptive?

You can help your organization in a few key ways. One is to simply think about your own organizational culture in light of the blur box. Sometimes, insights are very obvious. If a process is clearly hampering your ability to iterate, think about how to bring that up with the stakeholders. You're now armed with a conceptual model that can help you present solutions.

Some insights are more subtle and will take time to realize. For example, what is your team culture like? What will it take to get stakeholders to adapt to the realities of the blur box? These aren't simple questions. It takes bravery and buy-in to explore them. That's why I warned you not to buy a copy of this book but to buy two. It needs to be a conversation, not a mandate.

But if you believe what I believe, the really, really best thing you can do to help yourself, your organization, and me at the same time is to realize that we are standing at the threshold of a paradigm shift. The new rules are unwritten. The next big thing is coming. Between when I wrote this book and published it, a new movement has begun called Reimagining Agile (reimaginingagile.com). I don't know much about it yet, but it seems like that could lead to the next big thing.

We all need to communicate with each other. Ask questions, give advice, and learn from each other. I wrote this book for a very simple reason: I want to help others avoid personal failure in their software development struggles.

So keep in touch, whether it be emails or YouTube comments or LinkedIn, wherever we both happen to be. Share your insights with me and with others so we can get ahead of this new way of thinking.

# REFERENCES

Alleman, Glen. "Project Manager and Agile." *Herding Cats* (blog). June 29, 2011. https://herdingcats.typepad.com/my_weblog/2011/06/project-manager-and-agile.html.

Ambler, Scott W. *Agile Database Techniques: Effective Strategies for the Agile Software Developer.* New York: John Wiley and Sons, 2003.

Ambler, Scott W. *Agile Modeling: Effective Practices for eXtreme Programming and the Unified Process.* New York: John Wiley and Sons, 2002.

Ambler, Scott W. "Generalizing Specialists: Improving Your Effectiveness." Agile Modeling. Accessed January 19, 2024. https://agilemodeling.com/essays/generalizingspecialists.htm.

Ambler, Scott W., and Mark Lines. *Disciplined Agile Delivery: A Practitioner's Guide to Agile Software Delivery in the Enterprise.* 1st ed. Indianapolis, IN: IBM Press, 2012.

Ballard, Mary, and Robert Lineberger. "Video Game Violence and Confederate Gender: Effects on Reward and Punishment Given by College Males." *Sex Roles.* 41, no. 8 (2004), 541–558. https://doi.org/10.1023/A:1018843304606.

Bell, T. E., and T. A. Thayer. "Software Requirements: Are They Really a Problem?" Proceedings of the second International Conference on Software Engineering, October 1976. https://dl.acm.org/doi/10.5555/800253.807650.

Belling, Shawn. Comment on post by Henrik Mårtensson. LinkedIn. November 19, 2023. https://www.linkedin.com/feed/update/urn:li:activity:7130914426941030401.

Cockburn, Alistair. "Post-Agile Thoughts." *Heart of Agile.* April 22, 2019. https://heartofagile.com/post-agile-thoughts/.

Cohn, Mike. "The Definition of Ready: What It Is and Why It's Dangerous." *Mountain Goat Software* (blog). May 23, 2023. https://www.mountaingoatsoftware.com/blog/the-dangers-of-a-definition-of-ready.

"Context Switching Is Killing Your Productivity." Software.com. Accessed September 20, 2023. https://www.software.com/devops-guides/context-switching.

Davis, Alan M. "The Software Company Machine." *IEEE Software* 17, no. 2 (March 2000). https://doi.org/10.1109/MS.2000.10005.

"DOD-STD-2167A: Military Standard Defense System Software Development." U.S. Department of Defense. June 4, 1985. https://www.product-lifecycle-management.com/download/DOD-STD-2167A.pdf.

Driessen, Vincent. "A Successful Git Branching Model." *Nvie* (blog). March 5, 2020. https://nvie.com/posts/a-successful-git-branching-model/.

Faeth, Frank. "IT Project Failure Rates: Facts and Reasons," March 22, 2022. LinkedIn. https://www.linkedin.com/pulse/project-failure-rates-facts-reasons-frank-faeth.

Galen, Robert L. *Extraordinarily Badass Agile Coaching: Beginner to Mastery and Beyond.* RGCG, LLC, 2022.

"Gartner Forecasts Worldwide IT Spending to Grow 5.5% in 2023." Gartner. April 6, 2023. https://www.gartner.com/en/newsroom/press-releases/2023-04-06-gartner-forecasts-worldwide-it-spending-to-grow-5-percent-in-2023.

Green, K.C. "The Pills Are Working." *Gunshow* #648. January 9th, 2013. https://gunshowcomic.com/648.

Griffiths, David. "Learn Agile Estimation in 10 Minutes." May 9, 2014. YouTube video, 11:55. https://www.youtube.com/watch?v=Hwu438QSb_g.

Griffiths, Mike. "Implementing Agile Practices in an Un-Agile Organization." PMI Global Summit 2023. October 26, 2023. https://pmiglobalsummit.gcs-web.com/program/agenda#sess55107818.

Hakes, Tyler. "Ideal Days vs. Story Points: Which Is Better and Why?" *7pace* (blog). January 25, 2021. https://www.7pace.com/blog/ideal-days-vs-story-points.

Heisenberg, W. "Über den anschaulichen Inhalt der quantentheoretischen Kinematik und Mechanik." *Zeitschrift für Physik*. 43, no. 3 (1927): 172–198.

Highsmith, Jim. "Agile on the Precipice." LinkedIn. January 2, 2023. https://www.linkedin.com/pulse/agile-precipice-jim-highsmith/.

Highsmith, Jim. *Wild West to Agile: Adventures in Software Development Evolution and Revolution.* Addison-Wesley Professional, 2023.

Hubbard, Douglas W. *How to Measure Anything: Finding the Value of Intangibles in Business.* 3rd ed. Hoboken, NJ: John Wiley & Sons, Inc, 2014.

Jeffries, Ron. "Making the Date." *Ron Jeffries* (blog). November 10, 2005. https://ronjeffries.com/xprog/articles/jatmakingthedate/.

Jeffries, Ron. "Story Points Revisited." *Ron Jeffries* (blog). May 23, 2019. https://ronjeffries.com/articles/019-01ff/story-points/Index.html.

Jeffries, Ron. "Developers Should Abandon Agile." *Ron Jeffries* (blog). May 10, 2018. https://ronjeffries.com/articles/018-01ff/abandon-1/.

Kern, Jon. "Got Technical Debt?" Technical Debt. February 13, 2013. https://technicaldebt.com/got-technical-debt/.

Kern, Jon. "Ten Years of Agile: An Interview with Jon Kern." informIT. August 3, 2011. https://www.informit.com/articles/article.aspx?p=1739476.

Khan, Rash. "Being Agile vs Doing Agile, Why is it important to differentiate!?" LinkedIn. December 5, 2015. https://www.linkedin.

com/pulse/being-agile-vs-doing-why-important-differenti-ate-rash-khan/.

Kim, Larry. "Comfort vs Growth Zone." Medium.com. April 16, 2019. https://medium.com/marketing-and-entrepreneurship/comfort-vs-growth-zone-3f0b4f9e5638.

Kniberg, Henrik. "The Resource Utilization Trap." Crisp Agile Academy. November 3, 2014. YouTube video, 5:33. https://www.youtube.com/watch?v=CostXs2p6r0.

Kruchten, Philippe. "From Waterfall to Iterative Development—A Challenging Transition for Project Managers." *The Rational Edge*. 2001. Archived April 9, 2001 at https://web.archive.org/web/20010409202130/http://www.umlchina.com/ProjMan/Fromwater.htm.

Kuttruff, Oliver. "The Definition of Business Agility and How to Put It into Practice." *Workpath Magazine*. November 16, 2023. https://www.workpath.com/magazine/agility-definition.

Lao Tzu. *Tao Te Ching: A New English Version*. Translated by Stephen Mitchell. Harper Collins, 2009.

Lineberger, Robert. E. "The Blur Box Explored: Solutions for Integrating Adaptive Processes." Paper presented at Project Management Institute Annual Seminars & Symposium, San Antonio, TX, 2002.

Lineberger, Robert E., and Kevin C. Dittman. "The Blur Box: A Conceptual Model for Understanding Iterative Development." Paper presented at Project Management Institute Annual Seminars & Symposium, Nashville, TN, 2001.

Lineberger, Rob, and Chris Vestal. Inheriting Agile channel. YouTube. https://www.youtube.com/@InheritingAgile.

Lineberger, Rob and John Mendonca. "Methodology as Road Kill: The Decade-Long Assault on Quality Assurance." *Software Quality*. American Society for Quality. Spring 2001.

Malina, Peter. "Why Trust Is More than Agility." *Peter Malina* (blog). Accessed September 21, 2023. https://petermalina.com/posts/trust_vs_agility.

"Manifesto for Agile Software Development." Agilemanifesto.org. 2001. https://agilemanifesto.org/.

Marín-Pérez, Abraham. *Real-World Maintainable Software*. O'Reilly Media, Inc., 2016.

Mårtensson, Henrik. "Waterfall vs. Agile: Battle of the Dunces or A Race to the Bottom?" *Kallokain: From the Trenches of Business Management Consulting*. November 16, 2023. https://kallokain.blogspot.com/2023/11/waterfall-vs-agile-battle-of-dunces-or.html.

Martin, Gary. s.v. "Jack of All Trades." The Phrase Finder. Accessed January 19, 2024. https://www.phrases.org.uk/meanings/jack-of-all-trades.html.

Martin, Robert C. *Clean Architecture: A Craftsman's Guide to Software Structure and Design*. 1st ed. Pearson, 2017.

Meloche, Thomas. "A Future Without Agile." LinkedIn. November 21, 2023. https://www.linkedin.com/feed/update/urn:li:activity:7132714275269210112/.

Moody, Glyn. "How Linux Was Born, As Told by Linus Torvalds Himself." arsTECHNICA. August 25, 2015. https://arstechnica.com/information-technology/2015/08/how-linux-was-born-as-told-by-linus-torvalds-himself/.

Musser, Heidi, Jon Kern, Sanjiv Augustine, and Jim Highsmith. "Reimagine Agile: Back to Basics, Forward to the Future." Agile Alliance. November 14, 2023. https://www.agilealliance.org/reimagine-agile-back-to-basics-forward-to-the-future/.

North, Dan. "The Worst Programmer I Know." Dan North & Associates Limited. September 2, 2023. https://dannorth.net/the-worst-programmer/.

Olsen, Dan. *The Lean Product Playbook: How to Innovate with Minimum Viable Products and Rapid Customer Feedback*. 1st ed. Hoboken, NJ: John Wiley & Sons, Inc, 2015.

Perera, Sam. "Effort Estimating: Person-Days or Story-Points?" *Momenton* (blog). Medium. November 18, 2019. https://medium.com/momenton/effort-estimating-person-days-or-story-points-4c5301277423.

Reiber, D. "Bucking the Project." *Enterprise Solutions* (July/August 1999): 16–18.

Robinson, Murray, Shane Gibson, and Brendan Marsh. "#0077 - Brendan Marsh - What Really Happened at Spotify." March 31, 2023, in *No Nonsense Agile*, podcast, MP3 audio, 60:00, https://nononsenseagile.podbean.com/e/0077-brendan-marsh-what-really-happened-at-spotify/.

Rogow, Maury. "Growth Zone." LinkedIn. August 2023. https://www.linkedin.com/posts/mauryrogow_growthzone-growth-weekly-marketingtips-activity-7094742938831736832-MbMM/.

Rothman, Johanna, Becky Hartman, Mike Griffiths, Jesse Fewell, Betsy Kauffman, Stephen Matola, and Horia Slusanschi. "What is Hybrid Agile, Anyway?" Agile Alliance. January 4, 2017. https://www.agilealliance.org/what-is-hybrid-agile-anyway/.

Royce, Winston W. "Managing the Development of Large Software Systems." Lecture presented at the Institute of Electrical and Electronics Engineers WESCon, Los Angeles, CA, August 1970, 1–9. https://typeset.io/papers/managing-the-development-of-large-software-systems-zl45s18on/.

Rubin, D. R. "Don't Touch That Knob!" Symposium conducted at the 105th Annual Convention of the American Psychological Association, Chicago, IL, 1997.

Slater, Daniel. "Powering Innovation and Speed with Amazon's Two-Pizza Teams." AWS Executive Insights. Accessed January 19, 2024.

https://aws.amazon.com/executive-insights/content/amazon-two-pizza-team/.

Spolsky, Joel. "Evidence Based Scheduling." *Joel on Software* (blog). October 26, 2007. https://www.joelonsoftware.com/2007/10/26/evidence-based-scheduling/.

Stevens, Peter. "10 Agile Contracts." Agile Software Development. December 9, 2019. https://www.agilesoftwaredevelopment.com/posts/10-agile-contracts/.

"The Disciplined Agile® (DA™) Tool Kit." Project Management Institute. December 2021. https://www.pmi.org/disciplined-agile/toolkit.

*The Karate Kid*, directed by John G. Avildsen (1984: Columbia Pictures), DVD.

Thomas, David, and Andrew Hunt. *The Pragmatic Programmer: Your Journey to Mastery, 20th Anniversary Edition*. 2nd ed. Addison-Wesley Professional, 2019.

Verwijs, Christiaan. "The Rise of Zombie Scrum." The Liberators, Medium.com. March 29, 2017. https://medium.com/the-liberators/the-rise-of-zombie-scrum-cd98741015d5.

Vestal, Chris, and Rob Lineberger. Inheriting Agile. LinkedIn group. https://www.linkedin.com/groups/14330207/.

Watt, Alex. "Realistic Gym Workout Diagrams." College Humor. September 10, 2010. Archived March 22, 2014 at the Wayback Machine. https://web.archive.org/web/20140322074435/http://www.collegehumor.com/post/6283767/realistic-gym-workout-diagrams.

"Why Limiting Your Work-in-Progress Matters." *Planview Blog*. March 3, 2014. https://blog.planview.com/why-limiting-your-work-in-progress-matters/.

Wikipedia. s.v. "INVEST (Mnemonic)." Last modified July 18, 2023, 20:57 (UTC). https://en.wikipedia.org/wiki/INVEST_(mnemonic).

# FURTHER READING

Ambler, Scott W., and Mark Lines. *Disciplined Agile Delivery: A Practitioner's Guide to Agile Software Delivery in the Enterprise.* 1st ed. Indianapolis, IN: IBM Press, 2012.

Beck, Kent and Cynthia Andres. *eXtreme Programming Explained.* 2nd ed. Boston, MA: Addison-Wesley, 2005.

Benson, Jim and Tonianne DeMaria Barry. *Personal Kanban: Mapping Work | Navigating Life.* Self-published, CreateSpace Independent Publishing Platform, 2011.

Burnett, Michael. "The Age of Agile Must End." *UX Collective* (blog). February 12, 2023. https://uxdesign.cc/the-age-of-agile-must-end-bc89c0f084b7.

Davis, Alan M. "The Software Company Machine." *IEEE Software* 17, no. 2 (March/April 2000). https://doi.org/10.1109/MS.2000.10005.

Goldratt, Eliyahu M., and Cox, Jeff. *The Goal.* Gower Publishing, 1984.

Hubbard, Douglas W. *How to Measure Anything: Finding the Value of Intangibles in Business.* 3rd ed. Hoboken, NJ: John Wiley & Sons, Inc, 2014.

Larman, Craig, and Victor Basili. "Iterative and Incremental Developments: A Brief History." *Computer* 36, no. 6 (July 2003): 47–56. https://doi.org/10.1109/mc.2003.1204375.

Laster, Brent. *Learning GitHub Actions: Automation and Integration of CI/CD with GitHub,* 1st ed. O'Reilly Media, 2023.

Márin-Pérez, Abraham. *Real-World Maintainable Software.* O'Reilly Media, 2016.

Martin, Robert C. *Clean Architecture: A Craftsman's Guide to Software Structure and Design.* 1st ed. Pearson, 2017.

Martin, Robert C. *Clean Code: A Handbook of Agile Software Craftsmanship.* 1st ed. Pearson, 2008.

Olsen, Dan. *The Lean Product Playbook: How to Innovate with Minimum Viable Products and Rapid Customer Feedback.* 1st ed. Hoboken, NJ: John Wiley & Sons, Inc, 2015.

Pfieffer, Tobias. "Why Waterfall Was a Big Misunderstanding from the Beginning." *Journeys of a Not So Young Anymore Software Engineer* (blog). March 2, 2012. https://pragtob.wordpress.com/2012/03/02/why-waterfall-was-a-big-misunderstanding-from-the-beginning-reading-the-original-paper/.

"Measure Outcomes." Project Management Institute. January 2023. https://www.pmi.org/disciplined-agile/ongoing-goals/measure-outcomes.

"Organize Metrics." Project Management Institute. January 2023. https://www.pmi.org/disciplined-agile/ongoing-goals/organize-metrics.

Reinertsen, Donald G. *The Principles of Product Development Flow: Second Generation Lean Product Development,* Celeritas Publishing, 2014.

Schwaber, Ken, and Mike Beedle. *Agile Software Development with Scrum.* Prentice Hall, 2002.

Thomas, David, and Andrew Hunt. *The Pragmatic Programmer: Your Journey to Mastery, 20th Anniversary Edition.* 2nd ed. Addison-Wesley Professional, 2019.

# ACKNOWLEDGMENTS

You know a book is a labor of love when you are typing with one hand at 2:00 a.m. and cramming stale chips and salsa into your mouth with the other because your stomach started rumbling back during chapter 13. Or when you swallow your imposter syndrome and reach out to the people who have inspired you for decades—even when they don't know you. Or when you are asked by the speaker team at a major global conference to please remove your illicit promotional display with 16,387 cubic inches of strobing LED lights that you set up in the waiting area. Or when you reassure yourself that you can write for "just a couple more hours" and get some sleep before going to work the next day, only to realize it is Monday morning and you have to lead standup in three hours.

When you're in that kind of situation and you actually find yourself enjoying life at the same time, it is probably due to people like these:

It's always fashionable to acknowledge one's parents, but I have specific reasons to do so. My mother Kathy has been a public school teacher and librarian for over 50 years. Literally for as long as I can remember she's been handing me books to read and encouraging me to teach. My father Jim was an executive at a national insurance company who turned down a VP promotion and stepped away to found his own business in a volatile field. That venture thrived for decades until he bequeathed it to others and retired. Combined, they taught me the value of belief in self, independent thought, and taking action.

This book would be very different if not for the coauthors of the Agile Manifesto, who coalesced a lot of ideas that were simmering across the industry. They raised the flag as high as it could possibly be raised. In particular I'd like to thank Jim Highsmith, Jon Kern, and Alistair Cockburn for being very responsive to my questions and fact-checking the backstory of the Manifesto weekend. (Jon in particular for the detailed notes.)

I also want to acknowledge the people in the background leading up to that event, the "lightweight" practitioners who perhaps did not sign their name to the manifesto but nevertheless made the movement possible: Mike Cohn, Scott Ambler, Esther Derby, Glen Alleman, and the countless others whom I followed and/or chatted with in forums back in the dim mists of the past, when we tried to solve the world's software crisis.

Joan Vaughan, Susie Gothard, Nancy Yuochunas, Laverne Knodle, and the rest of Purdue University's Management Information division, thank you for mentoring me in the field of information technology even when I made foolish mistakes.

Kevin Dittman, John Mendonca, Jeffrey Whitten, and the faculty of Purdue University's Computer Programming Technology department—your rigor and expertise shaped these ideas into a presentable form. Getting my master's degree there was like walking through a gauntlet of loving velvet hammers that continually pounded and chipped away at any assertion I made, ensuring that the concepts stood up to scrutiny.

Kevin in particular gently prodded (i.e., forced) me to submit the blur box to the PMI International Symposium (now known as the Global Summit.) Without that encouragement, I never would have stepped onto the stage or written those initial publications. The Project Management Institute truly is one of the greatest project management knowledge repositories in the world. Everyone I have interacted with there has been professional and encouraging, even at times when my ideas run counter to the practices they recommend. It takes an open mind to let the devil's advocate step onto your own stage.

My beta readers, Samuel Morris Johnston and Baxter Crabtree, are both consummate software developers and authors. They take no crap and allow none to pass by uncontested. Sam in particular summarized many of the concepts I was not already familiar with (such as Dan Olsen's writings) and refused to be credited because of his humble nature. However I could not let that go by without acknowledgment here.

Julie Broad and the team at Book Launchers were instrumental in delivering a professional product.

The organizers of the conferences I went to that enabled me to interrogate (I mean, *meet)* many great agile practitioners. Sanjiv Augustine, Kimberly Andrikaitis, Bob Galen, Paul Barrett, and probably a hundred other people I'm overlooking.

My book army of enthusiastic supporters who helped make this happen. As Tobias says in *Arrested Development,* "There are *dozens* of us!" But I'd like to call out the early supporters, in chronological order, who went an extra mile and I think would be OK with being publicly named: Kerri Patterson, Chris Correale, Chris Vestal, Blake Corman, Tim Draegen, Ester Miranda, Anass BERRADA, and Tiffany Schneider.

But this book definitely could not exist if not for the long conversations about software engineering I had with Gary Yates. He is the quintessential chief architect. The initial concepts he shared gave me the ideal jumping-off point for my master's research and my subsequent journey through agile practice.

One final acknowledgment to anyone who reads the next page and does the thing.

Thank you all so much.

# NEED A LOT OF COPIES?

Because it is a conceptual model, this book works best when shared with others. I've encouraged you to buy multiple copies. So to make that easier, I have bulk pricing available if you buy ten or more copies. Please contact me at roblineberger.com and I will provide you with details about the discounts so you can distribute the copies you need to reach your people.

Printed in the USA
CPSIA information can be obtained
at www.ICGtesting.com
LVHW090425030524
778875LV00010B/761